"Come on Northern"

The fall and rise of Bradford Northern RLFC 1954 to 1965

GW00585854

Trevor Delaney

London League Publications Ltd

"Come on Northern"
The fall and rise of Bradford Northern RLFC 1954 to 1965
© Trevor Delaney. Foreword © Len Haley

The moral right of Trevor Delaney to be identified as the author has been asserted.

Cover design © Stephen McCarthy.

Front cover: Design based on the 1960s 'old' Bradford Northern match programme.
Back cover: An advert from the Bradford Northern programme for the last match played by the 'old' Northern.

A CIP catalogue record for this book is available from the British Library.

First published in Great Britain in August 2012 by:
London League Publications Ltd, P.O. Box 65784, London NW2 9NS

ISBN: 978-1903659-63-2

Cover design by: Stephen McCarthy Graphic Design
                               46, Clarence Road, London N15 5BB

Layout: Peter Lush

Printed and bound by CPI Group (UK) Ltd, Croydon, CR0 4YY

Foreword

During my career I played with and against some great players and characters and have many fond memories of my time here at Odsal. From 1951 to 1954 it was much easier playing with the likes of Joe Phillips, Jack McLean, Ernest Ward, Bob Hawes, Ken Traill, and Trevor Foster, to name just a few, than during the period that this book covers, when none of us were really up to their standard.

Playing against the 1952 Australians under floodlights before a crowd of nearly 30,000 was memorable. But the highlight of my career was defeating Huddersfield in the Championship semi-final top-four play-off in 1951–52 at Odsal before a crowd of over 56,000, and qualifying for the final against Wigan at Huddersfield Town's Leeds Road ground. Unfortunately, before the final we lost the services of our captain, Ernest Ward, due to a family bereavement, and this was a contributing factor in our defeat.

Over those dozen or so seasons, I suffered numerous injuries, including a dislocated shoulder, a broken foot, a dislocated elbow, a broken nose and both knee cartilages were removed at different times. Fortunately we had private medical treatment paid for by the club and this helped to get me back into action. Injuries did not adversely affect my work, as a wages clerk at large textile mill in Dewsbury, as my livelihood always came before part-time rugby. Such injuries were accepted as being part and parcel of a tough game, but I was sorry to have to miss my benefit match in 1962 against Leeds due to badly bruising a shoulder.

In the latter years it was difficult to know which new youngsters and trialists we would be playing alongside. But I was persuaded to delay my retirement in old Northern's final season, captained the side and helped with coaching once coach Harry Beverley left. More than anything else, I think the club folded due to the gradual change in management, following the retirement of Harry Hornby and with manager-coach Dai Rees moving to Halifax. The great players were never replaced and the future chairmen, Cyril Bunney and Jackie Barritt, one assumes, had to sell most of the better players, such as Jack Scroby and Milan Kosanovic, in order to balance the books.

During my career rugby league was, of course, a totally different game from today's (17-a-side) version, with substitutes and limited tackles. In those days, with contested scrums, although the defending side fed the ball you never knew which way the ball would emerge.

I think rugby league was then a much better spectacle. For instance, there were three or four wingers scoring over 50 and 60 tries a season, which has not happened since the start of Super League.

My favourite position was at stand-off half, and I have been asked to name a competitive Northern side from 1954-1963, with myself as captain. I have excluded the obvious stars from the 1952 Championship leading side, but included Tony Storey, and Bill Seddon and Brian Radford, both of whom played the large majority of their careers after 1954. There maybe a few surprises, but here it is:

Bill Seddon, Jack Doran, George Penketh, Ralph Winnard, Malcolm Davies, Len Haley, Graham Oddy, Phil Crabtree, Norman Mackie, Trevor Jones, Tony Storey, Brian Radford, Harry Griffett.

After reading this book I'm sure you will be able to pick an old Northern side which will be able to give my selection a good game.

Len Haley
Liversedge, March 2012

From making his senior debut with Northern in September 1951 Len Haley made approximately 300 appearances at full-back, centre and both half-back positions. He was a member of the 1952 Championship leading squad and captained the side for three seasons from 1956–57 and in the club's final season, 1963–64.

Len Haley's career with Bradford Northern

Season	A	G	T	Pts
1951–52	34	0	6	18
1952–53	29	0	4	12
1953–54	25	0	2	6
1954–55	35	0	10	30
1955–56	31	0	4	12
1956–57	33	0	2	6
1957–58	26	2	3	13
1958–59	22	0	4	12
1959–60	25	0	3	9
1960–61	7	0	0	0
1961–62	12	0	1	3
1962–63	4	0	0	0
1963–64	2	0	0	0
Totals	**285**	**2**	**39**	**121**

Includes tour games, but not Lazenby Cup matches and other friendlies.

Acknowledgements

This book was intended as a nostalgic account of my first ten years as a Bradford Northern supporter. Yet, in order to satisfy my curiosity and produce an accurate record, I had to examine local newspaper archives. I am beholden to the sports reporters of the period, whose match reports are accessible in West Yorkshire's public libraries. The local history librarians, together with *Blackpool Gazette* archivist, Carole Davies, have been extremely co-operative.

The records produced by Irvin Saxton's Rugby League Record Keepers' Club form the basis of my research. I have also referred to the painstakingly kept scrapbooks of actor Duncan Preston and those loaned to me by Gary Wilkinson.

Leading rugby league historian Robert Gate gave me his usual encouragement and suggested improvements to the original manuscript. Len Haley kindly wrote the foreword and assisted with queries regarding past players. Likewise, Phil Crabtree provided anecdotes of his playing career. Thanks also to Ralph Winnard for using photos from his collection.

I should also like to thank the following for sharing their memories and expertise: my brother, Terence, who took me to my initial game at Odsal; John Downes and Martin Bass of the Bradford Bulls Rugby League Heritage Project; Harry Edgar of the *Rugby League Journal* ; Ron Bailey, the former secretary of Featherstone Rovers; Jack Prickett, the former Odsal groundsman; Charlie Ebbage; Andrew Hardcastle; Bob Ismay; John Pitchford; Mike Healing; Park Avenue supporter, Tony Green; Northern supporter, John Hamer; Tony Capstick; Chris Shaw; rugby historian Graham Williams; and all at the Rugby League Heritage Project at Huddersfield University: namely, Professor Tony Collins, archivists Amy Devenney and Amy-Jo Cameron-Williams, and the indefatigable David Thorpe.

I am also indebted to Bryan Jowett of Assist Computers for rescuing the files on the project; and to Peter Lush and Dave Farrar of London League Publications Ltd for finally bringing this idea to fruition.

Trevor Delaney

About the author

This is Trevor Delaney's fifth book – the previous four have all been self-published. In 1984 he wrote *The Roots of Rugby League,* a pioneering work which looked at the history of the split in rugby football from a rugby league standpoint. This was then followed by *The Grounds of Rugby League* (1991), *The International Grounds of Rugby League* (1995), and *Rugby Disunion – Broken-Time* (1995).

In the mid-1980s he edited and published *Code 13,* a quarterly journal which specialised in the game's heritage.

In 1990, he was the first person to identify the original Rugby League World Cup, which was found in a ditch some 20 years after it disappeared while on display at a Bradford hotel. The renovated trophy is again presented to the top international side.

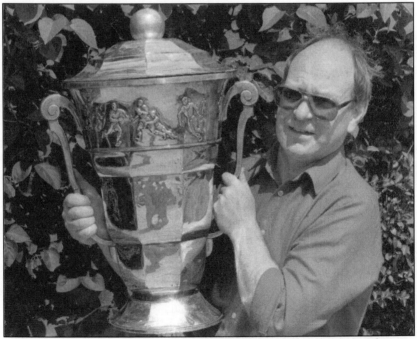

The author with the Rugby League World Cup which he helped identify.

Contents

Appendices

Adverts from Bradford Northern programmes in the 1950s.

1. 1946 to 1954: My early education
Odsal and Northern's Wembley triumphs

The Bradford Northern club, which in the Super League era became the Bradford Bulls, celebrated its centenary in 2007. This was meant to have been an off-the-cuff account of just one decade in those 100 years, the period from that eventful year in rugby league of 1954 to the collapse of the club in December 1963, the termination of its rugby league membership and subsequent re-launch in 1964. My story starts, as an eight-year-old, mid-way through the 1954–55 season – a season in which Northern topped the league in the middle of September. My regular attendance at games, though, only started in earnest – after the annual seaside holiday to the east coast – from early September 1956. From that date I can claim to have watched most of old Northern's home games but my memory has failed me on all but one or two of the most memorable incidents in each season – hence the need for extensive newspaper research.

Since the birth of the game in 1895, many rugby league clubs had gone out of existence, but none fell from the heights quite like the old Northern, situated in such a populous area, and with a history of recent success, particularly in the Challenge Cup. Northern's story is also unique in the manner in which the game rallied behind the new club both in terms of agreeing their early entry to the league and in the transfer of quality players to the new enterprise – decisions which were well rewarded from 1964 with new Northern's phenomenal away following.

In this period before full-time professionalism in the game's top tier, players had to hold down a day job or career as well as training two evenings a week. They were paid winning or losing pay and the possible bonus from a good Cup run, but unless they had been lured from rugby union with a sizeable signing on fee, the rewards were modest. Apart from illegal backhanders, players were rewarded for their loyalty to a club by a testimonial game. Spectators threw their loose change into a blanket as it was carried round the pitch and the beneficiary also received the gate receipts after expenses were deducted.

1

It was a time when the game was played mostly on Saturday afternoons with a 2.30pm or 3pm kick-off with the added joy of being able to read about every game played that day in West Yorkshire in the evening pink, green and yellow sports pages of the *Yorkshire Sports* and the *Yorkshire Evening News* and *Yorkshire Evening Post.*

This was a period of contested and untidy scrums, and it mattered as to who was blind-side or open-side prop or whether your side had a recognised specialist hooker. Unlimited tackles also affected the nature of the game and the physical make up of its combatants. Until 1964 there were no substitutions, even when an injury to a player could decide and ruin a game. It meant that players, unless seriously injured, had to play the full 80 minutes. The forwards, particularly, had to have stamina as the grounds in winter, and especially Odsal, were usually thick with mud.

In such conditions, goalkicking with the heavy leather balls was a difficult art, with the traditional toe end method still being used, apart from a few notable exceptions. One of the finest exponents of end-on goalkicking in this period was the Leigh, and former Dewsbury and Great Britain full-back, Jimmy Ledgard, who would later coach Northern. I can recall, as a 9-year-old, standing behind the posts at the scoreboard end at Odsal in September 1955 and mischievously 'betting' the Leigh supporters that Ledgard would miss with his goal attempt from the touchline.

Our family had always been a Northern and – in association football – Park Avenue one. Bradford City was almost a dirty word in our humble household. My father had followed Northern since the pre-war Birch Lane days, when goalkicking prop forward Charlie Litt apparently turned up to games on his motorbike. A postcard of the first side at Odsal in 1934 had always been a treasured possession; as was the souvenir brochure celebrating Northern's record of three successive Wembley appearances from 1947, with pen pictures of the famous players and the aerial shots of Odsal Stadium.

The tales of Northern returning to Bradford with the Challenge Cup were a part of my early sporting education. The names and exploits of some of Northern's all-time greats, such as the hefty prop, Frank Whitcombe, Willie Davies, Eric Batten, Ernest Ward, Trevor Foster, Ken Traill, Joe Phillips and Jack McLean, were already imprinted on my young mind. One of my earliest recollections is of passing Odsal Top on

2

a Saturday evening, possibly on our way home from one of my dad's Point-to-Point horse racing trips, and seeing the queues for the speedway – with numerous national flags flying from flagpoles down Rooley Avenue. In May 1954, this cavernous enclosure had held well over 100,000, then a world record rugby league crowd, for the Challenge Cup replay between Halifax and Warrington. I remember listening to the game on the radio. By now I was thirsting to be taken to my first live game of rugby league and to see inside Odsal Stadium.

One's allegiances to clubs and grounds, as Geoffrey Moorhouse pointed out in the foreword to *The Grounds of Rugby League,* are invariably decided from childhood. Odsal itself was always a major attraction, and, apart from rugby league, I would go there to watch many of the other events which were staged over the years. These included basketball with the Harlem Globetrotters, trotting, speedway, and stock cars – although, for these motor sports, it was more to see for myself what damage might be caused to the precious rugby pitch.

My first vivid memories of watching rugby league at Odsal centre on just three games, in February and March 1955. I can recall Billy Banks, the Huddersfield scrum-half, being congratulated for his performance as he left the pitch after losing to Northern 10–8; Northern's 27–3 win over Dewsbury under the floodlights; and Ernest Ward, then in Castleford colours, being ignominiously tackled into touch and onto the shale speedway track. Of the three events, it was Odsal's inaugural floodlights that made the most impact. Unfortunately, most clubs declined to play under them, only Leigh had also invested in lights, fearing some great disadvantage, but there was always the thrill of entering Odsal and watching Northern play the Australian and New Zealand touring sides at night.

The declining attendances at Northern's home games in this decade contrasted sharply with those at the Challenge Cup semi-finals, test matches and World Cup games; and the huge crowds, including over 83,000 in 1960, which I was able to be part of from the time that the Championship final was allocated to Odsal in 1957. In this period, Northern had only two five figure gates at the league games that I witnessed, against Leigh and Wakefield. By the early 1960s the visit of Trinity and Leeds saw the away support far outnumber the home faithful. Strange to imagine that in March 1953, for the visit of Huddersfield in the third round of the Challenge Cup, a crowd of

3

69,429 had been inside Odsal – with an atmosphere, no doubt, similar to those of the great Championship final gatherings. A little over 10 years later and only 324 spectators were dotted around the huge banking and terraces, which were made of rotting wooden sleepers and household waste.

The players' long walk down from the club house on the top embankment, where the dressing rooms were then located at Odsal, allowed me to mingle with the players and officials, before running in free fall down the ashes to the corner near the Old Stand. To the strains of, what I now know was, the stirring march *National Emblem*, the players entered the field near the corner flag. This had been the arrangement ever since the ground's opening in 1934, until it was changed in 1958 for the Championship final when the teams emerged at the side of that stand. Only when the smell of wintergreen mingled with the sound of boot studs on the shale speedway track did we fully appreciate the size of some of the visiting forwards. The fearsome sight of Workington Town's mighty pack, including Brian Edgar and the Martin brothers, readily springs to mind.

To my eyes, only Hunslet's myrtle green, flame and white design could rival Northern's white jersey with the simple red, amber and black hoops. It was always disappointing therefore to see your heroes emerge from the dressing rooms wearing – without a clear colour clash – the change strip of either all red or all blue, and occasionally all green. No doubt the heavy grounds in winter meant the traditional kit was at the laundry, but it always seemed, without their famous colours, Northern were at a psychological disadvantage before the kick-off.

When Northern were playing away, I often visited Headingley and Bramley's Barley Mow at a time when both clubs could offer first-class rugby. However, up to the early 1960s my memories are mostly of games at Odsal, as pocket money did not allow too many visits by Wallace Arnold coach to other grounds in the rugby league heartland. I can only recall visiting five away grounds to watch the old Northern; York's Clarence Street in 1956, when the home prop Vic Yorke kicked the Minstermen to victory and we nearly missed the coach back home; the Barley Mow, where youngsters were allowed to sit under the open railed fencing, and there was a 'penny on the ball' raffle to win a genuine leather rugby ball; Hunslet's Parkside, when a kick to touch by Bill Seddon was neatly fielded by yours truly with the obligatory shouts of "sign the lad on"; and watching Northern get truly thrashed at Lawkholme Lane, when Keighley had a useful side.

Only once can I remember leaving an old Northern game before the end. That was at Belle Vue in 1961 when the great Wakefield Trinity side – even without Neil Fox – inflicted Northern's second greatest defeat, 73–5. It was somewhere in the region of 55–5 when our party headed for the exits, with the light hearted rebuking from the home fans, and the cheers for yet another try ringing in our ears.

In those days, Trinity had one of the best club programmes in the league and my cousin in Wakefield used to pass them onto me whenever we visited. These gems were added to my small collection – then stacked near the enamel bread bin in the kitchen – which was being built up largely from writing to various club secretaries and enclosing the recommended stamped addressed envelope. Featherstone Rovers, Hull, Huddersfield and Barrow all replied, but St Helens quickly became my most respected club, when they not only sent me three or four of their pink, double folded, publications but also replied when I asked for the official programme for the Rugby League XIII versus France game at Knowsley Road in 1959, in which my Northern favourite, Milan Kosanovic, played.

At the time I started watching, there were only remnants left of Northern's great Wembley sides of the late 1940s under their manager-coach, Dai Rees and visionary chairman, Harry Hornby, an entrepreneur in ship breaking and engineering, who in the summer of 1950 spent a small fortune in signing five new Zealanders in a major transfer coup. Many members of the 1952 league leaders squad had either left – such as Bob Hawes, who returned later with the 1955 Kiwis and played in the second test at Odsal – or would soon be moving from the Odsal scene before I was able to become acquainted with either their names or their style of play.

Scrum-half Gwylfa Jones, who joined Northern in the 1946–47 season from Llanelli after playing Welsh rugby union trials; former Wyke hooker Norman Haley; former Ovenden centre Joe Mageen; and forwards Ron Greaves and Bill Shreeve fall into this latter category. Likewise, David Knopf's brief spell at Odsal was a total mystery to me, although he was the regular right-winger in the 1954–55 season before he returned to South Africa early the following season. As previously mentioned, Ernest Ward had already left to join Castleford, and I can

5

only vaguely remember Trevor Foster playing in his final game at Odsal in April 1955. In this same game, Coventry based Barry Tyler also made his last home appearance, although I have no recall of Trevor's close comrade on that day; nor of Northumbrian-born loose-forward Ken Traill. Signed from Hunslet in 1947, Traill played at Wembley in 1948 and 1949, was a tourist in 1950 and 1954, and played in all three tests against Australia in 1952. But his ball skills went unnoticed in the few games I witnessed before he moved to Halifax at the end of October 1955.

However, at the end of the 1955–56 season, I distinctly remember the former All Black, Jack McLean, scoring at least one of his five tries against Swinton, in his final game at Odsal before he retired and returned to New Zealand. His tally took him to the top of the league's try scoring chart with 60. My recollection of the play of that other great New Zealander, Joe Phillips, is not of his record goalkicking or defence splitting runs, but of a ploy which apparently brought him several tries. After indicating that he was about to kick at goal from a penalty award, and realising the defence was relaxed, he simply tapped the ball to himself and strolled in for a try. This manoeuvre was ended with the abolition of the tap penalty in 1960.

The squad that finished top of the league in the 1951–52 season but lost to Wigan in the Championship Final. Back row (left to right): Foster, Shreeve, N. Haley, Mageen, Bob Smith, Traill, Radford, Tyler; seated: Jenkins, Seddon, Hastings, Ward, Phillips, McLean, Hawes; front: L. Haley, G. Jones, Dickson, Greaves.

Wynne Jones, seen here scoring against Dewsbury at Odsal on 8 March 1952. (Courtesy Bradford Bulls Foundation RL Heritage Project)

Of those players in the 1951–52 squad, pictured in front of the Odsal clubhouse, only Radford, Smith, Jenkins, Haley and Seddon became familiar to me – all one club men. Brian Radford was signed in December 1948 when playing for Aberavon and made his debut in January 1949 at York, in time to appear at Wembley that same year. The versatile Bill Jenkins had been introduced to Odsal by an RAF colleague, George Troth, a former Northern winger, and made his debut against Hull KR in March 1948. Len Haley was signed for £250, after the former Cleckheaton rugby union and county trialist was banned from union for having played amateur rugby league for Overthorpe Rangers (Thornhill). He made his debut in September 1951 against Featherstone Rovers.

The sixth New Zealander, Bill Seddon, arrived in the 1951–52 season, when he played as an amateur in the 'A' team. His first game as a professional player was in the Lazenby Cup against Keighley at Odsal on 20 August 1952, when he scored a try and was hailed as a real 'find' because of his all-round ability. Three days later he made his full debut in a 40–11 home win over Bramley – the first time in the club's history that Northern had fielded an all New Zealand threequarter line – Hawes, Seddon, Hastings and McLean, with Phillips at full-back. Seddon returned home in May 1954, but rejoined Northern in October that year.

Although the club's problems grew from the late 1950s, any insight into the club's real plight was far from the mind of this writer in those days. As a teenager – apart from courting – the week seemed to revolve around the pending game, whether on a midweek evening or on the Saturday afternoon. Regardless of the increasingly disappointing results, and the many ribbings one had to endure for watching such a poor team, being one of Northern's hardcore of supporters was still something of a privilege.

Ken Traill and Alan Prescott leap for the ball in the 1953–54 clash at Odsal as Bob Hawes (2) watches. St Helens did the double over Northern that season. (Courtesy Tony Capstick)

When Northern's collapse finally came other visionaries were needed and cometh the hour, cometh the men in the form of Odsal legends Trevor Foster and the 'new' Northern's first chairman, Joe Phillips. Both spoke passionately about their plans to relaunch the club at a major public meeting at St George's Hall in April, 1964 – four days after my 18th birthday – which I attended along with my father and 1,500 other Bradfordians. And that summer a new era for the club began at Odsal. However, looking at the match reports and some of the attendance figures, it was clearly not all plain-sailing in the early months of that first season. The directors and coaching staff must have had many sleepless nights worrying about how to achieve the right blend of players, who would help secure the club's long-term support.

2. 1954–55: New recruits needed
Legend Trevor Foster retires

For the fourth time in the past few seasons, the clubs had failed to approve a proposal for two divisions – the latest scheme from the Rugby Football League (RFL) secretary, Bill Fallowfield, was very similar to the one which would ultimately be implemented in the 1962–63 season. In 1954 no one could possibly have envisaged that by the early 1960s Northern would not only be competing in such a lower division, but would also be languishing in the bottom position and failing to fulfil their fixtures.

The Odsal pitch had been reseeded during the summer, and Northern kicked-off the 1954–55 season with nine straight wins, including an 11–0 victory over Wigan at Odsal before a crowd of 15,000. By mid-September they were at the top of the Championship table and into the semi-final of the Yorkshire Cup, where they were only eliminated – 10–5 – after a great tussle with Hull at The Boulevard. Alas, after losing 10–2 to Widnes on 4 December before only 2,000 spectators – their lowest peace-time crowd since April 1934 at Birch Lane – over the Christmas holidays they slipped to 11th place after conceding their first league double to Keighley since the 1934–35 season. Northern lost 18–9 at Odsal and 6–5 at Lawkholme Lane.

Of the two games, Keighley were happier with the drier conditions at Odsal. The highlight was full-back Terry Hollindrake's 60-yard sidestepping run to the posts. It was the courageous Hollindrake's third penalty, in the 65th minute, which also won the game at Lawkholme Lane, where Northern put up a much sterner challenge after being ahead 5–2 at the interval. Although he suffered a broken nose, Hollindrake returned to help his colleagues withstand Northern's last-ditch effort to salvage the game, in which hooker Norman Haley made his final first team appearance.

Northern then entered 1955 with their sixth successive league defeat, when they went down 17–11 at York on New Year's Day. In this so-called festive game, winger David Knopf not only scored two tries, but also finished up with two black eyes. Former Wyke hooker, 22-year-old Dennis Hodgson, made his debut, and Carl Sharrock, who was

9

then serving with the Royal Signals, was given a run at centre, having earlier in the season played four games at stand-off.

In the return fixture at Odsal on the following Saturday, Northern lost 15–5 despite York being reduced to 12 men for short periods. The *Telegraph & Argus* sports editor, Jack Burns, reported that, when they entered the field, Northern had been greeted by a deathly silence. It was the first time in his long experience that he could ever remember this happening to a home side.

After two postponements due to snow and ice, against Wakefield and Batley, Northern's 12–9 win at Bramley gave them their first double of the season. Although Joe Phillips had a disappointing day with the boot, missing with six of his nine attempts, former Otley rugby union stand-off Eric Sutton used Northern's limited possession to good effect; and centre Len Haley gave Jack McLean, whose appearances had been limited due to injury, his best game of the season so far.

By the end of January Northern therefore had a 50 per cent winning league record – a fact which I was patently unaware of as I attended what, I believe, was my first game of rugby league. This was on 5 February 1955, when, as an inattentive eight-year-old, I was at Odsal when Northern beat Huddersfield 10–8 in a thriller; and Billy Banks, from the reactions of the spectators around me as the Welsh international scrum-half left the pitch, must have had an outstanding game for the Fartowners. By all accounts Jack McLean scored a spectacular 50-yard try; and Eric Sutton was being hailed as potentially the best half-back since the irreplaceable Willie Davies. It was only Northern's second league win in nine games since December, and the crowd of only 8,500 was a further indication of the Bradford public's apathy. This was the lowest for a Huddersfield fixture since before the war; the post-war average against the Fartowners then was 16,000.

Including the crowd of 56,476 at the Championship semi-final against Huddersfield, Northern's average attendance in the 1951–52 season was a record 17,791 (15,361 for league games only); but this dropped to 12,134 in 1953–54. Receipts for the year ending June 1954 were a record £56,797, which, after payments to the RFL and other clubs, produced a net income of £20,976. The club, however, made a loss of £1,781, after the players' wages and expenses, £11,048, and Odsal's upkeep were taken into account.

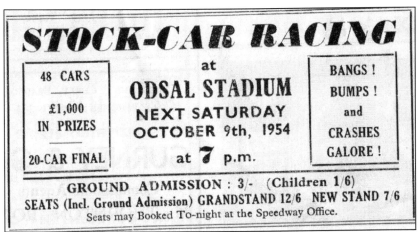

STOCK-CAR RACING

48 CARS	at	BANGS !
£1,000 IN PRIZES	**ODSAL STADIUM** NEXT SATURDAY OCTOBER 9th, 1954	BUMPS ! and CRASHES
20-CAR FINAL	at **7** p.m.	GALORE !

GROUND ADMISSION : 3/- (Children 1/6)
SEATS (Incl. Ground Admission) GRANDSTAND 12/6 NEW STAND 7/6
Seats may Booked To-night at the Speedway Office.

Stock-car racing was staged at Odsal to try to bring in extra income.

At the 46th AGM, held on 1 March 1955, vice-chairman Harry Woodhead explained to the nine other shareholders present that since 1934 about £18,000 had been spent on the troublesome playing area and during the previous year ground maintenance had cost £5,897. In an attempt to recoup some of this outlay the directors had been given permission to stage a further two stock car events in September and October. In the club programme notes they argued that they had inherited £8,000 of debts from the previous board; and that revenue produced from the occasional big game did not cover 25 per cent of the cost of preparing and maintaining the ground for such events.

Also, Entertainment Tax and the live televising of test matches, in direct competition with league games, were both putting excessive strain on all clubs. This meant that few funds were left for the purchase of new players.

Although no questions were asked at the meeting about the team's playing strength, the absence of any new recruits and Northern's recent poor form – a 24–0 defeat at The Boulevard had followed the Huddersfield win – had led to many complaints from supporters in the *Telegraph & Argus* letters page.

As the Challenge Cup transfer deadline passed Northern had made no new signings, but transferred 28-year-old Ron Greaves to Keighley. The former Abertillery rugby union prop was a member of Northern's Challenge Cup-winning side in 1949 and in the league leaders squad of

1952, but had been out of the game for some time – having made his last appearance in December 1953.

In view of Northern having lost seven of their previous nine league games, the 9–4 defeat of the holders, League Champions and current league leaders, Warrington, was the biggest shock of the first round of the Challenge Cup.Northern led from the first minute when a shrewd Traill pass sent centre Haley over and Seddon's superb conversion and two penalties gave Northern a deserved 9–0 interval lead. In a thrilling second-half Warrington had a 3–1 advantage in the scrums and whipped the ball from wing to wing, but they could not find a way past Northern's resolute defence.

Joe Mageen missed the second round home tie through injury, when Northern produced a lethargic display in losing 7–2 to Featherstone Rovers, and dangerman McLean was starved of possession. In the 77th minute Cliff Lambert scored the winning try for Rovers, for whom former Northern forward Bill Shreeve played a prominent role. Both clubs had agreed, if requested, not to allow the BBC to televise any part of the game, a decision that was fully justified because the tie was watched by 20,575 fans, easily Northern's biggest crowd of the season.

The following week, there were only 4,500 to see Castleford and the return to Odsal of transfer-listed Ernest Ward.The maestro scored a spectacular try and missed only two of nine shots at goal, including a last minute equaliser in the 23–23 draw. He had left Odsal after a 17-year association in November 1953, when a saga which lasted several months finally ended with Northern agreeing to Castleford's offer of £2,500. He made 391 appearances for Northern at full-back or centre, scored 117 tries and kicked 538 goals for a then club record 1,427 points. One of the most stylish rugby league players of all time, he captained Northern in their glory days and toured Australia and New Zealand with the British Lions in 1946 and 1950, the latter as captain. He also played full-back for England at rugby union during the war.

On Wednesday, 16 March Northern won the ball from only four of the first 24 scrums in the first 50 minutes of the floodlit game against Batley. However, once Neil Carter and Wynne Jones swapped positions at prop, they won abundant possession and Northern went onto win 26–4. Centre Ralph Winnard scored on his debut, but the former West Bowling junior injured his arm and was later moved to the wing

12

whenever the backs were switching from defence to attack. The son of Tom Winnard, Northern's international centre from the 1930s, this was his only first team appearance until 1956–57, due in part to National Service duties.

Rather than losing 17–15, Northern should have beaten Leeds at Headingley, as the top-four contenders were down to 12 men for the last hour of the game. However, Northern had no inside back to compare with either Lewis Jones or Jeff Stevenson, and their stereotyped passing could not force a victory in the thick mud. Their forwards failed miserably in the scrums and, apart from Ken Traill's scheming, which produced two tries, were also ineffective in the loose.

My first experience of Odsal under floodlights was on the following Wednesday, 30 March, when, sitting on the boundary fence, I witnessed Northern's easy 27–3 victory against lowly Dewsbury. Despite another scrum failure, thanks to the visitors' numerous blunders, Northern's threequarters had sufficient possession to score five tries. Up to that point, Dewsbury had won only four games, and in this match they conceded their 100th try and 500th point of the season – not that this seemed to upset the neighbouring Dewsbury supporter, who proudly wore her hand-knitted club scarf and good naturedly endured my childish taunts.

Forwards Neil Carter and Harry Griffett, the latter who had joined Northern in 1951 as an 18-year-old from the Hunslet Supporters' Club team, did more than enough to retain their places for the visit to Doncaster. However, with nothing to play for as far as the seniors were concerned, it was thought advisable that they should continue to give weight to the 'A' team's push for the Yorkshire Senior Competition's cup and league double. A former Batley junior, Carter had been signed after the Lazenby Cup game in August 1953, and made his debut on 27 March 1954 in a 36–13 win over Hull KR at Odsal, when Jack McLean's five tries took him past Emlyn Walters' all-time club record.

Northern's thrilling 22–15 victory at Tattersfield meant they remained unbeaten against Doncaster in league games, but it was not until the late stages – with Doncaster leading 15–11 – that they took control. McLean's power brought him another two tries, but it was the craft of both Foster and Traill, who also went over twice, which was the game's outstanding feature.

Northern then had a pointless Easter with defeats to both Warrington and Whitehaven. In a superb game at Odsal on Easter Saturday, in which former Wakefield Trinity second-rower, Tony Storey, had his best game of the season, Northern threw away countless chances in losing 13–8 to Warrington. Again deprived of possession, Northern had no schemer of the class of stand-off Gerry Helme or the elusiveness of centre Jim Challinor; the latter won the game with two brilliant tries. The crowd of 10,000 was considered to be extremely disappointing for such an attractive holiday fixture. Northern then travelled to Whitehaven on Easter Monday where they lost 12–4.

Before Northern's 30–25 win over 12-man Hunslet at Odsal on 16 April, which marked Trevor Foster's last home game before his retirement, Jack Burns commented: "One imagines that supporters will bid him an affectionate farewell, as not only has he graced the game as a player and coach, but his great-hearted displays, and scrupulous sportsmanship, have endeared him to followers of the code. No club ever had a better or more loyal player." Although Northern's general performance was as inconsistent as ever, the great man had a share in most of Northern's eight tries, including claiming the last one himself.

This was a feat I vaguely remember witnessing, while standing in my favourite spot near the side of the Old Stand. But I have no recall of Knopf's amazing run, which set up Bob Smith's second-half try. Despite being reduced to 12-men after only seven minutes, Hunslet actually managed to take the lead three times. But it was Trevor Foster's day, and at the end he was chaired off the field by Ken Traill, and his great friend and adversary, Arthur Clues.

On the following Wednesday at Belle Vue, Northern lost 31–12 to Wakefield Trinity. The game was thrown away in the first half-hour when Trinity's forwards scored four tries. After this game Trevor Foster retired from playing rugby. Since signing in 1938 he had made 430 appearances for Northern, scored 130 tries and kicked one goal. He represented Wales and Great Britain as well as touring Australasia in 1946. A try-scorer at Wembley in 1947 and 1949 and the club's joint record match try-scorer, with six against Wakefield Trinity on 10 April 1948, Trevor's contribution to Northern and the Bradford community is legendary. The Belle Vue game also marked Gwylfa Jones' last senior appearance and the end of Barry Tyler's distinguished Odsal career – before his close season move to Doncaster.

The 'A' team were still in the running to achieve a league and cup double and on the same night over 2,000 were at Odsal to see them beat Hunslet. They then moved to the top of the Yorkshire Senior Competition by beating Hull 18–7 at Odsal. Alan Winnard, the elder brother of Ralph and also a former West Bowling junior, kicked five goals. Harry Griffett and Jimmy Glynn scored tries before another 2,000 crowd. However, a defeat to Wakefield Trinity meant they finished second, behind Halifax. They then lost to Keighley in the league semi-final play-off at Odsal and lost in the cup semi-final at Wakefield.

Former Hunslet scrum-half, Roy Goddard, who made his debut against Bramley in March 1951 and had been Northern's first-choice scrum-half in 1953–54, missed both the latter games due to being suspended for five games because of illegal scrum feeding – clearly a heinous offence in those days. Ralph Winnard was still out injured, but a typical 'A' line-up around this time included the following, with the sub-editors struggling with Kosanovic and Scroby's names: Alan Winnard, Morgan, Jenkins, Gardner, Cawthra, Sharrock, Goddard, Fuller, Collins, Carter, Milan (sic), H. Griffett, Scrobie (sic), and loose-forward Glynn – the latter who was originally a full-back when he was signed in August 1952 after playing trials the previous season. Alan Winnard never made the first team, but later moved to Doncaster and Bramley, where he played and scored against Northern.

Unfortunately, the first team could not match the 'A' team's record, and their final position of 17th in the league was the worst for five seasons. Northern's inconsistency meant they needed to concentrate on team building if they were to win back the support they had lost during the season – down from an average 12,134 to 8,570 – and at the end of April 1955 they bid £2,000 plus a front-row forward for Castleford's centre Denzil Webster. But he preferred to move to York, where both he and his wife were teachers. At the same time, local junior product, Wynne Jones,who had made his debut against Huddersfield on 22 April 1950, was placed on the transfer-list at £1,000 after refusing the open-side prop position.

1954–55 Summary
Position in league: 17th of 31: P 36 W 17 L 17 D 2 - Pts 476–475
Average attendance: 8,570 (7,611 league games only)
Yorkshire Cup: Semi-final. Challenge Cup: Round two

Odsal legends

Above: Dai Rees
Right: Harry Hornby

Above: Russ Pepperall and Trevor Foster
lead the teams out for the Challenge Cup tie
against Huddersfield on 14 March 1953,
which attracted a record Odsal crowd for a
Bradford Northern match of 69,429.
(Courtesy Robert Gate).

Right: Frank Whitcombe in action for
Northern at Wembley against Halifax in
1949.

3. 1955–56: Two Kiwis leave
Exit Jack McLean and Joe Phillips

At the RFL AGM, on 9 August 1955, Belle Vue Rangers were voted out of the league, as a consequence of which, with the fixtures already having been published,the league table for the new season was to be worked out on a percentage basis.

At pre-season training, coach Trevor Foster welcomed a new signing, former Morley and Yorkshire rugby union hooker, Norman Mackie, and, among other players, three promising reserves were now in line for a first team place: Milan Kosanovic, Jack Scroby and Brian Hambling. A product of Hull junior rugby, blind-side prop Hambling had made his senior debut for Northern, against Castleford, in November 1952. But, due to being posted overseas by the Army at the back end of 1953, he made only eight appearances during his first two seasons and played no first team rugby in 1954–55.

Jack Scroby, an 18-year-old draughtsman, signed from that very productive nursery for Northern, Ovenden; while Yugoslav Milan Kosanovic also played in the Halifax League, with Pellon, before propping for Northern's 'A' team in the 1954–55 season, after trials with Halifax. It was not until April 1956 that he packed down at number nine with the first team, but he only ousted Mackie as the regular hooker at the start of the 1957–58 season.

The Lazenby Cup friendly against Keighley, won by Northern 23–22, was nominated as Trevor Foster's Testimonial game. It was ceremonially kicked off by the popular Yorkshire cricketer, Johnny Wardle. Trevor's fund was closed at £950 and he later received a cheque for £1,005. There were first appearances for both Mackie and Kosanovic; while 20-year-old Eric Hamilton, who had played occasionally in the previous two seasons before going overseas on National Service, impressed at half-back.

Northern had tried Joe Phillips at centre and Bill Seddon at full-back in the pipe-opener. This experiment was quickly dispensed with, however, and both were back in their customary roles in the 23–8 victory over struggling Liverpool City at Knotty Ash, where the poor state of the pitch was causing concern. There were first team debuts for Kosanovic, Mackie and Scroby, and Hambling made the first of his

42 appearances that season at blind-side prop. Ken Traill was a dominant force and, because Northern were never in danger of losing, they did not need to over exert themselves in the sweltering conditions.

Wynne Jones, although selected for the Liverpool game, had not yet re-signed for the new season and his fee was progressively reduced from £1,000 to £750. He started playing in October and asked to be taken off the transfer list in November. With the recruitment of Les Belshaw from Barrow for £1,000, Jones moved into the second-row for all, but two, of his 19 games during the season. Belshaw had played for four years for Old Thornesians before signing for the newly-formed Doncaster in 1951 and was a member of Barrow's 1955 Challenge Cup-winning side.

In the 40–14 win over Bramley at a sun-drenched Odsal, Northern secured possession from only eight of the 40 scrums – including only two in the second-half. However, the visitors were handicapped by their own ineptitude, as well as having their injured centre Harding a passenger from the 14th minute. Joe Phillips' bewildering running helped set up four tries for Jack McLean, as Northern ran in 10 tries, much to the supporters' delight.

Hodgson replaced Mackie for Hunslet's visit to Odsal in the Yorkshire Cup first round, and the fears that Northern would be punished in the scrums proved to be unfounded in a thrill-packed game watched by a crowd of nearly 9,000. Ken Traill's skilful leadership of his new forwards, plus the all-round ability of Northern's backs – seven more tries in the 27–23 victory – led the *Telegraph & Argus's* 'Oracle' to enthuse about the attractive nature of Northern's play and the likely return of bigger crowds to Odsal.

Early in September Brian Radford was transfer-listed at £750, but later in the month both he and Bill Jenkins asked to be taken off the transfer list after Northern had agreed terms with Batley for both the long-serving players. At that stage in their careers neither Welshman had been able to command a regular first team place, but decided that they still wished to remain at Odsal. There had been no enquiries for Wynne Jones, Ken Traill, listed at £4,000, nor for 30-year-old Gwylfa Jones, the regular scrum-half in 1954–55, who was listed at £500.

The first defeat of the season came at Headingley, where a 12-man Leeds, for most of the second-half, easily dealt with Northern's attacks. The only encouraging feature in the 24–12 defeat was the first-class performance of Jack Scroby in only his third senior game. This was Tony Storey's last game for Northern before the second-rower was transferred to Featherstone Rovers for £1,000, which was then Rovers' highest ever transfer fee. Having been at Odsal since April 1953, he moved from Featherstone to Warrington in December 1956 after taking up a teaching post in Newton-le-Willows.

For the Yorkshire Cup second round tie at Bramley, prop Rodney Thomas, a 21-year-old former Pellon junior, was promoted after only three 'A' team games; and Harry Griffett took over Storey's position in the second-row. Northern won only 16 of the 47 scrums, but the revised pack, which was well organised by Ken Traill, performed aggressively in the loose in Northern's 12–5 victory. Len Haley tore his ankle ligaments, and his enforced absence gave Sutton the opportunity to establish himself at stand-off. This was David Knopf's last senior game for Northern, having scored 30 tries in his 57 appearances, as he returned to Johannesburg following a short spell with the 'A' team after he recovered from injury.

The following day at Odsal, Northern easily beat Batley 31–13 with attractive passing in the second-half resulting in McLean going over for another four tries. Joe Phillips kicked three spectacular goals in the first quarter, but had to hand over to Seddon following a knee injury. Brendan Cope, a former Bradford junior who scored a try for Batley, later joined Northern on trial until the end of the season.

Unfortunately, Northern failed to use their wingers at Parkside, where Jack McLean took his only chance of the game to score Northern's points in a 16–3 defeat. Hunslet scored 10 unanswered points in the last 10 minutes to become the only side to then have a 100 per cent league record.

Northern took a long time to settle at Hull KR, but near the end they established a 15–8 winning lead, despite the lack of possession from the scrums and the 70th minute dismissal of scrum-half Roy Goddard. Not once so far this season had Northern won an equal share of the ball in the scrums and despite the recall of Mackie they again struggled in this area. However, they made amends with fine defensive work and entertaining back play, with Phillips the chief menace from full-back.

On the following Tuesday evening, Northern were unlucky to lose 23–16 in the Yorkshire Cup semi-final at Hull before a crowd of 16,000. The enthusiasm of the young pack meant only two points separated the sides for most of the game. Hull's first seven points were doubtful, including a try by international Harry Markham, who appeared to bounce the ball. It was only 18–16 with 14 minutes to go, but Hull held the ball for the last seven minutes and posted a further try. Due to business commitments in London, right-winger Bob Smith had cried off, but the ever reliable Bill Jenkins stepped in, and scored one of Northern's two tries. This was the last senior game for Roy Goddard, who, tragically, in December, 1956 had to have a leg amputated following a serious motor accident.

Scrum-half Eric Hamilton, who had earlier represented Cumberland against Lancashire, returned for the visit of Leigh. The Lancashire Cup finalists were averaging over 30 points a game, but Northern produced a great performance and won 35–16 before the season's second highest crowd – 10,500. Once again the youthful pack, under Ken Traill's leadership, was the cornerstone of the victory. It was reported that the crowds would roll up to Odsal if Northern could regularly produce this form.

Northern retained the same side at Station Road, where they were unfortunate to lose Hamilton with concussion after only 20 minutes. However, it was more the general lack of team effort that led to their 10–6 defeat to Swinton, and their failure to register a single try. Apart from some inexcusable tackling lapses, Northern then put in a much better performance in beating Workington Town 29–19 at Odsal, where there was brilliant co-operation between the backs. Bill Jenkins was a success at stand-off and Seddon outstanding at centre; wingers Bob Smith with a hat-trick and McLean with two, scored five of Northern's seven tries.

In a 20–10 defeat of Doncaster, Jack McLean then produced two 70-yard try-scoring runs in his hat-trick at Tattersfield, where Scroby damaged a shoulder in the first few minutes, but did not leave the field until 10 minutes from the end. Graham Oddy, an 18-year-old, former Ovenden scrum-half, made his debut, but his scope was limited due to a lack of possession. Unlike several of his contemporaries, during his time in the forces Oddy was able to get away regularly to assist the club because he was based mostly at a Halifax depot.

In Northern's 34–20 win against Castleford at Odsal, Ernest Ward was bamboozled by Bob Smith's kick and chase for a try; and Seddon went the length of the field for one of his brace. Unfortunately, stand-off Jenkins broke a rib after 63 minutes and was out of the game for the next five weeks. It was poignant that after playing so many great games alongside Ernest Ward at club and international level, this was 29-year-old Ken Traill's last game for Northern before he signed for Halifax for a fee of £2,750

Traill's departure allowed Jimmy Glynn to establish himself at loose-forward and he made his debut on the last Saturday of October, when Northern entered the top-four after beating Huddersfield 14–2 before their top crowd of the season, 12,000. The Fartowners' sixth successive defeat at Odsal was mainly due to their middle backs' poor performance, who squandered a 3–1 advantage in the scrums, but Northern defended stoutly. Joe Phillips, with a try and four goals, was Northern's most influential back; Wynne Jones was their best forward and made Radford's try.

Although Northern lost Len Haley after only 16 minutes, Featherstone Rovers deservedly won 21–8 to inflict Northern's first home defeat of the season. With the debut of Les Belshaw at open-side prop, Northern fared better in the scrums, but it was not until Phillips moved to stand-off in the last quarter that they really looked dangerous.

This proved to be scrum-half Eric Hamilton's last game. The former Cumbrian miner had rarely been able to travel to Odsal for training and in March 1956, after making only 16 appearances since his debut in 1953–54, he was loaned to Workington Town, with a view to him transferring to his hometown club. He later signed for Whitehaven in 1958–59.

The following Saturday, 12 November, there were no league games in the West Riding, because Odsal hosted the second test against New Zealand. Great Britain won 27–12 before a crowd of 24,443, who paid £3,998, the highest of the tour. As previously mentioned the tourists included former Northern favourite, Bob Hawes.

Northern's visit to Castleford saw the lead change hands seven times, and if the home side had not squandered abundant possession, they would have taken the points. Ernest Ward showed that he was still an expert at relieving pressure, but it was Joe Phillips' superior goalkicking which won Northern the game, 19–17.

With Northern's backs, with the exception of Jenkins, well below form, debutant wingman Brian Todd, a former Halifax junior, received only a handful of passes in the 11–6 defeat to the understrength New Zealanders. Played before a crowd of only 5,271, who paid £711, under the Odsal lights, the game was marred by numerous infringements at the scrum and play-the-ball, but scrum-half Graham Oddy still managed to impress. At the request of the tourists, schoolboys aged under 14 were allowed in free – an idea which Northern later used for under 15s, who were required to assemble at the bottom car park gate 15 minutes before the kick-off.

In late November 1955 clubs were keen to get their hands on a share of the £20,000 1954 tour profits, but Bill Fallowfield, the RFL secretary, said the money had been ploughed into gilt-edged securities and loans to clubs for ground improvements. Northern had benefited with a £5,000 loan towards the estimated £7,000 cost of reseeding the Odsal pitch, but the club would still have welcomed a cash handout. At Northern's AGM on 1 December 1955, the accounts for the year ending June 1955 revealed their worst ever year financially, with a loss of £5,815, making a debit balance of £12,207. In the 1954–55 season receipts had dropped to £21,466, producing a net income of £12,805. Because of the team's poor form, players' wages were down to £8,469, but ground repairs had cost £3,661 and there was a loss on transfer fees of £2,051.

Cyril Bunney, a top maker and spinning manufacturer, became vice-chairman. In the previous 18 months, Harry Hornby Junior, his namesake's nephew, and Frank Whitcombe, in September 1955, had also joined the board, and along with team manager Dai Rees, Harry Hornby Senior (the chief shareholder), Len Dobson, a former Northern player from the Birch Lane days, and R. C. Yablon, a local solicitor, they were both re-elected.

At Odsal, Northern had taken revenge over Hull for the earlier Yorkshire Cup defeat, being assured of their 14–6 victory once the youthful pack had tamed the mighty Hull six. Jenkins and Sutton produced some fine work, and Jack McLean continued his try-scoring exploits with another two tries.

Northern then left it late to beat Hull KR 31–13, and only moved in front when the visitors lost their full-back, Golding, through injury. Phillips and McLean accounted for 25 of Northern's points in this game. It was therefore no surprise when both New Zealanders were chosen to play for a Rugby League XIII against New Zealand at Odsal on

Wednesday 7 December, when the tourists were beaten 24–11 before a crowd of only 3,643; the second-half of this floodlit game was televised. Phillips and McLean then played at Wheldon Road on the following Monday, in a charity match for the dependents of Dennis Norton, who had collapsed and died during Castleford's game against the tourists.

Because of the failing light, the floodlights were switched on for the last 25 minutes of the 27–0 victory over Liverpool City, which was watched by the lowest crowd of the season, 2,400. McLean scored another three tries, one of which was made by Oddy, and Joe Phillips produced a brilliant display of goalkicking, despite the high winds and mud-covered ball.

Northern stayed overnight at Keswick on only their fifth visit to Workington Town, where they lost 26–8. This was mainly due to the speed of wingers Ike Southward and Ralph McCarten, and the superiority of the Harry Archer and John Roper half-back combination.

The proposed Saturday game at Odsal on Christmas Eve against York was postponed because the covering of straw was still frozen solid. But a thaw set in to allow Northern gain revenge for last season with a comfortable Christmas double over Keighley – 16–5 at Odsal on Boxing Day and 17–2 at Lawkholme Lane, the following day. Both games were played on quagmires of pitches.

At Odsal, where Keighley had agreed to a later kick-off in order for the second-half to be played under floodlights, a rare 3–1 scrum advantage in the first-half helped Northern to victory. Wynne Jones and Jimmy Glynn, who was outstanding in both games, frequently tore holes in the Keighley defence, while Jack McLean was the difference in the backs with two tries through his strong finishing. It was the first time that season that Terry Hollindrake, who earlier had been selected for Great Britain, had failed to score in a league game. At a rain-swept Lawkholme Lane, Northern had the advantage of the elements in the second-half after leading 5–2 at half-time through a McLean try. Two further goals from Phillips ended Keighley's hopes and there were late tries by Radford and Jones.

Northern had won only once at The Boulevard since the war – 5–3 in January 1947. Therefore, the Northern supporters who made the journey on 31 December 1955 were well satisfied up to half-time, when Hull led by only six points from two 'suspect' tries. However, in the second-half Northern, who were then fourth in the table, capitulated and a 28–4 defeat cost them the leadership of the Yorkshire League.

For the league game on 7 January, Wakefield Trinity's players would not agree to a later start in order to play the second-half under Odsal's lights. This had been agreed to by the clubs to avoid a direct clash with Bradford City's league game at Valley Parade and the FA Cup tie at Park Avenue, where 18,524 saw Middlesbrough progress 4–0. At Odsal, where the attendance was 6,000, Trinity's full-back Eric Lockwood damaged a leg after 20 minutes, but Trinity still managed to wipe off an early 10 point deficit before Northern ran out 34–10 winners.Youngsters Hambling, Glynn, and Oddy, all try-scorers on the day, continued to impress.

Northern then moved back into the top-four following their hard earned 15–5 victory over Batley at Mount Pleasant. This was largely thanks to the combined effort of the forwards and the Seddon-McLean combination. The left-wing partnership was then the most prolific in the league; Seddon had put on a yard or two of pace from the previous season.

As West Yorkshire continued to be gripped by snow and ice through much of January, 10 tons of straw had been used to protect the Odsal pitch. However, the game against Hunslet was abandoned after 69 minutes because the referee could not distinguish the players due to the muddy conditions, although Northern had changed their jerseys and the floodlights were switched on. Northern led 18–3 at that late stage and the result was allowed to stand. Sutton, who was then seen as mainly a reserve stand-off, played well at centre, and scored one of Northern's four tries.

The irresistible Jack McLean claimed his sixth hat-trick of the season in the 26–7 win at Bramley, where Phillips's initial breaks and Seddon's direct running added greatly to Northern's attack. After another strong performance, Brian Hambling was being tipped for international honours.

Northern thought the Thrum Hall pitch was unplayable, but Eric Clay, who was then considered to be one of the game's most promising referees, decided at noon that the game should go ahead. In Northern's 17–12 defeat to Halifax he disallowed 'tries' for both McLean and Seddon, added to which Mageen failed to touch down after crossing the line. There was said to be an amazing improvement in the work of Northern's forwards, who were up against the might of Halifax's pack, which consisted of mainly international players. But, in the end, Northern were outdone by Ken Traill, who produced brilliant passes to make two of Halifax's three tries.

In peace time, Northern had not failed to reach the second round of the Challenge Cup since 1935, and there was a sizeable following at Parkside to see them defeat Hunslet 10–9 – a victory achieved with little or no ball. After the first 10 minutes, Haley clung like a leech to dangerman Brian Gabbitas and Northern's forwards contained the home six with tremendous tackling. There were tries for McLean and Jenkins, and, with his second goal, Joe Phillips broke Ernest Ward's club record of 1,427 points. Harry Griffett finished with five stitches in a head wound and Hambling, recovering from concussion in St Luke's Hospital, only discovered that Northern had won at 10pm that evening.

After two weeks of league postponements, in the Challenge Cup second round against Rochdale Hornets, Northern's forwards made up for their poor scrummaging technique with excellent covering and forceful loose play at the Athletic Grounds. A crowd of 12,364 saw Northern triumph 5–2. Hornets had no one to match either Joe Phillips, for his outstanding covertackling, or the elusive Len Haley, who made the only try of the match for McLean 10 minutes from the close

Against Leigh in the league campaign under the Hilton Park lights, Northern defended heroically, after Haley retired in the third minute with a head wound, and only lost 7–2 in the dying minutes. Phillips gave a great exhibition of kicking, and completely overshadowed his opposite number, Jimmy Ledgard.

Hodgson fared no better at winning possession than Mackie, who had been dropped after the Challenge Cup second round. However, after being drawn against St Helens in the third round, it was considered that Northern had done enough to worry Saints coach, Jim Sullivan, who was present at the game.

Most of the league game at Belle Vue was played in Northern territory, but despite constant onslaughts Trinity only once found a way through Northern's defence. It was full-back Eric Lockwood's goalkicking which won the day – 11–10 – as both Scroby and Smith crossed for Northern, but Phillips only managed two goals from eight attempts.

Early in the game against Featherstone Rovers at Odsal, Bill Seddon breaks, supported by Jack McLean. Len Haley, in the background, went off injured after only 16 minutes. (Courtesy Robert Gate)

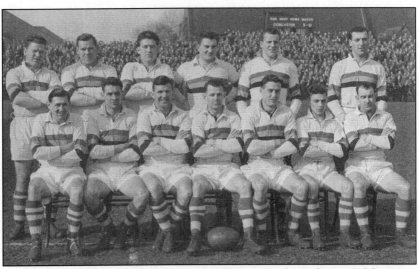

The side against Wakefield Trinity at Belle Vue. Back: Hodgson, Belshaw, Hambling, Glynn, Scroby, Harry Griffett; Front: Seddon, Bob Smith, McLean, Phillips, Mageen, Oddy, Sutton. (Courtesy Robert Gate)

Two successive rearranged league games were then played under the Odsal lights, on 14 and 19 March, against Leeds and York respectively. Leeds rested several key players, including scrum-half Jeff Stevenson, but still managed to produce a dazzling display of handling to outclass Northern 17–5. This fourth successive league defeat just about ended any hopes of a top-four spot and with it the players' £500 share out. Against York, Brendan Cope, the trialist from Batley, made his only first team appearance for Northern on the right-wing. York were unlucky to lose 9–4 because Northern had to rely on the sheer brilliance of Jack McLean, who scored another hat-trick of tries.

The keenly anticipated Challenge Cup tie against St Helens saw Northern quickly sell their allocation of 1,000 stand tickets plus a further 300 on the popular side. History was on Northern's side, having beaten Saints on all three occasions in post-war Challenge Cup ties. However, their coach, Jim Sullivan, had moulded Saints into the best team in the league and they had a league double over Northern in 1953–54, in the only previous post-war league meetings.

Because of the fixture congestion, there was no special preparation, apart from a massage and steam bath on the Wednesday, and a pre-match briefing on the Thursday. With scrum possession vital against the best pack in Lancashire, Northern persevered with Hodgson at hooker, and opted for the hefty Wynne Jones in the second-row over the faster and more elusive Griffett. However, any planning that Northern had made could not have prepared them for the 53–6 hammering that they suffered at the hands of the eventual Cup winners, before a crowd of 22,485.

Compared to their first round form, Northern's rugby was said to be, "like stale beer to champagne". While Saints were hardly ever out of top gear, several of their 11 tries were the result of terrible defensive blunders, and the fact that Northern finished with five injured players could not be used as an excuse for such a pathetic performance. Hambling had deputised for Dennis Hodgson in the second-half after the hooker's ear was split in two; Dai Rees described the injury as the worst he had ever seen. It was a sad end to Hodgson's senior Odsal career, in what was Northern's heaviest defeat for 22 years, since Hunslet beat them 57–2 at Parkside on 20 January 1934. Despite losing their hooker, McCabe, after threequarter time, Saints still managed to score 26 points in the final 11 minutes.

As the league season neared its conclusion, Halifax refused to play under the Odsal lights, because the 12–12 draw could well have been a top-four decider. The crowd of 9,000 was considered good for a 5.30pm kick-off. Only Northern and Leigh had floodlights at this time, which explained some team's reluctance to play under them. Ken Traill was strangely subdued against his old colleagues, and Northern won the majority of possession in the scrums – a rare feat against Halifax. Northern went in front for the first time after 71 minutes, but a penalty three minutes later evened the scores.

The most encouraging feature of the game, from Northern's point of view, was the play of former Cleckheaton rugby union scrum-half, Alan Lancaster, who, on his debut, had a hand in both of McLean's tries. In 1947, as a 15-year-old, Alan Lancaster was a founder member of Shaw Cross in Dewsbury, a club which became a prodigious nursery for young rugby league players, and produced many future internationals, including Mick Sullivan. In 2008 he was awarded the MBE for services to young people.

Their first league defeat at Featherstone since September 1934 dashed the faint hopes that Northern might secure a top-four spot. They led by six points after only eight minutes, but conceded six tries for only the second time that season in the league, and lost 26–12.

On Easter Monday at Odsal, they were then held to a 17–17 draw by Doncaster in a game which marked the debut of former 19-year-old Ovenden stand-off, Derek Davies, who was one of Northern's try-scorers. As well as having electric acceleration on the rugby field, in July 1959 Davies was clocked at 10.1 seconds for the 100 yards, when representing the Army versus Queens University, Belfast, and 10.5 in the Northern Ireland District Army Championships.

Odsal staged another major match when Halifax failed to impress in beating Wigan 11–10 in the Challenge Cup semi-final before a crowd of 51,889. They struggled in defence for threequarters of the game before Alvin Ackerley won 11 of the last 13 scrums. Stan Kielty had a hand in each of Halifax's three tries, including selling first-half try-scorer, Billy Boston, an outrageous dummy to send centre Geoff Palmer over for the crucial try.

Northern made eight changes for an 11–7 win over Huddersfield at Fartown, and played Kosanovic at hooker for the first time. Hundreds of the crowd left long before the end of this drab affair, which was lightened only by the brilliant wing play of Jack McLean and Mick Sullivan, both of whom scored 50-yard run tries.

The last home game of the season, against Swinton, had the added poignancy of being advertised as the final Odsal appearance for Northern's outstanding New Zealanders, Joe Phillips, Jack McLean and Bill Seddon. However, there was a disappointing crowd of 6,000 for such an occasion, which was marked by McLean scoring five tries in the 27–13 win, thus taking him to the top of the league's try-scoring chart with 60. Phillips managed only two goals from his 10 shots at goal, and was outshone on the day in this department by his opposite number, Jack Tobin. Northern looked to be heading for another defeat, but scored 21 points in a 17 minute spell in the second-half. It was also a memorable game for Norman Haigh who made his only first team appearance on the opposite wing to McLean.

Including his debut at York on 30 September 1950, Joe Phillips, a former junior rugby union international from Wellington, made 232 appearances for Northern scoring 661 goals and 47 tries for a total of 1,463 points. Both goals and points totals were then club records. Joe Phillips still holds two Northern records, with his four tries from full-back, scored against Halifax on 20 October, 1951 and his 14 goals in the 64–5 defeat of Batley at Odsal on 6 September 1952. After running a hotel business in Cornwall, Phillips decided to come out of retirement in September 1956, which resulted in Northern transfer-listing him at £3,000. However, he argued that he was a free agent and the dispute was only settled on 22 January 1957, when the Rugby League Council dismissed Northern's appeal against their earlier decision and sided with the player. He signed for Keighley on the same day.

Northern's greatest ever winger, Jack McLean, scored a record 261 tries in 221 appearances for Northern after making his debut at Bramley on 21 October 1950. This included a record 63 tries in the 1951–52 season. He scored a modest 11 tries in his first season, when the former All Black took a while to adjust to his new code, but then registered more than 50 tries – 63, 59, 52, and 60 – in four of his six seasons at the club. Only an injury in the 1954–55 season prevented even more.

On Thursday 19 April, Seddon attended a farewell party before his planned return to New Zealand. However, the following day he cancelled his boat reservation after Harry Hornby talked him into staying with the promise of a suitable business appointment. With the loss of Phillips, Seddon was seen as a valuable replacement at full-back and, although not in the same class as Phillips, an accurate enough goalkicker.

That Friday evening, the season ended at Clarence Street, where Northern, including all three New Zealanders, put in an indifferent performance in losing 21–6 in a rearranged game against York. Northern had very little to offer other than occasional breaks by promising youngster Lancaster, who nonetheless could not quite keep the experienced county player W. Riley in check. Therefore, after a promising start, in which they had been serious top-four contenders, the season ended on a low note, and the loss of McLean and Phillips, together with the departure of Storey and Traill, would be badly felt. The next week most of West Yorkshire was under six inches of snow and the Bradford Amateur Cup final between Queensbury and Wyke at Odsal on 26 April was cancelled.

1955–56 Summary
Position in league: 8th of 31 P 36 W 22 L 12 D 2 – Pts 622–455
Yorkshire Cup: Semi-final. Challenge Cup: Third round.
Average attendance: 6,881 (6,856 league games only)

Joe Phillips, supported by Jack McLean and Norman Mackie, makes a break during the 1955–56 season. (Courtesy Robert Gate)

Les Belshaw, who joined Northern from Barrow in the 1955–56 season. (Courtesy Tony Capstick)

Jack McLean hands off a Leeds defender at a packed Headingley, with
Bob Smith in the background.

Left: Graham Oddy, one of several former Ovenden juniors
who joined Northern. (Courtesy Tony Capstick)
Right: Malcolm Davies, who joined Northern from Leigh,
pictured in his Welsh jersey.

4. 1956–57: Malcolm Davies
Uproar as new Welsh flier sold to Leeds

Northern made only two pre-season signings of any note: Malcolm Davies and Trevor Jones. 28-year-old Davies, a former Glamorgan policeman, had scored 79 tries in 84 appearances for Leigh since turning professional in 1953, including a record 38 in the 1955–56 season. The former Penarth and Glamorgan county union player had been chosen for Welsh rugby union international trials along with Lewis Jones and was in the Welsh rugby league side against France in 1953. After a dispute with his club, Davies, who was over six feet tall, had threatened to quit the game and Northern, who were desperate to fill the gap left by Jack McLean's retirement, moved in quickly in the summer to pay Leigh a bargain price of £750 for him.

Trevor Jones, Batley's 26-year-old second-rower, was then signed for only £250, having been listed since December at £1,000. He originally played in the pack for Ossett in the Dewsbury League, but was selected at stand-off or centre when he played rugby union for the RAF Group Command while serving in Germany. Following trials with Dewsbury as a centre, he joined Batley in February 1952. He was still extremely mobile in the loose and was also a useful goalkicker. He was easily distinguishable on the field as he invariably wore a scrum cap. Jones was a try-scorer in the Lazenby Cup at Keighley on Tuesday 14 August, when Northern were well beaten 19–13. Full-back Seddon, who was easily Northern's best back, added two late tries and a conversion when Keighley eased up at the end.

Ken Ward, who had previously played with Doncaster, Halifax, Oldham and Leeds, was promoted from the 'A' team. But, apart from this friendly, the centre or full-back made only five senior appearances in his career at Odsal before announcing his retirement. Unfortunately, all were in a losing side because Northern were beaten in their first seven league and cup games in a disastrous start to the new campaign.

In the first league game of the season, on an afternoon of torrential rain, Ward partnered Malcolm Davies at Belle Vue, where Trevor Jones also made his full debut in a 10–7 loss to Wakefield Trinity. Derek Davies and Alan Lancaster impressed as a half-back pairing; and the former's brilliant change of pace made a try for right-winger Bob Smith.

Against Leeds, in the evening of Wednesday 22 August, the lead changed hands four times in the first 10 minutes and there was no indication that Northern were to concede 40 points at Odsal for the first time ever, in losing 40–14. Even when Bob Smith broke his collarbone after 15 minutes Northern only trailed 16–7 at half-time. However, as gaps began to appear Lewis Jones helped himself to a hat-trick of tries and kicked 11 goals from 13 attempts for a club record 31 points. On his home debut, Malcolm Davies scored a brilliant try, which must have been noted by the Leeds directors in the crowd of 10,500 – a figure which was not beaten in the league until the reformation of the club.

Due to their improved position in the previous season's table, Northern had to play Lancashire's top three clubs. However, they were made to look distinctly second rate in a 34–7 thrashing by the Challenge Cup holders St Helens at Odsal. With Belshaw injured, newcomer Trevor Jones was the only forward to match Saints' mighty pack, while winger Todd showed his more experienced colleagues how to tackle. This attractive Saturday fixture attracted only 5,500 fans, which hardly helped the club's perilous finances.

The need for team strengthening was again all too evident when Huddersfield ran in nine tries at Fartown on the following Wednesday, to inflict Northern's biggest league defeat, 45–10, since the war. Thus, during my family's annual holiday on the east coast, Northern had conceded 119 points, including 23 tries, and rewritten the record books. After all our fun at the seaside, the reports of those games made painful reading.

The following week, a loss of £781 and a debit balance of £4,786, on the year ending June 1956, was declared to shareholders at the AGM. In view of the declining gates, chairman Harry Hornby thought it was a satisfactory balance sheet; while director-manager Dai Rees said they realised two or three experienced players or personalities were needed to guide the promising youngsters, but there was a limit to the offers they could make to rugby league clubs or rugby union men.

Later, at an open meeting on 28 January, Dai Rees let it be known that, at the beginning of the season, Northern had a list of six Welsh rugby union players, to whom they had been prepared to pay up to £2,000, but every player they had approached had turned them down.

Northern's leaky defence yielded another five tries at Wheldon Road in the Yorkshire Cup first round, although they matched Castleford try for try – including four to the brilliant Malcolm Davies. However, they could manage only one goal,from 11 attempts by four players, and lost 23–17. It was felt that with better service Davies would have won Northern the game. The obvious need was for a first-class goalkicker to replace Joe Phillips, because neither Bill Jenkins nor Bill Seddon could be relied on for consistent accuracy. Former Wyke junior Fred Lee made his debut at scrum-half, the first of only five first team appearances, including one against the Australians, in some of which he was the goalkicker. He later moved to Castleford in 1957–58.

Matters went from bad to worse with the news that Northern's powerful centre, Joe Mageen, was refusing to play for the club again, after suffering verbal abuse from a small section of the Odsal crowd during the heavy defeat to Leeds. He was the game's most prolific try-scoring middle back as a member of Northern's 1952 Championship leaders' squad, and a medal winner with Northern's 1953 Yorkshire Cup side. As well as representing Yorkshire in 1954 and 1956, the former Ovenden junior made 202 appearances for Northern from 1949, and scored 69 tries. Mageen was quickly signed by Halifax for an undisclosed fee and made his debut against Dewsbury on Monday 3 September. He subsequently moved to Hull KR, and played there until he retired in 1959.

On the same night, before a crowd of only 1,400, Northern unveiled a speedster in 20-year-old Stan Rodwell, who scored four tries from the left-wing in a 20–8 victory over the reigning French Champions, Albi, who were on a four match tour. On the Wednesday, the former Wakefield junior, who had just finished his National Service, then made his full debut against York at Odsal, when Northern's "bad positioning, faulty covering and weak tackling" led to a 17–5 defeat.

Because he was attending a business course, Len Haley was fortunate to miss a 41–16 humiliation by Barrow at Odsal, where, with an international second-row of Reg Parker and Jack Grundy, some of the Barrow forwards seemed faster than the home backs. Northern's frail midfield defence was so mesmerised by the great stand-off, Willie Horne, and the Great Britain centre, Phil Jackson, that only one of Barrow's nine tries was scored by a winger. Barrow's jerseys that day were a striking cherry with a white V, so for many years I wrongly assumed they were the club's first choice colours. The Barrow supporter, who had kindly pointed out to me the intricacies of his side's play, failed to mention this fact.

Northern left the bottom of the table with a 19–7 win at Doncaster, where Derek Davies had some brilliant runs and Seddon, without the responsibility of captaincy, returned to form. However, this first league win of the season was achieved against very weak opposition. Therefore, the directors could not relax in their efforts to sign new players and that weekend they were busy scouting in South Wales.

Malcolm Davies, the league's most prolific try-scorer at this stage in the season, took some near impossible chances to score a hat-trick in a 21–18 defeat at Featherstone.Seddon was Northern's best defensive player, but managed only three of seven attempts at goal, while Rovers held their slim lead despite being without their hooker for the last hour.

After a blank Saturday, the following Wednesday, 3 October, a floodlit test trial, Great Britain versus the Rest of League, attracted a disappointing crowd of only 6,477 to Odsal. The RFL secretary, Bill Fallowfield, said it had been a "pointless exercise" and argued that genuine competitive games, and not the appearance of personalities, really interested the public.

On his first team debut, Douglas Maclean, the former Wyke centre and winger, scored a try in a 22–10 victory at Hull KR, where Northern produced their best performance of the season so far. Carter, Jones, and try-scorers Radford and Lancaster were prominent, and Seddon found his goalkicking boots to land five.

On Monday, 8 October, two games, watched by a meagre crowd of 1,084, who paid £112, were played under the Odsal floodlights as the authorities experimented with different methods of bringing the ball back into play after the tackle. First up was Leigh 26 Oldham 12, who played under the rugby union rules of immediate release, followed by Northern 14 Huddersfield 6, who were instructed to play-the-ball forward. Nine out of 10 spectators, who bothered to vote on their preference, opted for the latter of the two methods, which I recall produced more turn-over of ball than the normal game of rugby league, but much aimless kicking down field. 'Oracle' argued that the rugby union method was shelved over 50 years ago and it would be best to keep it on the shelf for another 50 years.

Despite losing 16–11 to Warrington at Odsal, Northern so impressed the 6,000 spectators that the players were given standing ovations at half-time and the final whistle in this exciting game. Northern would have won, but they had no player in midfield who could impose a steadying influence, and consequently Malcolm Davies was neglected on the wing.

Australia selected 10 test players for the floodlit game against Northern on 24 October, when only 3,000 spectators braved the elements. Bob Smith, who had scored four tries in the 'A' team on the previous Saturday, replaced Len Haley, who had injured a leg in training. Derek Davies was rested and Douglas Maclean given an opportunity at stand-off. Malcolm Davies was the best back on the field, his brilliant hat-trick of tries helped Northern to an 11–8 lead, which they held for 10 minutes thanks to sterling work by the forwards. However, the tourists then responded with 15 points in a seven minute spell to finish worthy 23–11 winners. Malcolm Davies's performance made him a strong candidate for a test place and he was selected for a Rugby League XIII, which lost 19–15 to the Australians on the following Monday evening under Leigh's floodlights.

The following Saturday, for their first home win of the season, Northern produced a brilliant display against Halifax, who were on the eve of flying out to France to play Albi and Carcassonne in the European Championship. Northern dominated Halifax's forwards; and with three tries to each side – Scroby, Jones and Lancaster crossed for Northern – it was Seddon's four goals which were the key factor in a well-deserved 17–11 win.

In October Northern's former international winger, Eric Batten, had been appointed as Batley's team manager, and his new charges gave Northern a fright at Mount Pleasant before conceding defeat, 12–9. It was 2–2 at half-time and Batley should have made more of their abundant possession, but they had no one of the class of Malcolm Davies, who scored two tries – the first in the 41st minute – from very limited chances. Batten's old colleague, Ernest Ward, who was on a month's trial at Mount Pleasant, was down to play at centre, but failed a late fitness test.

In an 18–7 home defeat to Hunslet, Milan Kosanovic had been selected at the expense of Mackie. However, up against the 1954 World Cup hooker, Sam Smith, he received little support from the rest of the reshuffled pack, apart from Radford and first-half try-scorer, Trevor Jones. Consequently, against Arthur Clues and his colleagues, the backs had few chances, but Rodwell and Lancaster had some promising efforts thwarted.

At Bramley there was still a problem with scrimmaging, but Northern produced some attractive back play to register their highest score of the season, 24–14. There were tries from Bob Smith, who scored two, Malcolm Davies, and Radford, and six goals from Seddon. This was all witnessed by this 10-year-old youngster, while sitting pitchside inside the Barley Mow's open boundary fencing.

This same result was repeated against Castleford at Odsal the following week, when Malcolm Davies scored another hat-trick, including a 70-yard 'special'. This was his 7th try of the season against Castleford, who led 9–7 at the interval. But in a dazzling five minute spell, Northern scored three tries to give the visitors the run-around. On his debut John Hanley, the former Bramley hooker, gave Northern plenty of possession.

On 31 November Northern did not play because the test match was staged at Odsal. In thick mud, Australia beat Great Britain 22–9. It was the highest crowd, 23,634, of the series, but the lowest receipts, just £4,172.

In the 17–5 defeat at the picturesque Clarence Street, Northern again won plenty of possession with Hanley at hooker. But York gave them a lesson in taking half chances and Rodwell was up against a very keen cover defence when openings came his way in the second-half. Centre Denzil Webster had a fine game, and York prop Vic Yorke kicked four goals to give the Minstermen a safe cushion.

In winning 17–10, league champions Hull produced the more intelligent kicking game in the Odsal mud, and this proved vital when twice Northern were poised to challenge with only five points separating the sides. The attendance of 3,000 was the lowest league crowd since the previous December. The average at that time was about 6,000 and caused concern.

By the end of the year Northern had to rearrange five games, including against Wigan due to them reaching the Lancashire Cup final, and had played fewer games, 17, than any team in the league. On 22 December the game at Headingley was abandoned after 24 minutes due to fog when Leeds led 5–0; while both Christmas games against Keighley, at Lawkholme Lane on Christmas Day and Odsal on Boxing Day, and the Huddersfield fixture at Odsal on 29 December were called off due to the dangerous state of the pitches because of frost and drifting snow.

Les Belshaw had been recalled for the proposed game at Lawkholme Lane, but by early January he was placed on the transfer-list at his own request at a fee of £1,000. Northern insisted that all players trained at Odsal and were prepared to help find him a house in Bradford, but his wife preferred to stay in Doncaster where he worked.

Due to their inactivity, the Northern players were given extra training before the 15–7 victory over Featherstone at Odsal, where the game became a "shambles" in the last quarter when five players were sent off by Eric Clay. Rovers were 7–5 ahead when Brian Radford scored a decisive try, which resulted in Lambert being sent off. He was then followed by Hanley and Radford of Northern and Hockley and Kirk for Rovers. Both players were given bans, Hanley for four matches and Radford for two.

In the second week of January 1957 the directors dropped a bombshell, when they apologised to the loyal band of supporters for what they termed "the compulsory sale" of Malcolm Davies to Leeds for a fee of £3,000. The scorer of 22 tries in 18 league and cup appearances, he had only recently moved to a house provided by Northern and was to start a new job as a representative the following week. A further blow was the announcement on 22 January that Northern had failed in their appeal in the Joe Phillips case. After being declared a free agent by the RFL, he signed for Keighley that day without, of course, Northern receiving a penny for his transfer.

The sale of Malcolm Davies prompted Northern to hold an open meeting on 28 January, when over 500 supporters crowded into the clubhouse, with others locked out, to hear the directors' report and to air their views on the future of the club. Northern were prepared to surrender the lease on Odsal, which had until 1968 to run, due to it costing £1,250 in rent, plus rates. The directors felt it unfair that as tenants they should have to pay for the upkeep of the stadium and the pitch. They complained that the club's pools had not been well supported, in stark contrast to such as Halifax, who were said to have 16,000 members in their weekly draw, and Wakefield Trinity, whose pools had cleared their £7,000 debts.

Following this, Northern gave a dismal display at Castleford, where they lost 13–0 and failed to score for the only time that season. Seddon sent out a wild pass for winger Frank East to race 60 yards for a try and also had an unhappy time with the boot. His opposite number, Albert Lunn, kicked five goals. This was Hanley's last game because, after his suspension and problems with a knee injury, he was taken off the playing register.

In the cup tie rehearsal against Dewsbury, Douglas Maclean was promoted from the 'A' team to his regular position of right-wing, where he established himself for a straight 16 games. Bryn Hopkins, the former Keighley second-rower who had been exchanged for Jimmy Glynn, who had been transfer-listed at £750, scored on his debut, but otherwise was rarely in the picture in Northern's easy 23–10 win. Northern breached the Dewsbury defence after only one minute and Scroby crowned a forceful display with an interception try.

The game clashed with the football derby at Park Avenue, which drew 22,010 fans. The Odsal crowd of only 1,700, who paid £135, was Northern's lowest since January 1943 when 1,500 watched a charity game against Halifax. Cyril Bunney blamed three factors: the derby game, poor opponents, and fans' disgust at the sale of Davies. In contrast there were 23,500 to watch Leeds beat St Helens 22–11 when Davies made his debut.

On the transfer front, in mid-January Brian Hambling was listed at £1,000, at his own request, because he was finding it difficult travelling from Hull to Odsal for training; and Les Belshaw and Eric Cooper, Wakefield Trinity's former Doncaster winger, upset their respective club's plans for a straight swop. Wynne Jones, however, was signed by Featherstone Rovers for £450. Including his debut in 1950, he made 153 appearances in his first stint at the club, and then returned on a free transfer in the 1962–63 season.

The first league double of the season came at Odsal with an 11–0 win over Bramley. Len Haley started the move which resulted in the first try for Maclean and then took a slick pass from Trevor Jones to score himself. Northern's Bob Smith and Bramley's Hammill were dismissed after a mass brawl and lecture by the referee. On the same day the 'A' team, who had won their previous five games, came a cropper at Wakefield, 51–5.

Northern then gave one of their pluckiest displays of the season against second-placed Barrow, who only secured their 7–2 victory at Craven Park through a 75th minute try by winger Danny

Leatherbarrow. Maclean had earlier dropped the ball over the line, while the "ever-improving" Winnard was narrowly foiled near the end after intercepting. It was a far cry from their mauling at Odsal in September against the Challenge Cup finalists.

In the thick Odsal mud, Northern progressed to the second round of the Challenge Cup with a comfortable 20–7 win over Dewsbury, who had a strong contingent in the crowd of 6,646. Northern took an early eight point lead, thanks to tries by Winnard in the 7th minute, and Radford in the 14th. The latter came after a 40-yard run and spectacular dive under the posts, but Dewsbury fought back and only trailed 8–7 at half-time. However, Northern's heavier forwards were always in command, before the wily Len Haley sent Rodwell away on a try-scoring run and textbook inter-passing between Seddon and Rodwell resulted in the winger's second try.

Ralph Winnard scores Northern's first try against Dewsbury in the Challenge Cup, with Douglas Maclean in support. (Courtesy Ralph Winnard)

On the same afternoon at Headingley, where Leeds beat Wigan before a crowd of 38,914 and hundreds more broke in for free, there was talk of setting a 38,000 limit for the second round tie against Warrington. At Leeds Malcolm Davies, who had lost much of his confidence following a thigh injury, could not command a place due to the return to form of George Broughton and the advance of young 'Del' Hodgkinson.

For the keenly anticipated visit of Wigan, who had won their previous 12 league games, Northern were unchanged, except for Smith who replaced Jenkins at centre. The ease with which Billy Boston scored his 46th try of the season in the fifth minute appeared to spell disaster. But afterwards he was kept well in check as Northern smashed Wigan's long unbeaten league record more easily that the final score of 14–5 suggests.

Mackie had his best game yet in both the scrums and the loose; and once Radford stormed over on the half-hour mark Northern never looked back. They scored four tries and, but for feeble goalkicking, would have won by a bigger margin in an 80-minute thriller. Wigan had conceded only four tries in their previous seven league games and so far that season only Hull, Barrow, Oldham and Australia had managed to cross their line four times in a game. After this performance, before a crowd of 6,000, there were unlimited steaks on offer for Northern's players while they prepared for the visit of Widnes in the second round of the Cup.

Unfortunately, it was snowed off on the Saturday and replayed the following Wednesday afternoon before a reduced crowd of 6,959. Despite being allowed out of school early, I still managed to miss the start of this exciting tie, due to having to retrieve my confiscated football rattle from the deputy head. The game ended in controversy when, with Widnes reduced to 12 men with the dismissal of centre Harry Dawson in the 62nd minute, referee R.L. Thomas, after consulting his touch-judge, awarded a 69th minute try to right-winger Peter Ratcliffe. However, photographic evidence clearly suggests that he was tackled short of the line by Seddon, in what was then the speedway pits corner. With tries from young wingers Rodwell and Maclean, plus a goal from Seddon, Northern only fell behind 10–8 in the last minute. However, defeat was always staring them in the face; Lancashire hooker Jack Hayes won the scrums 26–5 and their defence took a terrific hammering in a dour struggle.

In a 19–12 defeat at Hunslet, Clive Best, the 25-year-old Barrow full-back, made the first of four appearances during his month's trial. Domestic issues and the £300 fee convinced Northern not to retain the former Ebbw Vale man. He replaced the demoted Seddon at full-back and kicked two of his three goals from the touchline and the other from fully 50 yards; but he unaccountably missed from easier positions.Northern led 7–0 at one stage and 10–8 at half-time, but scrum failings and the loss of scrum-half Graham Oddy for the last 35 minutes, due to a head injury, made defeat almost inevitable. The game saw the dream two-try debut of Hunslet's 20-year-old centre Willie Walker, who later became a popular member of new Northern's original squad.

After playing in every game so far that season, Trevor Jones was replaced by transfer-listed Harry Griffett for a 9–3 defeat of Doncaster at a muddy Odsal, where Northern managed three quick tries in the second-half. Gordon Haley, a 22-year-old former amateur international, renewed his half-back partnership with elder brother Len from their Overthorpe Rangers days, made a steady debut, but tended to be too individualistic. Twenty-year-old Ralph Winnard was twice denied by his brother, Alan, after defence-splitting breaks. Best missed five kicks at goal, including one in front of the posts.

At Knowsley Road, St Helens ran out comfortable 23–6 winners after they scored four first-half tries and led 18–0 at half-time. Northern dominated possession in the second-half, and their work improved immeasurably; Winnard assisted Douglas Maclean to both Northern's tries and Trevor Jones made several solo runs. However, overall their orthodox methods presented few problems for Saints, whose crowd of 12,500 was the highest that Northern played in front of that season.

After impressing at St Helens, the following Wednesday evening Gordon Haley then gave the finest display by a Northern scrum-half so far that season in a 25–15 defeat at Leeds. He took over the kicking from Best, landed three goals with his instep style and was the game's outstanding player, despite Lewis Jones scoring 13 points. Bryn Hopkins suffered a knee injury after 34 minutes, but like the rest of the team, plugged away as Northern gave a spirited display, and twice hit back at 12–8 and 17–13 before the Challenge Cup winners eased to their 18th successive win.

After a few weeks self-imposed rest to regain his fitness, Seddon returned to the side for a somewhat fortunate 14–13 win over Dewsbury at Crown Flatt. He denied he was unsettled after being dropped against Hunslet and by the end of the season he proved his loyalty to Northern by turning down the option of a move to Batley. The highlights of a poor quality game was a dynamic try by "will-o'-the-wisp" Gordon Haley and a first hat-trick by the Dewsbury, and future

Northern winger, Horace Grainger, who nearly claimed a fourth try after kicking ahead.

The rearranged game against Keighley, under the Odsal lights, was brought forward to Monday 25 March, in order to rest the pitch for the Challenge Cup semi-final on the following Saturday, which caused the postponement of the game against Batley. It was Northern's fourth game in 10 days. They gave a lacklustre performance and lost 18–3, their first home league defeat of 1957. Keighley were faster all round and, to rub salt into the wounds, on his first return to Odsal Joe Phillips kicked six goals. This game marked Les Belshaw's 36th and final appearance for Northern because he was loaned to Leeds until the end of the season due to injuries at Headingley. He then joined Doncaster in September 1957, after the Dons had struggled to afford Northern's earlier asking price.

In an epic Challenge Cup semi-final at Odsal on 30 March, before a crowd of 49,094, Leeds beat Whitehaven 10–9 through a 75th minute drop-goal by scrum-half Jeff Stevenson. The referee, N.T. Railton of Wigan, had failed to award Whitehaven a penalty for what appeared to be a blatant play-the-ball infringement in the build-up to the kick.

Northern then journeyed to Lancashire on successive Saturdays and came away with mixed results. Their poor display at Central Park saw Wigan lead 27–0 at half-time despite having lost prop John Barton with a broken collarbone in the 23rd minute. Playing on the wing, Brian Radford had the unenviable task of marking Billy Boston, who crossed twice in the 38–5 revenge win, to take his try tally, at that stage of the season, to 55. Two minutes from the end Sutton sneaked over for a dejected Northern side, which included nine of the players who had won so brilliantly against the same opposition at Odsal in February.

The lead changed hands five times in the 18–17 victory at Warrington, where Mackie's excellent hooking allowed Seddon to exploit blindside weaknesses, and Gordon Haley again starred. The scrum-half kicked two superb goals from the touchline and then made the decisive try which put Northern into a 16–12 lead. Warrington, who had former Northerner Tony Storey in the second-row, could still have won the game, but left-winger Laurie Gilfedder failed with three late goal attempts.

Wakefield Trinity had refused to play under the Odsal lights, but after only one minute's play, with a 6.15pm kick-off, conditions were so

Keighley against Northern on 27 April 1957. Gordon Haley, Brian Radford and Neil Carter are in the background as Ralph Winnard gets the ball to the wing.
(Courtesy Ralph Winnard)

bad that the lights had to be switched on. Northern gave another depressing midweek display and lost 23–9, so Trinity registered their first league win at Odsal in 10 years. Smart work from Gordon Haley made a try for Sutton and the score to 10–9, but a revival never came.

At The Boulevard Northern led on merit until the 27th minute, when left-winger Ivor Watts latched on to a slack pass to race 75 yards for an interception try. Maclean had a try disallowed shortly after the interval when Northern trailed only 7–3, but thereafter the future Championship finalists took full control to win 23–3, including seven goals from their veteran full-back Colin Hutton, who punished Northern's inclination to concede penalties. After 78 minutes prop Neil Carter was sent off for the first time in his career, and received a two match ban.

Tony Beevers, a former Ovenden junior, made his first team debut at full-back in a 26–7 defeat to Huddersfield at Odsal, where overall Northern produced their third successive lethargic midweek performance. On his return, the sprightly Derek Davies scored Northern's only try, and the scores were level 7–7 on the hour mark, but Huddersfield scored five tries in the last 16 minutes to run out easy winners. The game marked Eric Sutton's 49th and final senior appearance prior to his transfer to Batley.

On Easter Saturday Northern travelled to Thrum Hall. They registered their fourth double of the season and only their second against Halifax since the war. In an 18–15 victory, Bill Jenkins scored a 75-yard interception try and his fellow winger, Tony Beevers, effectively won the game with three coolly taken goals after opportunist tries from Winnard, Smith and 'tearaway' Bryn Hopkins, who had become a powerful figure in the pack. His fellow prop, former Clayton junior George McLean, made his debut in this game.

Northern scored six tries – four of them made by Derek Davies – in a 22–18 win over Hull KR at Odsal on Easter Monday, a game in which 26-year-old Phil Crabtree, who was over six feet tall and weighed 16 stones, made his senior debut in the second-row. Inspired by his teacher, Northern's legendary stand-off Willie Davies, Crabtree's ambition to join Northern had been frustrated by National Service. But, after playing for Baildon RUFC and the 'A' team whenever he was home on leave, he was finally signed as a professional in 1952. A stalwart clubman, who played mostly at open-side prop, he remained loyal until Northern's demise.

At Lawkholme Lane on the following Saturday, Keighley scored two early tries and led 8–0, in what was looking like a celebratory send-off for New Zealander Neville Black. However, with the exception of try-scorer Geoff Crewdson, Keighley fell away badly after Northern hit back with a try by Gordon Haley and a 65-yard solo score from Bob Smith. At the interval Northern held a two point lead and further tries from Scroby, with two, and Winnard gave them a 23–16 revenge for the earlier floodlit defeat.

This disappointing season ended at Odsal on May Day, when a crowd of only 2,000 saw Northern beat Batley 22–12 after trailing 12–7 at half-time. In the second-half the visitors had no answer to Bill Jenkins. He scored a try, made another and kicked four goals. Northern therefore ended with four wins and their sixth double. However, this late flourish, which took them to 21st in the final league table, could not hide the fact that it had been one of their most depressing post-war seasons, with the average attendance of 4,691 being the lowest since the war.

Coach Trevor Foster scored a try in the 'A' team's 23–10 win at Leeds and the reserves finished on a high note by beating Wakefield Trinity 17–13, only their second defeat of the season.

Before the season's end the Northern directors issued a statement, in which they explained their decision not to accept the Corporation's new offer of a rent free period for three years. This would have been in exchange for charging £50 a day or 10 per cent, whichever was the greater, for any extra events at Odsal, except rugby league. However, having arranged to stage show jumping and the Harlem Globetrotters in the summer months, as well as speedway, Northern decided they would be out of pocket with the proposed arrangement with the Corporation. The reduction of entertainment tax in the April budget was most welcome, because over £2,000 had been lost the previous season because of this iniquitous tax. It would now mean more revenue from any big games at Odsal. For example, Northern would have received another £200 from the recent semi-final had it not been for this unfair levy on professional sport.

My first experience of a big game at Odsal was that year's Championship Final when league leaders Oldham – the only Lancashire side not to play Northern in the 10 years under review – dramatically beat second placed Hull 15–14 before a crowd of 62,199. Following the scenes at the 1954 Challenge Cup replay, Odsal's capacity had been set at 80,000, but the all-ticket restriction was eased by the police and nearly 17,000 paid on the day. All stand tickets sold out a week before the game and by the Thursday before the match it was estimated that 40,000 tickets, more than the previous year's attendance at Manchester City FC's Maine Road, had already been sold, including 14,000 in Hull, 12,000 in Oldham, and 6,000 at Odsal.

The Queen and the Duke of Edinburgh were visiting Hull at about the same time as the mass exodus to Bradford by road and rail, with 15 special trains scheduled to arrive at Forster Square and Low Moor from Hull and Oldham. For all the pomp and ceremony of Wembley, the clubs only received 8 per cent of the net gate. The participants in the Championship final were usually better off. For example, each of the finalists in 1957 received £2,705 (22.5 per cent of the net gate); Northern's share was £1,205. Expenses were £325, which included hiring the traditional Yorkshire brass band.

My pre-match ritual, for what, except for 1959, was an annual event until 1962, was to arrive shortly after the turnstiles opened two hours before kick-off, take in the atmosphere outside the ground and then marvel at the stadium filling up with thousands of supporters. Rooley Avenue was a hive of activity once the dozens of coaches arrived. It was difficult to avoid the ticket touts, the hawkers selling dodgy rosettes – which usually had a motif of the FA Cup – and pirate (unofficial) programmes. As a junior, I found a good view through the New Stand railings at the scoreboard end, which also avoided problems from latecomers. Despite the huge crowds, I always felt safe at Odsal – apart from the crush after the 1960 final.

1956–57 Summary
Position in league: 21st of 30 P 38 W 17 L 21 D 0 – Pts 479–672
Yorkshire Cup: First round. Challenge Cup: Second round.
Average attendance: 4,691 (4,558 league games only)

— **AT THIS STADIUM**

Two Dates to Remember . .

Friday and Saturday,
28th & 29th JUNE, 1957

HORSE
JUMPING
SHOW

Many World Famous Olympic Stars will be taking part

Show jumping was held at Odsal to try to raise extra funds for the club.

5. 1957–58: The Welsh flier returns
Tries galore but woeful marksmanship

At the RFL AGM it was decided that Leeds, as the leading Yorkshire side from the previous season, should play in the Lancashire League, to even up the numbers for the county leagues. This meant that Northern lost a potential five-figure gate, whereas their highest attendance against their four Lancashire opponents in this season was only 4,500, against Leigh and Warrington.

Northern did some sound business in the close season with the re-signing of Malcolm Davies from Leeds for only £1,000 and the acquisition of Halifax's 32-year-old right-winger Arthur Daniels on a free transfer. Davies's fee was later covered by a cheque from the Supporters' Club for £1,250. This was profit from the pools scheme which was making from £80 to £90 per week. Daniels, who had played against Northern at Wembley in 1949 and was a Lions tourist in 1950, signed for Northern after failing to agree terms with Huddersfield.

At Headingley, Davies had been unable to produce his best form after suffering a thigh injury and made only five senior appearances for the Loiners. Unfortunately, due to breaking his nose in an early season practice game, he missed Northern's first six games. This included a 31–19 defeat to Keighley in the Lazenby Cup at Odsal on Bank Holiday Monday, which saw the debut of former Bradford RUFC hooker, Brian Thompson.

Daniels made his debut at Huddersfield, where local 19-year-old full-back Brian Curry landed nine goals from 10 attempts in Northern's 33–15 defeat. In contrast, although Northern matched Huddersfield with five tries, three of their players failed to land a single goal, including two attempts from under the posts. With a three try spell in four minutes Northern led 9–5 after 22 minutes, but lacked the skill or stamina to match Huddersfield.

During the summer the playing area had been dug up, returfed in parts and was a fine sight for the first home game of the season. The 20–5 defeat to Swinton – a game dominated by the industrious Lions pack, which included future new Northern forward Ken Roberts – again emphasised the importance of a reliable goalkicker. Northern restricted the visitors to only two tries, but their full-back, Jack Tobin, kicked seven goals from seven attempts. The previous week Tony Beevers had landed 12 goals in the 'A' team's 69–10 thrashing of Bramley, but his only success on this day was when he converted Bob Smith's try.

Captain Len Haley injured his shoulder against Swinton and joined Malcolm Davies, Crabtree and Lancaster on the injured list. Reserve prop Bryn Hopkins returned to South Wales, although he later made the 400 mile round trip to play. Bill Seddon, whose appearances this season were limited due to a cartilage operation and the emergence of Tony Beevers, refused a move to Batley, after the clubs had agreed a fee of £400.

Workington Town's 13–3 defeat at Odsal was engineered by Northern's reserve half-backs and former Ovenden team-mates, Derek Davies and Graham Oddy. Davies, who made the first of Oddy's two tries and scored another, effectively cemented his position at stand-off, while Kosanovic also established himself as the first-choice hooker.

At Wheldon Road, Northern gained a merited 19–5 success despite conceding 21 of the game's 28 penalties. Derek Davies made two first-half tries for Jenkins and, with Kosanovic edging the scrums, Northern kept the rugged Castleford forwards in check. Walter Hemingway, a former Bradford junior who had been a member of the 'A' team since the start of the previous season, made his senior debut in this game.

Unfortunately, this marked Brian Hambling's final appearance in Northern's colours prior to his £1,000 transfer to his home town club, Hull, on 27 August. Since signing from Hull junior rugby in 1952, he had found it difficult travelling from Humberside for training, and he also felt that constantly switching between the front-row and second-row was not helping his progress. Although he had the misfortune to be carried off on his Hull debut against Hunslet, the transfer was a good move on his part, because he joined a squad that not only finished as Champions that season, but also reached Wembley in the Challenge Cup in 1959. Shortly afterwards, Les Belshaw returned to Doncaster. He had rejected a move to Batley.

Starting with a clear cut 28–12 win over Dewsbury in the first round of the Yorkshire Cup at Crown Flatt, reserve open-side prop George McLean began to establish himself as a first team regular. Northern's vastly improved attacking ability, spearheaded by Derek Davies's lightning acceleration, saw them score eight tries, including a hat-trick from the imperious Bob Smith. Shortly after half-time, Dewsbury got within five points, but Northern pulled away with well worked tries – wingers Jenkins and Rodwell took their chances with alacrity. Northern's only weakness was goalkicking, because they missed with nine attempts at goal.

This failure rate was repeated the following week at Odsal in a 36–22 league victory over the same opposition, when Northern fielded an all-Welsh threequarter line, Jenkins, Daniels, Smith, and Davies, with the triumphant four try return of the powerful running Malcolm Davies. Against a woefully weak defence Northern were capable of raising their game at will and cruised home with 10 tries – the first of Radford's tries came as early as the second minute. But complacency saw their own line breached on six occasions as Dewsbury reduced the 20–8 interval lead to six points. Northern then added four more tries, including Radford's second when the 31-year-old second-rower danced around six defenders in 10 yards.

Malcolm Davies's second spell at Odsal meant that 21-year-old Stanley Rodwell's first team chances were limited and he joined Batley on a protracted month's trial. He scored a try for Batley against Hunslet as late as 15 April 1958, but was not retained. After being crossed off Northern's register he re-signed for the start of the 1958–59 campaign, but made only one more senior appearance for Northern that season. Likewise, with a surfeit of scrum-halves on Northern's books, Fred Lee joined Castleford.

In their 37–7 defeat to Northern at Odsal, Leigh could only field a "shadow" side because injuries and influenza affected eight of their regulars. They then lost their former international full-back Jimmy Ledgard with a cut head after 12 minutes, following which Northern ran riot and scored seven tries in a 28 minute spell. Scroby celebrated his earlier 21st birthday with two tries and Derek Davies's sparkling form at stand-off allowed skipper Len Haley plenty of scope from full-back. Highlights of Northern's try-scoring, much to the delight of the overworked scoreboard operators, and the reactions of the 4,500 crowd, have survived on film.

This win took Northern to eighth position in the league table, and the following Tuesday evening at Odsal they qualified for the semi-final of the Yorkshire Cup for the sixth time in 10 seasons, with a 5–2 win over Featherstone Rovers before their then highest crowd of the season, 5,776. Northern had the better of the penalties, 22–11, but lost the scrums 20–11 and, with both defences well on top, it needed a scintillating break from Derek Davies to produce the match winning try for Malcolm Davies.

In Northern's 16–8 defeat at Wilderspool, Warrington loose-forward Laurie Gilfedder was the difference between two below strength sides with 13 points, including four penalties, and 18-year-old Jackie Edwards scored a "blinder". Due to influenza hitting the camp Northern fielded a much weakened pack. Prop Rodney Thomas made his first senior appearance since October 1955. Derek Davies was also a casualty, so the Haley brothers teamed up at half-back. Northern led 5–2 after 30 minutes and finished with a late flourish with an excellent try from Malcolm Davies. But, despite having three recognised goalkickers in the side, Northern's marksmanship again let them down.

However, the following week against Whitehaven, to add to his try in the 28–16 home victory, Bill Jenkins then proceeded to kick eight goals from 10 attempts, having landed only nine goals in his previous 10 games. Both sides scored four tries; it was one of only two games that season, the other was the 8–6 home victory over Hull KR, when Northern won because of superior goalkicking. Jenkins's 19 points was his best ever for the club.

The downside of this victory was that a leg injury caused Malcolm Davies to miss the floodlit Yorkshire Cup semi-final against York, which was watched by Northern's biggest home crowd of the season, 10,794. The rugged 2–2 draw might easily have been decided by master-tactician Riley, the York scrum-half, had he not opted for a tap-and-run rather than going for goal at a penalty. Northern then contrived to lose the replay 14–8, before a crowd of 9,019, who paid £1,152, having given York the runaround for much of the game. Bob Smith had a pass knocked down on the line, when he should perhaps have opted to score himself; added to this, Jenkins was tripped when he looked a certain scorer. Prop Vic Yorke kicked four goals from six attempts, while Northern had six misses until Neil Carter popped over the only goal of his career. York therefore qualified for their first final since 1936, only to lose to Huddersfield 15–8 at Headingley.

The lead changed hands five times in a 20–20 draw against Swinton, and once again missed goals cost Northern victory. They scored six of the 10 tries on offer at Station Road, but there was only a

52

solitary goal, from Jenkins. In the previous nine games Northern had scored 42 tries yet kicked only 23 goals from 60 attempts.

With the transfer of Brian Hambling and Les Belshaw, 24-year-old second-rower Harry Griffett became the third forward to leave Odsal in the space of seven weeks when he was transferred to Hull KR for £600. He had then made 65 appearances for Northern, but rejoined the club in the 1959–60 season, along with his younger brother, Terry. He scored two tries on his debut for Rovers having achieved the same feat on his Northern debut in October 1952.

After recovering from his cartilage operation, Bill Seddon played in the 'A' team against Huddersfield at Odsal on 12 October, but torn ligaments required him to have another three months rest. On the same day at Crown Flatt, powerful finishing by Daniels earned him a hat-trick of tries thanks to good approach work by Winnard and Derek Davies. However, Northern gifted Dewsbury two tries and had to settle for a 17–17 draw. Trevor Jones was dismissed shortly before the end, but his one match ban did not take effect until after the visit of league leaders Wakefield Trinity, who headed the table by three clear points.

In front of a 10,000 Odsal crowd, the thrilling 11–10 victory over the previously unbeaten Trinity was perhaps the highwater mark of old Northern's games that I witnessed. Leading 5–0 at half-time, they fell behind for the first time in the 70th minute. But their rampant pack, with Marston and Scroby outstanding, refused to accept defeat and Malcolm Davies's second try, in the 76th minute, brought them victory. Partnered by centre Bob Smith, who missed only one game that season, Malcolm Davies had therefore taken only eight games to climb to the top of Northern's try-scoring chart with 13. All three tries – Winnard got the other – were scored in the corners; and, without a recognised kicker, Scroby took on the task and landed one magnificent effort. For the half-back partnership of Derek Davies and Graham Oddy, it was their seventh successive victory.

This sequence came to an end at Thrum Hall, before a crowd of 13,153, where both prop George McLean and Halifax's Charlie Renilson scored their first senior tries in Northern's 16–8 defeat. Kosanovic bossed the scrums, but Northern were hampered when both their second-rowers, Hemingway and Hopkins, were injured. Northern only trailed 8–5, but Halifax, for whom full-back Garfield Owen failed to score for the first time that season, were worthy winners.

53

Northern's Christmas dinner in the Odsal clubhouse 1957: Brian Radford is in the foreground with Len Haley to the right. Other players visible on the right are Bill Seddon, Rodney Thomas, Gerald Handley, Milan Kosanovic, Trevor Jones and Ralph Winnard. Among those in the picture on the left are Trevor Foster, Bob Smith, and Tony Beevers.
(Courtesy Bradford Bulls Foundation RL Heritage Project).

Right: Loose-forward Jack Scroby fends off former Northern favourite, Ken Traill, in the game at Thrum Hall.
(Courtesy Robert Gate)

54

In the final week of October, on the day that he was due to play rugby union for Yorkshire against Cumberland, Northern clinched the signature of the Roundhay RUFC captain and England trialist second-rower, Norman Feather, for a signing-on fee in the region of £1,000. He was a member of Yorkshire's County Championship final side in 1956–57, during the season he had changed his mind about joining Halifax.

Feather went straight into the side that lost 12–3 to Hunslet at Odsal on 2 November – the first home defeat since the opening game against Swinton. Like the rest of the team, Feather faded as the game progressed and was subsequently given two weeks in the 'A' team to adjust to playing his new code. It was 0–0 at half-time, but Northern relied too much on individual efforts and, with an abundance of possession, Hunslet scored their 12 points in an eight minute spell. This was Mackie's last game for Northern because he later announced his retirement due to an elbow injury – but he subsequently turned out for Wakefield Trinity 'A' team.

Wakefield Trinity made unmerciful amends for their recent defeat at Odsal by thrashing Northern 37–6 at Belle Vue. Northern's lamentable defence was torn to shreds by inside backs Ken Rollin, Aubrey Houlden, and Neil Fox as Trinity ran in nine tries. Malcolm Davies and Daniels both got on the scoresheet, but they came up against a brick wall in full-back Eric Lockwood, who saved four certain tries. Although there was no solace on the field, a few hours later the players celebrated Derek Davies's 21st birthday at his father's Fountain Head Inn in Pellon.

In a 15–12 home win over Hull, Northern prospered from shrewd distribution by third choice scrum-half Alan Lancaster, who had been utilised mostly at centre and stand-off in the 'A' team. Clever approach work by Derek Davies, Hemingway and Radford resulted in tries for Bob Smith, who scored twice, and Len Haley. The latter swore that he had another perfect try disallowed after a 70-yard solo effort. A highlight of the second-half was a 45-yard break by prop Neil Carter, but it was his solid foraging which really helped win the day.

Feather returned for the visit to Bramley, where Northern had their third successive away loss, 24–15, and were behind from the third minute. A lack of cover by the back-row forwards let them down; and they had no one with the leadership qualities of Bramley's veteran scrum-half George Langfield. Previously, Northern had only lost once at the Barley Mow in over 20 years.

Consequently, Radford reluctantly took over the loose-forward spot and only Jones, Kosanovic and Feather kept their positions in the pack for Northern's 20–2 defeat to Featherstone Rovers at Odsal. The game was evenly poised at 5–2, but after their forwards had done the heavy graft, Rovers struck on the hour mark with 10 points in three minutes, by exploiting Northern's weakness around the base of the close up scrums. Dogged by back trouble, this was Neil Carter's final first team game. He had made 64 appearances since making his debut in the 1953–54 season.

During February, Harry Hornby, who had been Northern's charismatic chairman since October 1945 after joining the board in 1937, announced he would be retiring on health grounds. He would then be able to spend most of his time in the Bahamas and Beverley Hills, where he usually spent the winter. He was made a Life Member of the club at the AGM on 5 December 1957, when Northern reported a loss of £2,028 on the year ending June 1957, with a deficit of £4,877. This was despite a drop in players' wages and expenses of £800; a profit on transfer fees due to the sale of Malcolm Davies, Joe Mageen and Wynne Jones; and £2,032 having been received from the Development Fund. The new chairman, Cyril Bunney, believed that the worries over the playing area had been overcome. Unfortunately, this was not the case, as it took until the late 1960s for the problems with the drainage system to be rectified.

Scroby was back at loose-forward for the visit to Craven Park, where Northern lost 7–3 to a depleted, but grimly-determined, Hull KR, whose prop forward Grice suffered a broken nose after only 30 seconds. Northern failed to take their chances in the heavy conditions. Bob Smith twice broke through without support and Feather narrowly failed to score near the end. Second-rower Phil Crabtree suffered an ear injury but had recovered for the visit to Whitehaven, where no Yorkshire side had won that season.

In a pulsating game at the Recreation Ground, Northern were unlucky to lose 24–19 after twice recovering from Whitehaven rallies. Whitehaven lost centre Eppie Gibson through injury for half the game and withdrew John Tembey from the pack. But they still managed to score the winning converted try, engineered by Billy Banks, in the 75th minute. Despite Hemingway having to deputise at loose-forward for the travel sick Scroby, the pack gave a sterling display, thanks to the promptings of Gordon Haley, who also crossed for a try, after a blind-side move, at the Kells end.

A 31–5 confidence building victory over Doncaster drew only 2,300 spectators to Odsal, the lowest crowd since January 1957. Len Haley replaced Jenkins at full-back and Winnard returned at centre, but it was Derek Davies's devastating midfield bursts which brought him two of Northern's nine tries and helped create others, including a hat-trick for Malcolm Davies. Former Northerner Les Belshaw was in the Dons' pack.

Northern fielded an unchanged side in losing 10–0 to Keighley at Odsal on Christmas Day, when Derek Davies bruised his back and Daniels fractured his fibula. This lethargic team performance meant that Len Haley moved to stand-off, Jenkins replaced Daniels, and Beevers came in at full-back when Northern gained revenge, 21–19, on Boxing Day. There could be no grumbles about either result. At Lawkholme Lane Northern took a 10 point lead after 22 minutes and were in total control with Malcolm Davies scoring a first-half hat-trick of tries.In the two games, in which former Northerners Bill Shreeve and Jimmy Glynn played in their pack, Joe Phillips claimed 17 of Keighley's 29 points.

Northern ended the holiday programme at Odsal with a 35–12 trouncing of Castleford, the fourth game in eight days for both teams, in which they scored six tries in a 13 minute spell just after the interval. This included two by Radford who had swopped positions with right-winger Hemingway. Before being injured, Malcolm Davies claimed five of Northern's 11 tries, which was their highest try-scoring feat in a match for five years. Amazingly, Northern had the same number of unsuccessful attempts at goal. Beevers missed five kicks, Jenkins three, Gordon Haley two and Scroby one, in yet another woeful display of goalkicking.

Without their leading try-scorer – Douglas Maclean took over the left-wing spot – Northern then produced arguably their best result of the season by surprisingly beating Leigh 13–4 at Hilton Park. After defeating the league leaders St Helens on New Year's Day, Leigh were expected to easily keep their undefeated home record against Yorkshire clubs intact. However, behind a dominant pack, in which Norman Feather went over for his first try in rugby league, Gordon Haley marked a top-class performance with a brilliant solo effort. Some tenacious defence, with Beevers a fearless last line, meant that Northern gained their second double of the season.

Malcolm Davies returned for the visit of York and his single try in the unexpected 13–11 defeat took his total to 30 tries for the season, behind Halifax's Johnny Freeman who was on 38. Although they managed to cut back an eight point deficit, Northern failed to force home their constant attacks and were let down by their backs. One reason for this inconsistent home form was put down to the size of Odsal and the sparse crowds. As an example, Gordon Haley had played "blinders" at Leigh and Whitehaven, but the home supporters had yet to see such a performance, and the player put it down to Odsal's lack of atmosphere.

Bill Seddon made a successful return to the first team after injury, with three goals from six attempts in an 18–3 win at Doncaster. Jenkins's two tries took his points total past the century mark for the first time since moving to Odsal in 1948. Emergency left-winger Derek Davies had some inspired moments, the highlight was a 55-yard try-scoring dash.

The victory was tinged with sadness due to the death, the previous day, of director Frank Whitcombe. The former Odsal great, who had been Northern's representative on the Rugby League Council and a member of the important Cup and Rules Revision Committee, had recently put his name forward for consideration as manager of the forthcoming tour of Australasia. At the Rugby League Council meeting on 11 February a minute's silence was held as a sign of respect for his memory and the victims of the Manchester United Munich air disaster.

A rehearsal for the Challenge Cup tie, the game against Bramley on 25 January was postponed with five inches of frozen snow on the Odsal pitch. In January Northern had turned down an offer from Leeds for Derek Davies who, having completed his first week of Army training with the Duke of Wellington Regiment, was unable to travel to Workington, where Northern lost 9–0 in the Derwent Park mud. Facing wind and rain, they managed to restrict a Town side with top-four ambitions to one try in the first-half, but they had no stamina left on the turn around to take advantage of the conditions. Seddon was Northern's hero, often pulled off last-ditch tackles and stopped Ces Thompson from scoring after he had crossed the line.

Northern versus York at Odsal in 1957–58. Top: Winnard escapes the clutches of Foster, supported by Beevers; below: Bob Smith and Winnard create an overlap for Jenkins (No. 2). Note the railway sleeper terracing, lack of crush-barriers, and decrepit loudspeakers at the Low Moor end.
(Both photos courtesy Ralph Winnard)

In beating Bramley 15–9 at the Barley Mow, Northern extended their unequalled record of successive peace-time wins in the first round of the Challenge Cup, in which they had last lost in 1935. Bramley, on the other hand, had failed at the first hurdle in the previous 10 seasons. The postponed tie was played on Wednesday afternoon, when referee Clapham had a difficult time in keeping tempers under control and dismissed stand-off Geoff Dudley in the second-half. Bramley led 7–2 at half-time, but Northern fought back with fine tries by Brian Radford and Malcolm Davies before Gordon Haley produced a brilliant match winning effort. Unfortunately, captain Len Haley dislocated his shoulder in creating Radford's try and missed the rest of the season. With an attendance of only 2,344 Northern lost £100 on the tie.

Before the lowest Odsal crowd of the season, 2,000, Northern just about merited their 8–6 win over Hull KR, although seconds from the end the Rovers' wingman, Brian Shaw, was foiled only inches from the line after a 70-yard run. Returning to action after a three month absence prop Bryn Hopkins had a hand in both the tries from Kosanovic and Jenkins.

In losing their second round Challenge Cup tie 11–8 to Rochdale Hornets, Northern's 'goal-kicking curse', one goal from six attempts, again struck at the Athletic Grounds, where Seddon missed the easiest of chances with Northern 6–3 down. Then, almost immediately, Hornets scored a converted try from centre Norman Short, despite a flying tackle from Seddon. This effectively won the game, although Northern, who were on a £20 win bonus and encouraged by a vocal following of over 1,000 fans, dictated play near the end. The Army authorities had been sympathetic to Northern's request for Derek Davies to be flown over from Northern Ireland for the game, although fellow serviceman Jack Scroby was again unavailable. The impressive Malcolm Davies and Jenkins scored Northern's tries, while Bill Seddon sustained another injury to his kidneys, which meant hospitalisation and a prolonged absence. The tie's only redeeming feature was a 9,317 crowd, which produced receipts of £1,188.

Although it was the second coldest spell in March for 20 years, lasting all of 19 days – only March 1947 was colder – amazingly none of Northern's scheduled games were lost due to the weather. In the Parkside mud, the result was 10–7, but Northern nearly forced a draw near the end when Gordon Haley split the defence only to stumble when a pass to Malcolm Davies might have guaranteed a try. With Radford concussed in an early tackle, Northern deserved at least a point; Feather, Crabtree and Scroby worked valiantly in defence for the majority of the second-half.

In early March at Swinton, Malcolm Davies opposed Brian Smith of York in the first tour trial, which was abandoned after 68 minutes due to a snowstorm. The game, which ended 22–10, was watched by only 1,500 hardy souls. In similar blizzard conditions at Odsal everyone, except the referee, thought the game against Halifax on 8 March should have been abandoned. The field markings were obliterated by the second-half whiteout. In a 5–4 defeat winger Douglas Maclean bounced the ball while scoring, but overall Halifax had the smoother combination in the backs with the two packs about even. Brian Thompson made his debut at prop.

Northern were totally outclassed by Warrington at Odsal, where Northern's backing-up was abysmal against a side that was yards quicker and deservedly won 19–5. Gordon Haley's frequent breaks went unsupported, and although Beevers landed a brilliant goal from the touchline he missed with three easier attempts. Having earlier played for the Dukes in the Army Cup final, Derek Davies made a welcome return, and played in the last eight league games – six of them in 23 days in April.

On the day of the Challenge Cup semi-final at Odsal, when a crowd of 31,517 saw Workington Town beat Featherstone Rovers 8–2, Northern travelled to The Boulevard, where no visiting side had won that season, to face third-placed Hull. Reserve forward Brian Thompson had the unenviable task of opposing Great Britain's hooker, Tommy Harris, who, along with loose-forward Johnny Whiteley, had recently been selected for the Lions tour of Australasia. Northern led early on after two opportunist tries from Malcolm Davies, but Hull's forwards were far too strong and mobile; Northern finally capitulated 28–11 after conceding eight tries.

Prior to entertaining Northern on a cold Easter Monday at Mount Pleasant, Batley had suffered a 61–12 thrashing at Wakefield on Good Friday and a close defeat at Rochdale on the Saturday. After their full-back, Philip Walshaw, had kicked Batley into a 6–5 interval lead with his 99th goal of the season, Northern finally ran out comfortable 21–6 winners. Playing down the slope they scored four unanswered tries against weary opponents. Scrum-half Gordon Haley created golden opportunities for his colleagues as a result of which Malcolm Davies claimed an easy hat-trick.

The following day at Odsal Davies scored four more tries to head the league's try-scoring chart at that stage of the season on 43, one ahead of Wigan's Mick Sullivan. Ralph Winnard also helped himself to a hat-trick in a 31–22 victory, to take his tally to four in the two holiday games, and 19-year-old, reserve loose-forward, Alan Dawes, also strolled in for a try on his debut after selling a cheeky dummy. Alan and his brother Ken had both been coached by Donald Ward, when the former Northern half-back was player-coach at Wyke. The former Keighley Albion right-winger, Gerald Handley, also made his senior debut in the latter game and did enough to retain his place. Fielding a makeshift side, Batley had therefore suffered their fourth defeat in five days. Their only bright spot came from Philip Walshaw, who kicked his 100th goal of the season. His consistency must have been the envy of the Odsal officials, as they watched Beevers again struggle with the boot, and the Batley full-back, who also impressed with his touch-finding, was high on their list of possible signings.

Malcolm Davies, along with Winnard and Dawes, also scored in a 24–21 defeat to Huddersfield at Odsal the following Saturday. Huddersfield had suffered three defeats over Easter, but Northern were in a benevolent mood in a typical end-of-season affair as indicated by the 11 tries scored. Despite Dawes being concussed for threequarters of the game, Northern were well in control, but faded badly in the last quarter to gift the game to the Fartowners. This match was watched by a Canadian Football promoter, who was considering introducing rugby league forwards to his code of football. However, he went away impressed with the play of backs Gordon Haley and Gerald Handley.

In a 26–13 defeat to York, the fourth meeting between the two sides that season, Northern trailed 11–2 at half-time at Clarence Street after winger Peter Foster had scored two tries in the first 12 minutes, and hooker Brian Thompson had kicked the first of his two goals. Northern rallied with tries from Daniels, Malcolm Davies and Smith to reduce the deficit to 16–13, but York finished well with two late converted tries.

The future scorer of nine tries against Doncaster 'A' (on 13 September 1958 from stand-off), former Ovenden junior, 18-year-old Geoff Higgins scored a brilliant solo try on his debut at scrum-half to clinch a hard fought 21–13 win over Bramley at Odsal. Making his 52nd successive appearance, Bob Smith dislocated his shoulder, an injury which caused him to announce his retirement from the game before the start of the following season. Since signing from Abertillery in February 1950, this stylish centre and winger had made 163 appearances and scored 86 tries, including 22 in the 1951–52 Championship leading campaign.

In losing the final game of the season 38–23 at Post Office Road, Northern could not contain the Featherstone pack or match the astute touches of loose-forward Harry Street. It was ironic, that after the lamentable goalkicking throughout the season, Bill Jenkins should land seven goals from nine attempts. It took his tally to a mere 47 as the leading kicker, while Malcolm Davies finished with 46 tries.

In another disappointing season, in which they missed the regular influence of Derek Davies and Jack Scroby due to National Service commitments, Northern finished 20th in the league. Both Malcolm Davies and Milan Kosanovic had established themselves as full international prospects. But, for next season, there was a crying need for a settled pack formation, and, of course, a reliable goalkicker. In all games, including the Lazenby Cup, Northern had scored 163 tries yet kicked only 85 goals.

On the financial front, at the Yorkshire Committee in mid-March, Northern had unsuccessfully volunteered to play in the Lancashire League, as did hard-up Dewsbury, for the following season's league fixtures, enticed by the prospect of the suggested grant of £1,000 as compensation for the extra travelling. As it was, Leeds again qualified for that role, which again deprived Northern, and other Yorkshire clubs, of their potentially largest gate. At a special meeting at Odsal on 15 April the directors explained that the ground was still costing around £4,000 a year to maintain and they were responsible for £10,000 in guarantees to creditors. The club received a 10 per cent share of the revenue from the big games at Odsal, but many of the old railway sleepers that made up the terraces were rotten and there was a need for investment in concrete terracing.

Regardless of its shortcomings, Odsal was granted the Challenge Cup semi-final over Headingley, due in part to its seating capacity, including track seats, of 9,400, with 4,420 of these under cover; and had the Wembley final between Wigan and Workington Town been drawn then the replay would have been at Odsal on the following Wednesday evening, with a crowd limit set at 80,000.

Despite high unemployment in Workington, which affected the level of their travelling support, there was still an attendance of 57,699, who paid £11,214, for the Championship final, when a powerful Hull side beat Town 20–3. Unfortunately, after leading 3–0, the beaten Wembley finalists were reduced to 12 men with the loss of Ces Thompson in the 28th minute with a badly twisted ankle. It was a sad sight to see the second-rower stretchered off, and, as this seriously affected the outcome of the game, it again supported the arguments for substitutes in major games where an injury could be verified by a doctor.

1957–58 Summary
Position in League: 20th of 30 P 38 W 16 L 20 D 2 – Pts 574–594
Yorkshire Cup: Semi-final replay. Challenge Cup: Second round.
Average attendance: 4,651 (4,268 league games only)

6. 1958–59: 10th in the table
Gates still slump despite late season success

Chairman Harry Hornby's decision to retire heralded a new era in the club's affairs. His shares, plus the property of Odsal Speedway, were taken over by the directors, which meant that no one shareholder could then have a controlling interest; and Northern would no longer be directly involved in promoting speedway at the stadium. Jackie Barritt, who had been chairman of Batley for the previous 16 years, had joined the board at the end of May and was installed as chairman of the selection committee. An amateur sportsman in his youth, he captained Batley Cricket Club and played half-back for the Batley and Roundhay rugby union clubs. He had been chairman of the Yorkshire Senior Competition for the past 12 years, was then a member of the RFL's management committee and had been an international selector since 1952. He ran a bakery and confectionary business in Batley.

In late May 1958 a new Bradford Northern Development Fund was registered, following a disagreement between the directors and the Supporters' Club. The new committee was chaired by Fred Wood, the managing director of Yorkshire Engineering and Welding Co, and the vice-chairman was director Trevor Foster, who had joined the board in February. Other members included Doris Beard, the club's assistant secretary, and H. Bairstow, the only supporter not to have resigned over the dispute. He was registered as the new pools' promoter. For the new season, the Development Fund bought a set of kit for 30 players for £300. A new Supporters' Club was later formed with Trevor Foster as chairman.

The previous season, Northern had had a number of fruitless attempts to find a more reliable goalkicker. They had shown interest in Workington Town's 29-year-old full-back Stanley Thompson, the holder of Dewsbury's goalkicking record, who later joined Batley. In March they denied reports that they had offered over £3,000 to David Bell, Hull & East Riding's goalkicking full-back. The England rugby union trialist apparently had refused a similar offer from Hull KR. Swinton refused Northern's request to take their full-back, Jack Tobin, who was then on offer at £1,000, on a month's trial. Finally, in July 1958, they signed Batley's centre or full-back Philip Walshaw, at what was described as "a reasonable fee, due to the success of the pools". He had been listed at £1,000 at his own request in September 1956 and broke Jack Perry's club record with 115 goals in the 1957–58 season. It was the second time Jackie Barritt had signed the player; he had paid the former Wakefield League junior £200 to turn professional with Batley in 1951.

Walshaw kicked three goals from seven attempts in the 25–17 Lazenby Cup defeat on Tuesday 12 August at Lawkholme Lane, where Daniels raced almost the full length of the field for Northern's first try as they recovered from a 13–0 deficit. And it was the winger's 35-yard drop-goal that took them into a 17–15 lead, before Keighley scored 10 points in the last five minutes. The new play-the-ball rule, whereby a scrum had to be formed if the acting-half-back was tackled in possession before another player had touched the ball, was judged a success in opening out play.

The league programme, with Leeds again featuring in the Lancashire League, started with the tonic of a 15–13 win at Salford, where Kosanovic dictated the scrums and Jack Scroby, who was on leave from the Army, along with Derek Davies, was powerful in the loose. Quick thinking produced a duo of tries for Len Haley and one for Radford. Two of the tries were a direct result of superb runs by scrum-half Gordon Haley. Close eyes were on Walshaw's goalkicking and he managed three from five attempts, in contrast to Salford's kickers who could only manage two from seven.

Both Scroby and Davies had to return to Northern Ireland and therefore missed the 15–7 home victory over Leigh on the following Wednesday evening. Although slightly beaten in the scrums, none strove more conscientiously than Kosanovic, while Malcolm Davies, the scorer of two tries, turned in his most accomplished performance so far. On his return after a long layoff through injury, Len Haley was the architect of two tries, and Walshaw found the mark with vital goals late on to settle matters.

The following Saturday, Northern were in with a shout against the reigning league champions at Odsal; they trailed Hull by only 8–5 after 55 minutes. However, a hesitant defence and lack of stamina allowed the Airlie Birds to score three tries in an eight minute spell in the last quarter to win comfortably 21–8. Trevor Jones and Brian Radford had midfield breaks ruined by lack of support and both try-scorers, Malcolm

Davies and Handley, were neglected on the wings. Gordon Haley's failure to link with his colleagues ruined much of his brilliant individual work, although he continued to impress with his touch-finding and eager cover tackling.

Northern's "pathetic and puerile" work at Crown Flatt on the Tuesday saw them lose 21–12, after they opened up the Dewsbury defence as early as the sixth minute and later appeared to have the game in their grasp. Kosanovic gave them a 26–16 advantage in the scrums, but their leaden-footed forwards' play was so unimaginative that Dewsbury were able to manage without their injured stand-off Brian Foley for the final 15 minutes. The game's most conspicuous figure was referee F.G. Howker from Rochdale, who lectured both sides and awarded 30 penalties.

As a result of this inept performance, four changes were made for the Yorkshire Cup tie against York at Odsal, including the inclusion of stand-off Derek Davies and loose-forward Jack Scroby, who were again flown in from Northern Ireland at the club's expense. Try-scorer Kosanovic again won the scrums, but Northern surrendered the lead three times after leading 12–8 at half-time. Although he kicked four goals, flat-footed Walshaw's slowness into the tackle was exploited by nippy opponents, who scored seven tries to Northern's five. The final score of 31–23 flattered York, and meant that Northern had won only two of their last 13 games against the Minstermen.

Northern's mediocre form continued at Craven Park, where they lost 19–14 despite scoring four tries to Hull KR's three. Trailing 17–6 at half-time, in the second-half, which was marred by brawls and fisticuffs, they had enough possession and territorial advantage to have won the game. However, between them, Walshaw, with five, and Jenkins missed with seven kicks at goal, which cost Northern the match. For right-winger Gerald Handley, who made a good impression in his six appearances, this proved to be his last senior game. After his National Service he returned to Odsal in 1961–62 season, but did not make the first team squad.

Len Haley resigned the captaincy that he had held since September 1956 because he felt the extra responsibility was affecting his form. Jenkins then celebrated his promotion to the role with a first-class display in a 26–16 defeat against Warrington at Odsal, where Northern turned a nine point deficit into a one point lead, within nine dramatic minutes of the restart. On his senior debut, hooker Gerald Welsh, who had recently been signed from Burton Sports Club in Leeds, edged the scrums and Walshaw kicked five goals from five attempts. However, Northern lacked the sort of leadership shown by loose-forward Harry Major and Warrington's greater pace and mobility – including some Brian Bevan magic – saw them score six tries in inflicting Northern's fifth successive defeat. This marked Stan Rodwell's last first team appearance. He scored 14 tries in 31 appearances, not including the four he scored on his debut against Albi.

Injuries to several York players in the last 15 minutes could not detract from Northern's well-merited 20–3 win at Clarence Street, where the new half-back pairing of Gordon Haley and Alan Lancaster was a great success. Jenkins landed three of his four goals from long distances and Welsh maintained the form shown on his debut. Beevers had stepped in for Walshaw, who, it was now revealed, had been nursing a thigh strain for most of the season. Lancaster was later listed at £600 and had a month's trial at Dewsbury, but was not transferred.

The return of Kosanovic was the only change for the visit of Doncaster, whose spoiling tactics kept them in the game for long periods until they were overcome 26–16. Jenkins gave an inspirational captain's performance with two tries and six goals, but for which Northern would have struggled. This was Bryn Hopkins' final game before he announced his retirement.

The 11–11 draw at Mount Pleasant, where Northern gave an inept display, meant that after the first nine league games they were in 13th place in the table with nine points and had scored and conceded the same number of points, 137. Northern were fortunate to come away with a point because Malcolm Davies's try was disputed and Batley's full-back, Stanley Thompson, hit the post with a penalty kick in the closing stages.

The dismissal of Hunslet's Harry Poole and Kelly, early in the second-half when the scores were level at 7–7, appeared to indicate that a shock Northern victory was on the cards at Odsal. The game marked the debut of former Stanningley loose-forward, Steve Hey, who had earned rapid promotion after only four reserve outings. However, his opposite number, Brian Shaw, inspired an amazing comeback and Northern were finally humbled 17–7. To add to Northern's woes, Kosanovic, who had been named in Yorkshire's shadow side for the game against Lancashire later in the month, was also dismissed in the 68th minute and was later banned for one match. Fortunately, Geoff Higgins struck up a strong relationship with Len Haley and kept his place at scrum-half until the end of the season.

Welsh deputised for Kosanovic for the visit to Post Office Road, where Northern did well to hold Featherstone for the first 35 minutes. However, they then faded badly, with atrocious handling in the second-half, to lose 29–5. Peter Baddeley, the Doncaster second-rower, made the first of two appearances during his month's trial, but was not signed as Northern's offer was less than Doncaster's £750 valuation.

Five players were dropped for the visit of Hull KR, when Kosanovic dominated the scrums and Steve Hey gave a five-star performance as Northern scored five tries to four in a gallant 20–17 defeat. On his senior debut, 20-year-old centre George Penketh, along with half-backs Higgins and Oddy, was one of a trio of former Ovenden juniors who deserved to be retained. After trials with Halifax, he had played in the 'A' team since the end of 1957. This was Rovers' first win at Odsal since November 1935, ending a run of 16 successive defeats. Defensively, Walshaw had again been cruelly exposed and this was his final senior game of the season.

In his place, Bill Seddon made a pleasing return after injury, with strong tackling and smart link-ups in a welcome 17–15 win at Doncaster, where Northern conceded three tries in the first 15 minutes. There was eager support play from Higgins, and Penketh was again prominent, but it took a 67th minute try from Malcolm Davies, who cut inside three defenders, to clinch matters. Up to this point of the season he had been well below his best form. With stiff competition for places at half-back, this was Gordon Haley's final game prior to his transfer to Dewsbury.

Northern's confidence was further boosted by a skilful 10-try rout of Dewsbury at Odsal, where there were hat-tricks for both Malcolm and Derek Davies in the 38–13 victory. The improved teamwork and support play of Penketh and Higgins augured well for the future. But the game was watched by only 2,500 fans with receipts of just £210. The extra expense of flying Davies and Scroby from Northern Ireland ate into this figure.

In November Batley lost interest in signing transfer-listed Ralph Winnard at Northern's asking price, and Dewsbury offered less than

£500. He was then in competition with Penketh and Jenkins for one of the centre berths, but then played every game in 1959–60 and remained at Odsal until 1962.

Northern earned a bonus for their defeat at Belle Vue, where they troubled Trinity with tenacious tackling in a 13–8 defeat. Although Northern won only two of the 13 second-half scrums, they still led for four-fifths of the game after holding a 5–0 interval lead through a brilliant 75-yard try by Daniels. He also pulled off a try-saving tackle on Ken Hirst after racing across to the opposite flank. Great Britain prop Don Vines got his marching orders late in the game, before Neil Fox's last minute drop-goal took his seasonal points tally to 150.

Kosanovic missed the 16–12 victory over York at Odsal, because he was playing for a Rugby League XIII which lost 26–8 against France at St Helens. York, who missed Vic Yorke, who kicked four goals in the game at St Helens, pulled back an 11 point deficit in the second-half. However, Northern fought a spirited rearguard action to inflict the first league double over the visitors since 1952–53. In a side which was now moving the ball with some skill, Penketh and Daniels were becoming Northern's most potent attacking force, while the marked improvement in the goalkicking from the previous season was emphasised by the fact that two of Seddon's five goals were landed from the touchline.

Keighley were expected to bring at least 1,000 fans for their visit on 29 November, but the game was cancelled due to fog. How many would have travelled is debatable because Wakefield Trinity, with 4,500 versus Hunslet, and Dewsbury, who mustered 453 versus Bramley, both had their lowest crowds of the season. The eight games in Yorkshire averaged only 2,500.

Although still without Derek Davies and Jack Scroby, who were needed for an Army rugby union game the following Monday, Northern were rapidly gaining in confidence and they gave their best display of the season in inflicting Halifax's first home defeat – 23–18 – in over two months. Most of their five tries were the result of superb moves prompted by Len Haley and Higgins, and first-class finishing by Malcolm Davies and Daniels. The latter's strike rate had doubled since the arrival of Penketh. An important score in the second-half went to Trevor Jones, who raced through a huge gap created by a back-flip from Higgins.

70

Northern then climbed to 11th in the table following a 27–12 home win over Whitehaven, who had nine regulars absent. At one stage the Cumbrians held a nine point lead before Northern, led brilliantly by two-try Len Haley and the ever-improving Steve Hey, responded with 21 points without reply. Trevor Jones also picked up two smart tries in the treacherous snowy and foggy conditions. The game marked Brian Radford's 300th senior appearance, in what was his well-deserved joint testimonial season with Bill Jenkins. Although the board introduced a scheme of allowing free entry to the New Stand in bad weather, the attendance was still only 2,000. So far the nine home league games had averaged attendances of 3,600, with the away games 1,000 higher.

Apart from the return of Scroby, who replaced the reliable and industrious Walter Hemingway in the second-row, Northern fielded an unchanged side for their visit to Hilton Park. But they were no match for the Leigh forwards. Kosanovic lost the scrums by a ratio of 3–1 to Lancashire's hooker, Walt Tabern, and the side crashed to its heaviest defeat of the season, 31–9. It was a miserable afternoon for Northern, because Jenkins (ribs), Crabtree (torn buttock muscles), and Penketh, who played most of the game with a cracked jaw, all sustained injuries which kept them out of action for several weeks.

The club's financial position was also under strain, with under £600 received from the three games since the start of November and the need to pay off one or two past items of heavy expenditure. To ease the crisis the RFL granted them a £3,000 loan, and later in December Northern finally agreed to the terms of the Corporation's three year rent free offer, which they had declined in 1957. The AGM on 30 December 1958 was attended by only five directors and seven shareholders, and no balance sheet was produced. It was admitted that the £7,000 received from the pools in the previous 18 months had gone on running costs due to bad gates. At another meeting, on 25 March, 1959, the accounts for the year ending 30 June 1958 showed a loss of £2,410 and a deficit of £7,390. Total receipts had been £26,895 (£15,511 net after payments to the RFL and other clubs) but no profit was made on show jumping and other non-rugby league events. Wages rose to £8,054, ground maintenance cost £2,527 and Northern paid out £1,189 more in transfer fees than they received.

Northern against Hunslet at Odsal 1958–59, which marked Steve Hey's senior debut. Back: Jones, Radford, G. McLean, Feather, Kosanovic, M. Davies, Hey; front: Higgins, L. Haley, Beevers, Jenkins, Walshaw, Daniels.
(Courtesy *Rugby League Journal*)

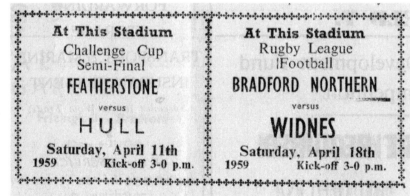

At This Stadium
Challenge Cup
Semi-Final
FEATHERSTONE
versus
HULL
Saturday, April 11th
1959   Kick-off 3-0 p.m.

At This Stadium
Rugby League
Football
BRADFORD NORTHERN
versus
WIDNES
Saturday, April 18th
1959   Kick-off 3-0 p.m.

Adverts from the programme promoting two of the end of season matches at Odsal.

Douglas Maclean (left), George Penketh and David Walton, pictured at Odsal in March 1959. (Courtesy Bradford Bulls Foundation RL Heritage Project).

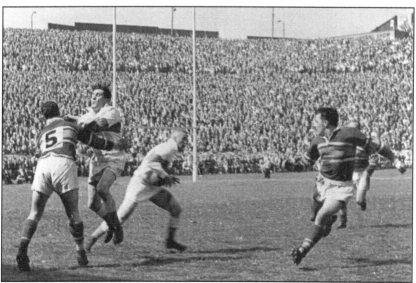

As he is tackled by Hunslet's Willie Walker, a future new Northern signing, St Helens centre Duggie Greenall slips a pass to Tom van Vollenhoven in the 1959 Championship final at Odsal. Greenall joined Northern as player-coach for an ill-fated spell in 1960–61.

Commenting on Wakefield Trinity spending a rugby league record of over £22,000 on new players in one season, the chairman, Cyril Bunney, admitted that "Northern did not have 22,000 shillings to spend". Looking to the future, however, the directors felt they were winning the uphill battle of unearthing young talent. Hey, Higgins and Penketh were a trio with great potential, and the 'A' team were having a particularly good season.

Northern picked up six points over the Christmas period with a double over Bramley, 36–16 and 17–9, and an amazing 31–6 win at Fartown. Compared to the care-free game at Odsal on Christmas Day, when Northern ran in eight tries, the meeting on Boxing Day was a stern tussle in the mud. Kosanovic, beaten 2–1 in the scrums at Odsal, gained the majority of possession at the Barley Mow, where the burly George McLean was really in his element in a dominant pack led by Trevor Jones. At Fartown, after leading 12–0 at half-time, Northern ran Huddersfield ragged with some brilliant handling of a greasy ball. Malcolm Davies scored a hat-trick – including an obstruction try –to take his tally over the holiday period to six, while, in the three games, Bill Seddon kicked 15 goals. Since returning from injury, the New Zealander, who had drawn winning pay from eight of those 10 games, had put in some outstanding performances. He was solid in defence and provided plenty of flair in attack. Unfortunately, both Derek Davies, who was admitted to Bradford Royal Infirmary with a shoulder injury against Huddersfield, and Jack Scroby, with an ear injury against Bramley, were Christmas casualties.

Norman Mackie, who had retired with elbow trouble in 1957–58 season, turned out for Wakefield Trinity 'A' in December 1958, with Dai Rees arguing that he had no complaints because Northern had recently recruited forward David Walton from the Wakefield League.

Northern started the New Year, in 13th position, with the first of five consecutive defeats. After giving Salford a 10 point half-time lead at Odsal through slipshod covering, Northern rallied brilliantly with three tries in 11 minutes. This should have won the game because Salford were tottering, but Seddon missed two kicks from under the posts and Salford hit back near the end to win 15–9. On his return after injury, Jenkins never looked comfortable, but neither Hey, who had a sparkling game, nor Kosanovic, who did his work in the scrums, deserved to lose.

After two cancellations due to snow and ice, at Warrington and at home to Castleford, Northern then made a trip to Whitehaven. Clive Brook, a 21-year-old former Lockwood centre, made his senior debut at the Recreation Ground. He did a lot of the forwards' tackling in a 15–3 defeat. His fellow centre Winnard also showed toughness, which many of the pack lacked. With more possession the backs would have had more than a first-half try by Malcolm Davies, which levelled the score at the interval. However, despite committed work from Hey, the rest of the pack faded in the second-half as Whitehaven upped the tempo to win comfortably.

The margin of defeat, 22–7, at The Boulevard flattered Hull. The game was decided in a 10 minute period before and after half-time. Tommy Finn scored a hotly disputed try with Seddon claiming he had held him up over the line; and then Len Haley's pass was snapped up by Ivor Watts as Northern were pressing. The home six, superbly led by Johnny Whiteley, had the edge, but Northern's pack, urged on by captain Trevor Jones, atoned for recent poor form with a tenacious performance. Northern's hopes of a top gate were dashed when a frozen pitch forced a cancellation against Halifax. It would have been the first game at Odsal in five weeks.

Beevers deputised for influenza victim Seddon for the visit to top-four candidates Widnes, whose 14–10 victory was their seventh on the trot. The Chemics were nine points up in 18 minutes and Northern never managed to make up this leeway, despite scoring the same number of tries – from Malcolm Davies and Hey. Daniels did not have the speed to finish on two occasions and Higgins stumbled on the run-in when he had effectively beaten the defence. In the end it was full-back Arthur Pimblett's three penalties which decided matters, but Northern were glorious in defeat.

Northern's 11–2 setback against Huddersfield in the first round of the Challenge Cup at Odsal not only blemished their previously referred to record, but it also made the rest of the season's outlook appear bleak. In the previous post-war clashes with Huddersfield the winners had progressed to the Challenge Cup final, in 1947, 1948 and 1953, but this sequence was to be broken. In a dour struggle, watched by a crowd of 6,470, Northern's pack all but burnt out the Huddersfield six, although in Jack Fairbank the Fartowners had the game's outstanding forward. With the half-time score only 2–0 down, once winger Aidan

Breen had scored in the corner, the matter was decided by a special try by 33-year-old Ernie Ashcroft, although the centre's task was made easier by Daniels' fatal inclination to seek the interception.

Northern then ended their league campaign with a flourish in losing only three of their last 12 games. This sequence commenced with a seven-try, 29–15 home victory over Batley, who were no match for Northern's backs, even though Malcolm Davies and Derek Davies were both absent through representing Wales in Toulouse on the Sunday. The latter was the travelling reserve, and was only eligible through having a Welsh born father. Making his first of only three appearances that season, Douglas Maclean sharpened up the service from stand-off and Daniels helped himself to a hat-trick of tries as well as making another. The game saw the debut of 21-year-old Jack Doran who joined the club as a trialist in the 'A' team in December 1958 before signing as a professional in April 1959. The former Victoria Rangers winger, who was over six feet tall, had few chances on the right flank, where he was opposed by former Northerner Eric Sutton, but proved he was not short on courage.

Northern then blooded 21-year-old David Walton, a hard-working, former Wakefield Trinity front-rower, in an 18–8 Odsal success against Keighley, who wilted in the final quarter after holding territorial advantage. Leading 6–5 at half-time, Northern held the visitors for the first hour with tenacious defence and then scored 10 points in the last 13 minutes. Malcolm Davies defied a damaged ankle to score a vital try and Trevor Jones plunged over from Higgins's back-flip.

The following Wednesday, a leaderless Northern gave a feeble display against Castleford, who enjoyed their first taste of floodlit rugby, and were humiliated 23–9. Bob Taylor, who later moved to Odsal in 1960–61, provided power in the centre which no Northern player could match. In the return fixture on the Saturday, Northern totally rejigged their backs and gained their revenge, 12–11, although Castleford had a try disallowed in the last minute after leading by seven points early in the game.

Halifax then played their first ever game under the Odsal lights on the following Monday, 16 March, when they beat Northern 13–10. The 4,000 spectators were kept enthralled by the closeness rather than the quality of the game, in which each side incurred 14 penalties – Bill Seddon and Peter Briers each landed five goals. Halifax had a 2–1 scrum advantage, but Northern went ahead five times and Higgins had two runs which were foiled only inches short. Reserve scrum-half, Bryn Jones, later a member of new Northern's original squad, got the match's only try with a solo effort.

On Easter Saturday Northern earned a well-deserved 15–15 draw against second placed Hunslet at Parkside, where only Hull and Oldham had taken a point that season. Hunslet had exerted themselves at Headingley the previous evening before 27,000 spectators. But this could not detract from Northern's spirited display after they saw an 8–2 lead, following tries from Penketh and Doran, change to 15–8 down in the five minutes before half-time. In this spell the powerful 19-year-old, former Pontypool left-winger, John Griffiths, scored a try on his Hunslet debut, and full-back Bill Langton's three goals took him to the head of the league's goalkicking list with 150 for the season. Intelligent prompting by Scroby and mighty midfield surges by George McLean helped turn the tide as Hunslet were kept scoreless in the second-half. Northern's fans enjoyed the sight of Brian Radford racing 45-yards for the vital try after Scroby had scooped up a loose ball on his own 25-line and created the opportunity.

On Easter Monday, unpredictable Northern fielded the same side, except for Walton who replaced Hey at loose-forward, and again succumbed to Huddersfield at Odsal, this time 18–7. Northern held the upperhand at the start, when on at least three occasions their forwards were forced back after bulldozing their way over the line. But in the 11th minute a counterattack resulted in them conceding a try and thereafter Huddersfield's mobile back-row tightened their grip, which allowed left-winger Aidan Breen to race in unopposed at the corner for the second of their four tries. Northern's backs made little headway because of their forwards' reliance on barging tactics, and only once did they manage to breach a resolute defence, when Daniels crossed.

The following day at Keighley Northern won 12–11. This started a run of five successive wins until the end of the season. At half-time two Terry Hollindrake penalty goals were all the Lawkholmers had to show for their continuous pressure. Northern led 9–4, with a try from Penketh and three goals from Seddon. A converted try from winger Roy Bleasby then levelled matters before Hollindrake's fourth goal gave Keighley the lead for the first time. However, in the dying minutes, a grand try from Derek Davies gave Northern two valuable points against

Yorkshire opposition. With Leeds deciding to return as a Yorkshire club next season, Northern were then striving to clinch at least ninth place in the Yorkshire League, in order to retain their current fixture status against the middle five Lancashire sides.

They confounded all expectations in beating fifth-placed Wakefield Trinity 12–9 on the Saturday after Easter, after trailing 7–2. Trinity badly missed Neil Fox and Don Vines who were both on duty with Great Britain in Grenoble. Bill Seddon made several try-saving tackles before creating the try of the match on the 25th minute. After making a breathtaking break, the full-back kicked over Gerry Round's head, caught the ball before it had bounced, and sent the supporting Higgins over for a converted try, which levelled matters at half-time. It was curtains for Trinity when Derek Davies scored another spectacular try in the 64th minute, after prop Brian Radford and reinstated second-rower Norman Feather had made 70 yards between them. Before Odsal's largest crowd of the season, 7,500, Kosanovic was a tower of strength in the scrums and the loose. This was despite suffering from mild concussion for two-thirds of the game.

Northern's scheduled home game on 11 April against Featherstone was postponed because Rovers were at Odsal in the Challenge Cup semi-final. Playing behind a mighty pack, half-back George Matthews scored a hat-trick of tries in Hull's 15–5 success, watched by a crowd of 52,131.

Before the home game against Widnes, the club doctor and future director, Dr Harry Fidler, had Northern's players vaccinated against a polio outbreak in the city. The eighth-placed Chemics had won four on the trot, but Northern's 18–12 victory was more pronounced than the scoreline suggests. A highlight was the manner in which Higgins opened up a bewildered defence with his trademark back-flip for Trevor Jones to romp over from a scrum close to the line. Unfortunately, Malcolm Davies suffered a nose injury early on, which appeared to upset his confidence.

Northern's team spirit reached new heights at a waterlogged Wilderspool, where skipper Trevor Jones celebrated his 100th senior appearance for the club in Northern's 14–6 victory over ninth-placed Warrington. In gaining revenge for the earlier home defeat, Northern owed a huge debt to Bill Seddon, whose all-round performance, including four goals and some intelligent touch-finding, easily outshone test full-back Eric Fraser.Higgins scored the first try and created the other for Kosanovic, while George McLean used his 17 stones to good effect in the forward skirmishes, where Scroby and Hey also shone. This meant Northern could boast of wins against all their five Lancashire opponents. This was hailed as their best performance, because no other Yorkshire side had taken a point off the Wire at Wilderspool all season.

In a dreary end-of-season match at Odsal, Northern beat Featherstone 20–8, but victory was not certain until three minutes from the end when Radford sparked off a 10 point scoring burst. Although he only restarted playing in November after injury, Seddon took his points tally for the season to 147.

Northern's fifth successive win – their best sequence all season – clinched 10th place in the league and guaranteed that for the following season they would retain fixtures against the second-flight Lancashire clubs. Their current team spirit and form certainly supported the official view that better times were ahead at Odsal and that they were deserving of better support. Unfortunately, Northern had reserved most of their better performances for their away games – 20 of their 42 points were gained away from Odsal – and had suffered five defeats at home against teams they had managed to beat on their own grounds. Consequently, although their stock had not been higher for several seasons, the late surge came too late to make any impression on attendances. The 19 home league games attracted an average of 3,526, a new post-war low.

During the close season two of Northern's most experienced backs, Arthur Daniels and Bill Jenkins, announced their retirements. 31-year-old Bill Jenkins's decision to retire was prompted by his promotion at Enfield Rolling Mills, where he worked as a chemist. His final first team game was against Halifax at Odsal in March, although he scored two tries in his joint testimonial game with Brian Radford and Keighley's Ernest Redman at Odsal in October 1959. Such was his versatility that he played loose-forward and every back position, except scrum-half, in his 241 appearances; scored 80 tries and 105 goals for a total of 450 points. He later received a cheque for £175 from his joint testimonial fund with Brian Radford. Since his signing from Halifax for the start of the 1957–58 season, 34-year-old Arthur Daniels scored 35 tries in his 61 appearances.

Derek Davies and Brian Radford, the latter who had played for Wales in 1952, were in a Welsh International XIII which played three games against St Helens from 18 to 23 May in Llanelli, Pontypool and Cardiff.

Odsal's third Championship final saw St Helens beat Hunslet 44–22 in a classic before a Whitsuntide bank holiday crowd of 52,560, who paid £9,890. The great Tom van Vollenhoven, who had recovered from a thigh injury in the semi-final against Oldham, scored a hat-trick of tries which included one of the most spectacular ever seen at Odsal. Unfortunately, the BBC failed to archive the footage of this remarkable score and I did not see the game. It was the one final I missed. I was on a school trip to Edinburgh, where a wily newspaper seller on Princes Street convinced two naïve youths that the Scottish sports paper had a report and pictures of the game, when there was not even the result.

1958–59 Summary
Position in league: 10th of 30 P 38 W 20 L 16 D 2 – Pts 593–563
Yorkshire Cup: First round. Challenge Cup: First round.
Average attendance: 3,745 (3,526 league games only)

7. 1959–60: Scroby sold for record fee
Northern slip 16 places in the league

Before the start of the season, the directors attempted a membership drive, because the number of season ticket holders in 1958–59 had dropped to only 247, paying £479, from the high of 1,534, paying £2,963, in the 1952–53 season. However, their cause was not helped when the disappointing news broke in late August that Halifax had signed Jack Scroby for a club record £7,500. While the fee, which was to be paid in instalments, helped to reduce the club's deficit at a time when Northern were struggling to keep their heads above water, the departure of their best forward was a major blow to the hopes of sustaining the previous season's progress and regaining lost support.

Northern had turned down a previous transfer request, but apparently the directors could not believe that Halifax would pay such a large asking price. As Scroby was still on National Service with the Duke of Wellington Regiment, with whom he had represented the Army in all the previous season's major rugby union games, including playing twice at Twickenham, director Trevor Foster had flown out to Northern Ireland to get his signature on the transfer forms. Since signing as a junior from Ovenden in 1955, Scroby had made 103 appearances. He made his debut for Halifax in the Yorkshire Cup win over Wakefield on 29 August.

Northern's only pre-season signing was of Wyke forward Ken Dawes, who later in the season made his only first team appearance, alongside his brother Alan. But Dai Rees's scouting mission to South Wales in September resulted in the signing of former Abertillery and New Brighton second-rower Gray Robbins who had represented Monmouthshire and the Army in rugby union. The 23-year-old had impressed in two trials with the 'A' team and was available immediately after his discharge from the forces.

The season began on 10 August at Lawkholme Lane, where Northern beat Keighley 19–18 in the Lazenby Cup, thanks to a 78th minute try by Winnard, converted by captain Trevor Jones. But photographic evidence clearly suggests that centre Terry Hollindrake had a perfectly good try disallowed, which effectively cost Keighley the game. Substitutes were agreed on for the second-half, but only Northern made use of them.

In the opening league game at Odsal, Northern trailed 15–10 at half-time and had to come from behind three times to beat Workington Town 20–15. In a courageous, hardworking pack, Steve Hey vied with Town's Ces Thompson as man-of-the match. Both men set up two tries and scored one themselves. Northern's forwards took control in the second-half with converted tries from Kosanovic and Jones.

At Bentley Road, on Thursday 20 August, Northern crashed to their first ever league defeat to Doncaster, 17–16, despite scoring four tries to three and always appearing to have the edge. Then, on the following Saturday, after being in the game for the first hour, Northern were thrashed 35–6 at Warrington. Nineteen-year-old stand-off Bobby Greenhough created six of Warrington's seven tries by punishing Northern's weakness around the base of the scrum. Welsh had an unhappy time deputising for the injured Kosanovic, and lost the scrums 25–7. Northern leaked 25 points in the last quarter.

Scroby's move to Halifax took place around the time that Northern beat Keighley 13–11 at Odsal, where Seddon kicked five goals from seven attempts. Keighley gave away 23 penalties and following a loose-arm offence, at a scrum in front of the posts, Seddon won this tedious game with the last kick of the match. The only highlight was a 70-yard try-scoring run from Keighley's second-rower, Geoff Crewdson, in the 15th minute. Loose-forward Fred Ward made a quiet debut for Keighley following his record £3,000 transfer from Leeds.

Northern's 23–10 home defeat in the Yorkshire Cup was never in doubt once Hull built up a 16–2 interval lead. In a 10 minute spell half-backs George Matthews and Tommy Finn shared four tries as a result of the ball-handling skills of Tommy Harris and Brian Hambling. Unfortunately, Derek Davies's lightning pace never bore fruit due to poor handling by the backs and two of Hull's tries resulted from Northern mistakes.

This was Malcolm Davies's last game in the first team because, due to a loss of form and confidence, he played out the rest of his stay at Odsal with the 'A' team. In October he was placed on the transfer list at £500 and turned down a move to Dewsbury before he signed for Bramley in mid-November, having scored 97 tries in his 90 appearances. He scored against Northern on Christmas Day 1959, at the Barley Mow, and retired as a player at the age of 33 on 21 March 1960. He continued as Northern's pools promoter until May 1962, a role he later fulfilled with great success at Keighley. On his return to Wales he set up a glass and china wholesalers in Barry and went on to serve his local community after he retired.

Northern then had a dramatic 12–10 home win over Widnes, following a Seddon penalty in the 78th minute, having scored seven points in the last six minutes. Bradford junior Peter Nunns made his debut and replaced Malcolm Davies on the left-wing. Apart from Seddon, who kicked three goals from four attempts, Northern's backs had little to offer. Brian Radford and try-scorers Hey and Hemingway were Northern's best forwards.

In a 19–19 draw at Whitehaven, left-winger Clive Brook made a try-scoring return to the side in only his second senior game, having made his debut on the Recreation Ground in January 1959. Along with Winnard, he produced some devastating tackling. Seddon, who kicked five goals from six attempts, started the rally which brought Northern 15 points in the last 23 minutes; star forward Steve Hey scored in the dying minutes after a defensive error. On the final whistle, acting captain Len Haley went within inches of scoring.

Kosanovic missed the game at Whitehaven due to a leg injury, and Welsh deputised, but the following Wednesday, 16 September, he travelled to Hull as reserve for Yorkshire's game against Cumberland. This coincided with his second unsuccessful transfer request. He had been persuaded to stay by Cyril Bunney in 1958–59, and Dai Rees said that Northern had turned down a £4,000 offer from a West Riding club earlier in the season – most likely Halifax or Wakefield Trinity. The popular Yugoslav then had a superb game for Yorkshire in their 47–15 defeat of Australia on 28 September at Belle Vue. Propped by Don Robinson (Leeds) and Jack Wilkinson (Wakefield Trinity), as well as winning possession, he was very active in the loose and went over for a try. On 11 November he again played for Yorkshire in their 38–28 win over Lancashire, and edged the scrums 19–15. He was then chosen for the reserve squad for the second test against Australia at Headingley, as understudy to Hull's Tommy Harris.

After missing three games in January 1960 due to severe influenza, Kosanovic again requested a move, and Northern finally agreed to list him at £4,000, and would have accepted cash or a player exchange in any position. The 26-year-old was rumoured to be unsettled due to a lack of income because of Northern's poor performances. However, before the Challenge Cup transfer deadline he turned down a definite move to Barrow, who offered him a house and job, because he preferred to continue living in Halifax. He always appreciated the help that Northern had given him in developing his rugby career and continued to give the club good service until his subsequent transfer to Wakefield Trinity in 1961.

Anyone of six players could have been sent off in the ugly 19–10 defeat at Leigh; but Brian Radford was made the scapegoat by referee Wilson and was dismissed in the 74th minute. He subsequently missed two matches due to suspension. Seddon, whose five goals pulled Northern back to 11–10 behind after 53 minutes, was also booked along with George McLean. Hey was again the pick of a hard grafting pack, and his form had brought him to Wigan's attention.

Gray Robbins made his senior debut in a convincing 23–13 victory over out-of-form Halifax at Odsal. He and Alan Dawes formed an effective second-row partnership, and Kosanovic celebrated his Yorkshire selection against Australia by dominating the scrums. Northern stormed to a 23–5 lead after 49 minutes, against a Halifax side, handicapped by an injury to centre Geoff Palmer, who slipped to their sixth successive defeat.

With nine points from their first eight games Northern were in 13th place in the league, but their 16–15 defeat at Headingley on 3 October started a run of eight successive league defeats. Against all the odds, 11-man Leeds won the game thanks to a 76th minute try to young centre Peter Parker. Northern led 10–5 at half-time and could easily have had more tries against subdued opposition, for whom hooker Bernard Prior went off injured on the half-hour mark. Leeds also lost centre Derek Hallas in the second-half, but they still managed to stage a thrilling rally. Northern could still have won but full-back Walshaw, deputising for the injured Seddon, sliced a not too difficult penalty in the last minute.

Seddon missed a 30–6 home defeat to Hunslet on 10 October, because he was getting married. Hey was prominent in both of Doran's tries, but a sluggish Northern, who trailed 11–3 at half-time, were no match for Hunslet's powerful forwards, particularly Brian Shaw, Geoff Gunney and Don Hatfield, or their pacy backs. Geoff Shelton, Jim

Stockdill and 18-year-old debutant scrum-half, Roland Astbury, each scored two tries.

The "gloomy days at Odsal" continued with a 29–8 home defeat by Featherstone Rovers, who gave Northern an object lesson in teamwork. Once 19-year-old Terry Clawson gave Rovers the lead with a second minute penalty, their half-backs, Don Fox and Joe Mullaney, were rarely out of control. Fox toyed with a high-tackling defence to score two tries, and full-back Jackie Fennell kicked six goals. Grand work by Len Haley and Gray Robbins led to Hey scoring Northern's second try shortly after the break to take the score to 10–8. However, with the return to the field of their injured prop, Frank Moore, Rovers scored 19 unanswered points.

Following this game, 27-year-old George McLean, who had been the regular open-side prop since his debut in April 1957, told officials that he would not play for the club again due to a disagreement. He was transfer-listed at £500, later reduced to £250. He was allowed to assist his former junior club, Clayton, but returned to the first team in the 1960–61 season.

Workington Town full-back Syd Lowden's three penalty goals were the difference between the sides at Derwent Park. Northern scored four tries to three, but lost 19–14. The team's new pack formation, with the return of Jones and Hemingway and Dave Walton replacing George McLean, worked well, and Kosanovic won the scrums by a ratio of 2–1. However, Northern trailed Town 19–3 after an hour, until a stunning try by Walton sparked a late rally in which they scored three unanswered tries. Just as the home crowd sensed an easy victory, Walton set off on a remarkable 50-yard run; he brushed aside three men to score the game's best try. Then Doran and Penketh, with his second of the match, scored further unconverted tries.

A crowd of 1,500 braved the elements at Odsal to see a Northern select beat Keighley 40–34 in the Radford-Jenkins-Ernest Redman testimonial floodlit game on 26 October. Halifax's Johnny Freeman scored a hat-trick for Northern, and his team-mate John Thorley also gave his support. Walton kicked four goals and Bill Jenkins returned to score two tries. There was a first appearance for 22-year-old, former Huddersfield rugby union scrum-half, Denis Broadbent, who scored one of the 18 tries.

The Lazenby Cup side 1959–60. Back: Winnard, Malcolm Davies, Doran, Walton, Hemingway, Kosanovic, McLean; front: Seddon, Penketh, Higgins, Trevor Jones, Len Haley, Hey.
(Courtesy Bradford Bulls Heritage Foundation RL Heritage Project).

The backs take a breather at half-time in front of the old stand against Hull KR in March 1960. This was a familiar sight at Odsal until the speedway pits were adapted into makeshift dressing-rooms. Left to right: Derek Davies (on his haunches), Brian Smith, Doran, Winnard, Penketh, Higgins and Seddon. The forward bench is on the right. (Courtesy Duncan Preston).

Northern in training before the Challenge Cup tie against Castleford in 1960. Left to right, Trevor Jones, Alan Dawes, Welsh, Kosanovic, Marston and Hemingway. (Courtesy: Tony Capstick).

Over 83,000 packed into Odsal for the 1960 Championship final. (C.H. Wood)

Batley had not won at Odsal since 1935, but their 11–10 victory over a leaderless Northern was well-merited. On his first team debut, Denis Broadbent had an unenviable task behind a beaten pack, in which Kosanovic had a recurrence of his shoulder injury. Penketh snatched another brace of tries, including one in the last minute, but Seddon's conversion attempt from wide out struck the angle of the crossbar and post before bouncing back into play. On this performance experienced players of above average ability were badly needed.

Although they finally conceded seven tries, Northern then produced one of their best performances of the season against an Australian side which included seven of the test team which had beaten Great Britain 22–14 at Swinton. The Wednesday night floodlit game at Odsal was watched by a crowd of only 4,126, who paid £536, easily the lowest of the tour. The fans who had come were surprised to see Northern open the try-scoring when Penketh cut through to score his fifth try in three games. Northern's enterprising play could well have seen them hold a healthy half-time lead, but in the second-half the tourists, led by the balding but dynamic Brian Clay, and including the great Reg Gasnier, cut loose to win 29–8. However, Northern lost scrum-half Geoff Higgins with a broken leg, which put him out of the game for three months.

Alan Lancaster replaced Higgins for the visit to Post Office Road, where Featherstone Rovers, fresh from their Yorkshire Cup Final success against Hull, monopolised possession in a 16–5 victory. Northern's spirited defence kept the score to 8–2 at half-time, but they were pedestrian on attack and had no forwards to compare with Terry Clawson and Mick Clamp or backs with the initiative of Don Fox and Ken Greatorex. Lancaster tried hard behind a beaten pack, but Northern had little to offer as a combined force.

The club then signed open-side prop Peter Marston on a free transfer from Keighley. He was originally signed by Leigh from Bradford RUFC and had experience with Salford before joining Keighley in August 1956. He made 12 of his 54 Keighley appearances in 1958–59, but had since been unable to command a first team place. Following the transfer-listing of George McLean, Northern were hoping that Marston could add weight and experience to their scrummaging. He went straight into the first team at Hunslet, where Northern slipped to yet another defeat, 16–4.

Although Marston grafted hard and the team as a whole tackled vigorously, they had no one to match Hunslet's tearaway loose-forward Harry Poole, second-rower Terry Robbins or lively scrum-half Alvin Newall. In another disappointing game for Northern, there were also injuries to Penketh (cheekbone) and Len Haley (ankle), which caused both players to miss the next two games. This seventh successive league defeat plunged Northern to 24th place in the table.

There was finally some good news with the signing of York's highly-rated six foot right-winger, Brian Smith, who had scored 112 tries for the Minstermen. He had been transfer-listed at £1,500 and Northern stepped up their original £750 offer to agree terms; the Supporters' Club later presented the club with a cheque for his purchase. He was a sports teacher in his native Halifax, and found it difficult to travel to York for midweek training. After scoring four tries in six games early in the season, he lost his place at Clarence Street to the South African Hugh Gillespie. Smith was a physical training instructor at York Imperial Barracks when he signed for York, and had scored 30 tries in his first season of senior rugby, 1953–54, a feat he repeated in 1957–58. As previously mentioned, on 12 March 1958 he played in the first tour trial at Swinton, opposite Northern's Malcolm Davies, and was also named for the test trial at Headingley on 19 March 1958. In July 1957 he had been transfer-listed at £3,000.

Playing on the left-wing, Smith scored on his debut away to Hull KR on 21 November, but an ill-disciplined Northern again lost, 14–10, after leading 4–2 at the break. Derek Davies returned after playing in five 'A' team games and Norman Feather made his first appearance of the season in the second-row at the expense of Trevor Jones. Just after the break, Rovers shot into a 14–4 lead through the inspiration of hooker Alvin Ackerley, before Northern pulled back late tries from Smith and Doran; both wingers showed real determination in scoring.

Northern finally got back to winning ways with a 19–8 victory over Castleford at Odsal, where, once Marston had crossed in the fourth minute, they never lost the lead. However, they failed to convince the crowd of 1,500 – Northern's first gate under 2,000 since the pre-war Birch Lane days – that they had turned the corner. The visitors were the more impressive side until they lost their top try-scoring winger, Doug Iredale, after 30 minutes with an ankle injury. As Derek Davies was still struggling to find his old form, Northern tended to neglect their wingers. However, Doran still managed to score and Brian Smith saved his line frequently with fast recovering defence.

After being given a free transfer by Hull KR and playing in Leeds junior rugby, second-rower Harry Griffett had returned to Odsal earlier in the season, mainly as an on-field coach to the 'A' team. But his performances had been so impressive that he was promoted to face Halifax's formidable pack, including Jack Scroby, at Thrum Hall. Halifax finally won 14–11. They led 9–6 at half-time, thanks to tries by Johnny Freeman, after three minutes, and two by Alan Snowden, whose second came after a length-of-the-field move in the 30th minute. Using their abundant possession, Northern then pounded away at the line until Alan Lancaster dummied around the blind-side to score a 68th minute try, which Trevor Jones converted to level matters at 11–11 with his fourth goal of the match. Derek Davies was back to his sparkling best with many devastating bursts, but it was Halifax's youthful backs who finally triumphed. Bryn Jones helped make the winning try for centre John Burnett in the 72nd minute.

Northern's 30–15 defeat at Lawkholme Lane resulted from a totally inept display. Keighley's forwards, led by Fred Ward, were well in command. The home side posted six tries before Northern made the final score look a little more respectable with a late 10 point rally. This spiritless, disorganised performance immediately preceded the AGM, which was perhaps a good time for the directors to explain where the club was going.

Six of the previous season's regulars, soon to be seven, had retired or been transferred. The only experienced replacement, for whom Northern had paid a fee, was Brian Smith. Also, with only five wins from 17 games the 'A' team did not seem to have many players worthy of promotion.

At the AGM on 15 December 1959, the directors reported a loss of £2,622 for the year ending 30 June 1959, with a deficit of £10,013. The total gate receipts of £30,550 from all events produced a net income of £12,592, although the show jumping in the summer lost £1,250. Players' wages fell by £792 to £8,285. The above figures did not, of course, include any income from the transfer of Jack Scroby, but Jackie Barritt said that they were surprised that Halifax had agreed to pay as much as £7,500. Donations from the pools had again been substantial and the club also appreciated the Corporation's help by reducing the rent. Due to the state of the wooden terracing, estimates had been obtained for a small amount of concrete terracing, four or five steps, at the Rooley Avenue end, near the New Stand, but this made no impact on the ground's overall condition.

Northern's programme notes for the game against Huddersfield made reference to the problems created by the BBC's televising of test matches, in direct competition with league games. The BBC had paid a fee of £1,250 for the privilege. However, the decisive test at Wigan had attracted only 26,809, the lowest of the series, while the aggregate attendance at the previous Saturday's 14 league games was a mere 30,750. Leeds, 2,519, York, 1,911, and Bramley, 430, had all returned their lowest post-war attendance.

Even without any live television, however, Northern also had their lowest post-war crowd, so far. On a wretched day at Odsal there were only 1,100 spectators to see Northern fade badly against the Fartowners. They had taken a 10 point lead in the first quarter through tries from Penketh and Derek Davies, both converted by Trevor Jones. But Northern had no one to compare to scrum-half Tommy Smales and their 18–10 defeat was all the more unpalatable because Huddersfield played with only 12 men in the second-half due to an injury to forward Mick Clarke.

This was Brian Radford's last game for Northern following his decision to retire and make way for younger men. In this, his 12th, season he had missed only two of the 22 league games. During his career, including his debut in 1949, he made a total of 339 appearances, scored 50 tries, and played in every forward position except hooker. He was the sole survivor from the 1949 Challenge Cup winning side and his departure from Odsal left only Bill Seddon and Len Haley from the squad which topped the league table in the 1951–52 season. He later received a cheque for £175, the proceeds of his joint benefit fund with Bill Jenkins.

The club were unsuccessful in their approach to sign 1958 Lance Todd Trophy winner, Rees Thomas, who had been released by Wigan. They were hoping the scrum-half's experience would help a youthful squad, but he preferred to rejoin Swinton, his original club.

Due to Kosanovic having influenza, third-choice hooker Brian Thompson played in both Christmas games against Bramley. After losing 20–6 in the mud at the Barley Mow on Christmas Day, the same

Northern side scored a remarkable 33–2 victory at Odsal on Boxing Day. The pack, led by Marston, completely turned the tables. Derek Davies sparked the constant attacks which brought seven tries, two each for Harry Griffett and Doran, and one apiece from Marston, Hemingway and Smith, in the biggest win of the season. Both Bramley's former Northerners, Malcolm Davies – with a try – and Alan Winnard, with 11 points, scored in these holiday games. The attendance at Odsal was 1,500, while Bradford City, who were undefeated in 11 games, had 18,033 for the visit of Grimsby Town.

At Fartown, Northern's forwards played so well in the second-half that the first away win of the season looked to be on the cards. However, top-four contenders Huddersfield made sure of their 18–12 victory with the last move of the match. Northern's loose-forward Alan Dawes was convinced that he had scored a legitimate try in the first-half. But it was Northern's lack of discipline – Frank 'Spanky' Dyson kicked five penalties, mostly from under the posts – that really cost Northern the game.

On 9 January Bradford City beat Everton 3–0 in the third round of the FA Cup before 23,550 at Valley Parade, while at the same time on the other side of the city, only 1,000, who paid £75 – a new post-war low – turned up at Odsal to see Northern beat Doncaster 13–7. A solo try from Derek Davies was one of the few highlights. The game marked the visitors' 22nd successive defeat of the season, but they had an outstanding forward in Alan Hepworth – a future new Northern recruit. Seddon had a hectic time, as a new penalty rule brought him more into the action, but his goalkicking disappointed. Hooker Brian Thompson was handed the job and slotted over a penalty in his ninth and final senior game.

After the fixture at Castleford was postponed due to the weather, in what proved to be Harry Griffett's final senior game, Northern were beaten 9–5 by York in the Odsal mud. This was due to the scheming of half-back Jeff Stevenson, whose scintillating, side-stepping run set up York's only try for Dennis Flannery, who went in under the posts. The Great Britain skipper also led his forwards brilliantly when Northern looked to be gaining the upper hand. Northern's midfield defence was suspect, but there were many strong runs from Doran and several breaks by Derek Davies, who that day had been watched by Leeds officials prior to them asking Northern to name their price for the 23-year-old.

Northern's directors, who had turned down a big offer from Leeds in January 1958, took only two minutes to reject the approach for Odsal's brightest prospect. He had left the Army the previous week and later returned to Aldershot to play for the Duke of Wellington Regiment in the Army Rugby Union Cup Final, when he scored a try in the 14–0 win against the First Battalion Welsh Guards. As he was not then on the transfer list, Jackie Barritt was angry at the Leeds offer and the effect it might have in possibly unsettling Northern's star player.

As the Challenge Cup register closed there were no new signings or transfers. Northern had great hopes of signing 32-year-old, former test centre, Duggie Greenall, from St Helens and were quite prepared to meet the £1,000 transfer fee. They admitted to "tempting him with other incentives", but ultimately the prospect of having to travel from St Helens swayed his decision and he surprisingly signed for local rivals Wigan. Northern were put off by the £4,000 fee placed on Wakefield Trinity's full-back Don Metcalfe, and were also disappointed to miss out on the signing of the 24-year-old Trinity and former St Helens prop, John Lindley. He opted to sign for Castleford and played against Northern in the first round of the Cup. As previously stated, Milan Kosanovic turned down a move to Barrow, and there was no approach for Trevor Jones, who had recently been transfer-listed at £1,000 at his own request.

The game at The Boulevard was abandoned after 75 minutes due to blizzard conditions, and the final score, 16–7, in Hull's favour was allowed to stand. Northern trailed by only four points at half-time, but within five minutes of the restart the home pack dominated, with the Drake twins scoring three of Hull's four tries. Tongan centre, Nan Halafihi, had his best game since his recent signing from Doncaster and he and Wanklyn formed a dangerous right-wing partnership. Northern's captain Ralph Winnard grabbed a late 60-yard interception try before referee Ron Gelder called a halt because he could no longer distinguish the forwards.

In the return fixture at Odsal on the following Saturday, Northern earned the 'gallant losers' tag for their gutsy show in a 14–13 defeat. With Welsh deputising for Kosanovic, who had tonsillitis, they scored three tries to two and Hull full-back Peter Bateson's deciding goal came from a hotly-disputed penalty. Northern trailed by seven points on two occasions in the second-half, but brilliant defence from Seddon and Davies kept them in the game. On his return after missing 13 games, Geoff Higgins scored one of Northern's tries – the others came from Smith and Marston.

Northern's first away win of the season was their 8–4 defeat of Castleford in the first round of the Challenge Cup. In a rugged game, in which there were several flare-ups, Northern produced most of the attacking ideas and gave little away in defence. They struck in the 16th minute following an interception by the brilliant Davies. The stand-off's quick pass to Winnard put Smith away 75 yards out, and the winger outpaced five defenders to score the first of his two tries. Seddon's conversion from wide out gave Northern a deserved five point lead before Higgins hoodwinked the defence to hand Smith his second touchdown.

Following a devastating burst up the middle by Castleford centre Bob Taylor, Northern were hungry for more points, and just before the break Marston went close after a barnstorming run. In the final quarter, a try seemed imminent when Castleford's full-back Albert Lunn burst onto a reverse pass to race 30 yards, but he was halted by a last-ditch tackle near the line. Lunn then landed penalties in the 65th and 71st minute, but Northern's defence held firm until the final whistle, when both sets of forwards were busy exchanging blows. The incident was swiftly quelled by referee F.J. Howker, who earlier had booked Kosanovic.

A Northern supporter sent each player a 10 shilling note for their efforts, with the promise of a similar reward if they beat Swinton in the second round. After only 3,725 had watched the first round tie, Northern officials had hoped for a more lucrative draw than a trip to Station Road.

Meanwhile, in a 9–9 draw in the league at Mount Pleasant, Northern went into home territory only once in a pointless second-half. With a monopoly of the ball, Batley tested Northern's defence until their second-rower Don Platt scored his side's first try in six games. Northern had few opportunities, but were ahead twice, through an interception try by Doran and Seddon's goalkicking. His second goal was hotly-disputed after one touch-judge signalled 'no goal', but then changed his mind.

Northern's 13–9 defeat by Swinton, watched by a Station Road crowd of 8,189, will be remembered for a controversial try by centre Mike McGillicuddy in the 55th minute, which virtually decided a thrilling encounter. Northern were trailing by the two first-half penalties from loose-forward Albert Blan, when Seddon's clearing kick was charged down and McGillicuddy followed up to be awarded the try. All in the press box thought he had knocked on before grounding and the player himself later admitted that he had definitely infringed. There was a late fright for Swinton, when Derek Davies put in a perfect cross-kick for Doran to crash over in the corner in the 75th minute. When Seddon, who earlier had handed over the goalkicking to Jones after some bad misses, converted brilliantly from the touchline, the home side were clinging to an 11–9 lead. Albert Blan then kicked his fifth goal right on time.

Swinton only looked really dangerous when full-back Ken Gowers moved up into attack, although right-winger John Stopford threw away a certain try when he fumbled a pass from prop Dai Moses, who had made a spectacular interception and 40-yard run. Special mention was given to Marston, who broke his nose and gave a great hearted display, in a pack which held more experienced and heavier opponents – among whom was second-rower Peter Norburn, who was the only surviving member of the side which lost to Northern in the Challenge Cup in 1951, when he played on the wing. Apart from the controversial try, two needless penalties, for off-side, under their own posts also contributed to Northern's Cup exit.

The following week at Odsal it was a case of 'after the Lord Mayor's Show' because Northern sank to fifth from bottom of the league with a "dire display" in being humbled 14–2 by Hull KR, who the previous week had lost to Doncaster. Northern's problems were rooted in their failure to win much possession. County hooker Kosanovic was without his regular props – Walton and debutant Ken Dawes replaced the injured Marston and Feather – which meant that Rovers' experienced front-row of Grice, Ackerley and Coverdale had a field day in the scrums. Apart from Seddon and Smith, who tackled courageously, no other players produced the form which in the previous month had raised supporters' hopes of a rise up the table. The final score did not truly reflect the visitors' superiority.

Boosted by the return of fearless pack leader Marston, Northern not only earned a point, 5–5, against Warrington at Odsal, but almost forced a victory. Warrington had the edge in speed and ideas, but were hanging on at the end of a tough game, which referee Howker failed to control. Kosanovic scored Northern's try and Seddon's goal took him to a personal best, including the Lazenby Cup, of 70 for the season. The new second-row partnership of Gray Robbins and debutant Terry Griffett were subsequently retained. Like his elder brother, Harry, earlier in the season the 21-year-old former Leeds junior had also been crossed off the Hull KR register, in his case after playing trials with Bramley. He had served with the Dukes in Kenya and recently been demobbed from the Army.

Following this game, Cyril Bunney chaired a board meeting which agreed to some major changes to the management of the club. After a period of almost 24 years as first team coach, Dai Rees was relieved of his duties and replaced by Trevor Foster. Along with Rees, who was now given the role as stadium manager, Foster had been co-opted onto the board in February 1958 because of his football expertise. He was put in sole control of team matters, but worked in conjunction with the selection committee of Jackie Barritt, Rees, and Bunney. At the same time, Doris Beard, who had been assistant secretary for the past eight years, was appointed as successor to Eric England, who had joined the staff from leaving school in October 1938. As the only woman secretary in professional rugby league, she almost immediately had to deal with staging the Challenge Cup semi-final on 9 April and the Championship final on 21 May.

Under their new coach, Northern's unchanged side got their first away league win of the season, and their only league double, with a deserved 15–11 victory at Widnes. Although the home side had territorial advantage, Northern's revitalised pack stood up well, and loose-forward Alan Dawes had a particularly impressive game. Despite Derek Davies again below his best form, Northern's backs had the greater strike power, and all three tries came from fine teamwork. Penketh gathered a Smith cross-kick for the first; prop Walton's amazing interception and 50-yard gallop gave the supporting Davies the second; and Smith claimed the third after fine work from Higgins and Seddon. The latter converted two and kicked his only penalty attempt in the 79th minute. Northern only looked in danger of losing because of inconsistent decisions by the referee, and Arthur Pimblett's four penalties from nine attempts. After their recent good form, Northern were then thrashed 29–4 by Leeds in front of the season's second best home crowd, 5,250. Leeds, whose following easily outnumbered the home fans, built up a 13 point lead after 14 minutes, and were never tested in scoring five tries without reply. The standard fell in the second-half when there were some skirmishes.

There was then a week's break due to the Challenge Cup semi-final at Odsal, where Wakefield Trinity beat an understrength Featherstone Rovers 11–2 in front of a crowd of 55,935, with receipts of £10,348. A police spokesman said that traffic around Odsal was normal from just after kick-off, although 279 coaches and 3,500 cars were parked in the immediate area of the stadium.

Northern then played four games in a week, but lost three of them over the Easter holidays. On Saturday 16 April, Leigh winger Jim Humble scored a hat-trick in Northern's 19–17 defeat. But Steve Hey, on his return after a groin injury, almost scored the winner in the last minute. Seddon kicked four superb goals but missed with a vital 'sitter'.

On Easter Monday, Brian Smith scored a try on his first visit to Clarence Street since he signed from York, in Northern's 10–3 defeat. At a sun-drenched Odsal on Easter Tuesday, Northern trailed Wakefield Trinity 22–4 at half-time, but rallied to 28–17 as Trinity eased off in the energy sapping conditions. The highlight of an entertaining afternoon for the 7,500 crowd was Fred Smith's swerving run, which took him through half the Northern team, before he scored under the posts at the Rooley Avenue end.

In the Odsal finale against Whitehaven, Northern were behind 8–3 after 12 minutes, but led 16–10 at half-time and scored seven of the 11 tries and won 29–20. It was a typical end-of-season affair, in which serious defensive work was at a premium. Northern therefore finished with a 50 per cent return against their Lancashire League opponents.

On the following Wednesday at Belle Vue, Trinity fielded what some believed would be their Wembley line-up and beat Northern 28–5. They thus retained the Yorkshire League title, a competition in which Northern finished second from bottom, above Doncaster. Northern played better than the score suggests, and were handicapped with Steve Hey hobbling after 25 minutes. But Trinity turned errors into points and scored eight tries, including two from Fred Smith who equalled his club record total of 37. Neil Fox missed with all seven shots at goal, while Gerry Round kicked two from under the posts, but missed with another four attempts.

With nine players unavailable through injuries, Northern season's ended with a 26–9 defeat at Castleford, after they threw away a 9–4 interval lead. Walshaw's kicking and the hardworking loose-forward play of Winnard, who, along with Doran, had played in all 43 games, including the Lazenby Cup, were Northern's only redeeming features.

Northern's dire season saw them drop from 10th to 26th place in the league, above Liverpool City, Blackpool Borough, Dewsbury and Doncaster. It was their worst finish since their first season at Odsal, 1934–35. On rare occasions they had looked promising, but the general standard had been mediocre and they were in desperate need of at least two experienced men in both the backs and the forwards to guide the youngsters. The average attendance from the 21 home games, including the visit of the Australian tourists, was a new low of 3,010 – a season's total of 63,202.

There were far more than that at the Championship final, but yet again the event was ruined as a spectacle after Wakefield Trinity centre Neil Fox was injured in the early stages and spent the rest of the game limping on the left-wing. Consequently, Wigan ran out easy 27–3 winners before a crowd officially returned at 83,190, who paid £14,763, the second biggest rugby league crowd ever in this country, excluding those at Wembley. Such was the throng that spectators were even entering the ground at half-time and dozens, near to where I was standing, were overcome by heat stroke. Once again the call went up for investment in Odsal, with the need for three party talks to involve Northern, Bradford Corporation and the RFL. Architect C.E. Horsfall, Halifax's chairman, felt that replacing the Old Stand and providing dressing-rooms underneath any new structure was a priority.

1959–60 Summary
Position in the league: 26th of 30 P 38 W 9 L 26 D 3 – Pts 450–643
Yorkshire Cup: First round. Challenge Cup: Second round.
Average attendance: 3,010 (2,879 league games only)

8. 1960–61: The Duggie Greenall fiasco
Boardroom upheaval hits Odsal

This season Northern's new chairman, Jackie Barritt, also chaired the Rugby League Council and the International Board. In this World Cup year three of the games were eventually allocated to Odsal, including a possible play-off final. The original programme envisaged midweek floodlit games at Leeds United's Elland Road and Hull City's Boothferry Park, but these were later changed following the Football League's intervention.

Northern made a profit of £3,596 to the year ending 30 June 1960, due to a net balance of £4,583 on transfer fees, including the £7,500 for Scroby. The deficit was thus reduced to £6,435, and the club owed Hammond's brewery £3,000. The Development Fund had raised £3,300 in the previous year and at the AGM in October 1960 it was revealed that Northern were then losing £200 to £300 each week. The pools was the club's only salvation. To boost the club's crowds, pensioners could buy a season ticket for £1 which also gave them access to the New Stand.

The 'A' team coach, Len Higson, who had been at Odsal since 1935, retired, and was replaced by former scrum-half Donald Ward. The elder brother of Ernest, he played in the three successive Challenge Cup finals, 1947 to 1949, alongside Willie Davies. Northern held an open trial in June, in which 30 players from Bradford, Wakefield, Leeds and Pontefract took part and five were asked to join in pre-season training.

By this time Northern had finally persuaded Duggie Greenall to join them as player-coach. They had been watching developments since March, when he was transfer-listed at Wigan after being unsettled due to playing too much reserve rugby. A product of St Helens schools, in a Saints career spanning 14 years, he made his international debut in 1951 against France and was renowned for his lethal tackling. He was looking for a public house in Bradford but, due to staffing difficulties at his hotel in St Helens and the previously anticipated problem of having to make the regular journey over the Pennines, his stay at Odsal lasted only four games before he announced his retirement. The whole episode did nothing for either the club's or the player's reputation, and the £500 transfer fee was money Northern could ill afford to waste.

Northern also signed Rochdale Hornets full-back Eddie Trumble on a two month trial, and the former Leigh junior converted Doran's try in the Lazenby Cup game at Lawkholme Lane, which Northern lost 29–5. The unlucky Steve Hey curtailed his holiday at Skegness to play, but broke his collarbone and joined Penketh, who had a fractured forearm, and Seddon who had a cartilage problem, on the injury list.

The poor performance by the pack saw Welsh, Walton and Jones dropped for Northern's first ever visit to Blackpool, where Trumble and Greenall made their full debuts. Borough were one of the four clubs to finish below Northern the previous season and therefore the 18–0 defeat at the St Anne's Road Stadium was a real danger signal. Northern's need for new blood was clear when they lost the first of five games in August. Kosanovic won enough ball from the scrums, but Higgins rarely varied his tactics and Greenall never exerted his experience or authority.

Prop George McLean returned to Northern's ranks in the 'A' team against Batley on the following Monday, but injured his foot. Jack Doran scored a try in this game. He then played his third game in five days when Featherstone were the season's first visitors to Odsal on Wednesday 17 August, before a crowd of 3,100. Inspired by the trio of Colin Clifft, Don Fox and Terry Mullaney, Rovers ran in 20 points in the final quarter to win 27–5. In a scrappy game, in which hookers Willis Fawley and Kosanovic were repeatedly warned for scrum offences, Northern's goalkicking weakness returned. Trumble did not come up to expectations as a kicker.

However, against Batley at Odsal, Trumble snatched a neat try and kicked two fine penalties to give Northern a 7–2 lead at half-time. Unfortunately, after a brilliant goal from halfway by the visitors' full-back Jimmy Lawton, Northern could not cash in on Greenall's flair and poor finishing on the wings cost them the game, 14–7.

Smith and Higgins were dropped for the visit to Hull KR. Both Winnard, with a fractured finger, and Doran, who had a damaged mouth, were both on the lengthening injury list, and Greenall was unavailable due to business commitments. Down by five points in the first minute, Northern drew close at 11–7 thanks to a brilliant converted try by Derek Davies. But the defensive work had taken its toll. Rovers ran riot in the final quarter, and scored nine tries to win 33–7.

The 1960–61 Lazenby Cup side at Lawkholme Lane. Back: Walton, Doran, Trumble, Marston, Trialist, Brian Smith, Hey; front: Welsh, Trevor Jones, Winnard, Higgins, Derek Davies, Len Haley. (Courtesy John Hamer).

Billy Boston chases a loose ball in the World Cup decider at Odsal. (Courtesy Robert Gate).

The first round Yorkshire Cup tie was partly played in a tropical thunderstorm at Odsal. The half-time score was 10–4 to Castleford. Strong work from Jones, Walton and Robbins then raised hopes of a Northern revival. But once Castleford's scrum-half, George Brown, had gone through weak tackling for two tries the final result, 25–7, was never in doubt. There was a general lack of teamwork, and Duggie Greenall was surprisingly quiet, in his last game for Northern. He failed to arrive at training on the following Thursday and his non-appearance at Barrow resulted in him being transfer-listed at £500. At the same time, 20-year-old Geoff Higgins was listed, at £1,500, at his own request after being dropped, but he later won back his place.

In Greenall's absence, Brook took his place at centre and scored one of Northern's four tries in an impressive 18–5 victory, having led 6–2 at half-time. It was only their second win at Barrow in 24 years. Northern's play, with acting captain Trevor Jones outstanding at loose-forward, bore little resemblance to the season's previous games. The handling was quick and precise, and the defence held firm. For Rochdale Hornets' first league visit to Odsal since 1938, Northern produced more dazzling play, which at times astonished their loyal supporters. In a 20–9 victory, the pack was in control and the attack worked smoothly. Davies's lightning bursts and intelligent centre play by try-scorer Trumble were complemented by Smith's finishing speed and two tries.

Northern's good form continued in a 16–7 defeat to Leeds at Odsal, where the top crowd of the season, 5,500, saw them gain abundant possession and take a deserved 7–4 half-time lead. Leeds were stunned and frustrated, but their more accomplished backs – Derek Hallas, Fred Pickup and Lewis Jones in particular – sealed the game in the last half-hour when Northern's forwards began to fade.

Northern then travelled to Workington on the following Monday. Town lost their hooker, Bert Eden, after only four minutes with a dislocated shoulder, the price of scoring the first of their six tries. But even when home centre Bobby Ryan went off with a head wound, Northern never looked like scoring a try and they only had a 30th minute penalty from Walshaw to show for their efforts in a 28–2 defeat.

Because of the World Cup tournament no league games were played on the following Saturday, when Great Britain beat New Zealand

23–8 at Odsal in one of the opening matches. Unfortunately, high admission prices and live television coverage of the second-half reduced the crowd to only 20,577, with receipts of £4,729. It was disappointing for Northern who had pulled out all the stops to make the day a success.

Several of the Australian World Cup squad were at Odsal to watch Northern's 18–17 defeat by Castleford, on the following Wednesday under lights. The referee, H. Pearce, from Leeds, needed a police escort at the end of a stormy game, which saw the dismissal of Trevor Jones and Castleford's Bert Sayer. Northern, with a 3–1 scrum advantage in the second-half, might well have won had not Walshaw missed an easy penalty. But Castleford still managed to pull off a win, despite their new full-back, Peter Briers, who had played a trial in Northern's 'A' team before signing from Halifax, being injured for much of the second-half. After this game Eddie Trumble was crossed off the Northern register.

Pack leader Ralph Winnard returned at loose-forward and Seddon at centre for the visit by York, who were well led by Jeff Stevenson and their new signing from Keighley, Fred Ward. He scored two tries in their 16–13 victory. Northern played some entertaining rugby in the first quarter and led at half-time through tries by wingers Smith and Doran, but they did little in the second-half. York were far superior in the latter stages and scored the winning try in the 75th minute.

In the disappointing deciding game of the World Cup Great Britain beat Australia 10–3 before an Odsal crowd of 33,026, with receipts of £9,133. Despite a foul day, this was still the biggest crowd in the north of England bar one. In anticipation of a large crowd, a safety wall had been built around the speedway pits, but the all-ticket restriction was lifted once the pre-match sales were assessed. For example, although 2,790 seating tickets had already been sold at Odsal, Leeds returned 997 of their allocation of 1,000 ground tickets. Apart from Northern's games both teams had trained on the pitch and the incessant rain soon made the ground heavy with mud. If the game had been drawn the play-off final would have been under lights on the following Monday, instead of which Great Britain beat a Rest of the World side 33–27, in a game which included 16 tries. The attendance was only 3,908, and the tournament made a small profit of £478. The expenses were £40,000. Northern received £1,505 from the three games allocated to Odsal.

Batley were having their best season for many years, and had won 12 points from their opening 10 games. However, their atrocious handling presented the game to Northern, 15–7, at Mount Pleasant. Although Batley attacked for threequarters of the game, Northern led 10–7 at half-time through converted tries by Doran and Nunns, and gained the initiative in the last 15 minutes with fast direct play. This resulted in a try by Brian Smith, who was the most dangerous back on display, closely followed by Broadbent, who drop-kicked his second goal of the season.

In the 10–10 draw against Keighley at Odsal, Hull KR's transfer-listed trialist, 28-year-old Doug Holland partnered McLean in the front-row and was among Northern's best performers. He was then transfer-listed at £750 and Northern later signed him, for an undisclosed fee, in November. The former St Helens and Liverpool City prop or second-rower was signed by Rovers from Workington Town in December 1958 for £2,000. He had played for Lancashire against Yorkshire under the Odsal lights in October 1954 and was in a Rugby League XIII against France at Headingley in April 1958. He continued as a licensee in Hull during his time at Odsal.

Eddie Trumble impressed as a trialist for Keighley in the game at Odsal, but he was still not retained by the Lawkholmers. Northern led 10–0 at half-time and it appeared they would coast to an easy win after Keighley lost their 17-year-old centre, Albert Eyre, for the second-half. However, Keighley's 12 men scored 10 points in four minutes midway through the second-half to draw level. Unfortunately, full-back Phil Walshaw had not proved to be the answer to Northern's hopes and this was his final first team game before he was given a free transfer to Bramley. He had made only 23 appearances, and had kicked, by his high standards, a modest 52 goals.

With better finishing at Featherstone, Northern could have held a comfortable interval lead rather than trailing 5–4. There was little to choose between the teams until the 62nd minute, when centre Ken Greatorex raced 75 yards after he intercepted to hand a try to Willis Fawley. This heralded a collapse of Northern's defence as Rovers ran in 18 points in the same number of minutes to triumph 23–4.

In a 12–2 home win over Hunslet, Northern gave a debut to 23-year-old South African trialist winger, John de Klerk, who was looking for a rugby league contract having played a handful of games with St

Helens and Widnes. He was part of an influx of South African rugby union players who came to Britain to play rugby league in the late 1950s and early 1960s. His appearance helped to moderately boost the crowd to 2,400. Northern surprised the Parksiders with some crisp handling and led by two converted tries, to Smith and Nunns, at half-time. Thanks to Northern's defensive work Hunslet had only a Billy Langton penalty to show for their efforts and their frustration boiled over near the end when a free-for-all resulted in eight players being cautioned. De Klerk made several useful runs, but had only three more first team outings, all away from Odsal, before playing out the rest of the season in the 'A' team. He then moved to Huddersfield.

The first of these appearances was at Lawkholme Lane, where Northern lost 18–5 to a Keighley side which had not won in their previous 11 games. Northern were a spent force long before the end and had no answer to the strong running of Brian Todd and Roy Sabine in the centre of the field.

Following his signing from Hunslet, after three trial games, Welsh second-rower, Terry Robbins was down to play for Northern against Barrow on 26 November but the game was cancelled because the Odsal pitch was waterlogged. He made an impressive debut in a 7–7 draw against Castleford at Wheldon Road, where the pack produced their best performance of the season so far. A Geoff Higgins drop-goal near the end levelled the scores. Northern had deserved to win; they had given the home defence a gruelling time for most of the game.

Northern led 3–2 at half-time at Crown Flatt, after which Dewsbury blotted out half-backs Davies and Higgins and produced a great rally to win 7–3. Although Northern had the game's most dangerous winger in try-scorer Smith, and two hardworking forwards in newcomers Holland and Robbins, they lacked a leader and tactician.

Following this game there was the shock announcement that coach and director Trevor Foster had severed his connections with the club due to a disagreement on a non-rugby related matter, of which he said "there was no hope of reconciliation." For a short time he advised Keighley on scouting issues and then moved to Leeds to become their 'A' team coach. It later emerged that his position had been made untenable because he had been asked to act as a financial guarantor against the club's bank overdraft. He had joined the board on the clear understanding that his contribution would be only on rugby related matters. A special meeting was later held, on 25 January 1961, to discuss the club's overdraft, at which fellow director and stadium manager Dai Rees also resigned for the same reason. He later became a director at Halifax, the club which he played for in the 1930s. As Len Dobson, Northern's oldest serving director, from 1928, had died in late October, this meant the board was severely depleted.

Only 950 supporters turned up to Odsal in the week before Christmas as Northern, with Winnard at full-back for the injured Seddon, scored a fortunate 11–8 win over bottom club Doncaster. The visitors dominated for most of the game and led 8–5 after 65 minutes. Then, entirely against the run of play, Northern exposed the Dons' lack of cover for Doran to score two late tries. By mutual consent, Smith and Doran switched wings during the game, Smith reverted to the right-wing position he held at York, and this arrangement was maintained until his departure.

After the postponement of the Christmas Day game at the Barley Mow, on the Boxing Day Monday at Odsal Northern won an attractive game 9–8. The highlights were powerful up-the-middle bursts by Terry Robbins and his turn of speed to score; and a brilliant run by Holland to set up Smith's try. On his return after injury, Seddon missed at least five goalkicks.

Northern ended 1960 with an uplifting display against the league leaders at Headingley. The final score of 19–3 flattered Leeds, who only managed to get on top in the dying minutes. Before the day's biggest crowd, 11,981, Northern's backs defended well, but lacked their opponents' finesse. Terry Robbins and Holland again produced superb performances, the latter's only mistake in an otherwise faultless display was his lobbed pass to George McLean, which led to an easy interception try for South African flyer Wilf Rosenberg. This was the first time I can recall seeing Northern in action on television, because highlights from the game, including Geoff Higgins' try, were shown that evening on BBC North news.

Based on this performance, the club match programme confidently predicted that Northern would move up the league table in January, when three successive home games were scheduled. The game on 7 January against Hull KR was unfortunately postponed at midday due to the dangerous state of the frozen Odsal pitch. However, the following week a frost-covered Odsal was declared fit for the first ever visit from Blackpool Borough, whose journey was delayed due to dense fog in Lancashire. This caused the kick-off to be delayed for five minutes and a substitute referee from Bradford took charge of the game. As was the visitors' custom, on a visit to a new ground, before the game their captain and full-back, Jack Lowe, presented Northern's captain, Doug Holland, with a six foot long, 20 pounds stick of Blackpool rock. The niceties over, Borough then proceeded to thrash Northern 35–6, their biggest defeat for four years.

Borough, who had won six of their first seven games, had only just recovered from a disastrous losing run. However, future Great Britain scrum-half Tommy Bishop, a try-scorer in the first-half, proved to be more than a handful. Their adventurous style of play led to left-winger, Tony Wilkshire, taking full advantage of Brian Smith's second-minute hip injury to claim four of Borough's seven tries. All the visitors' tries were scored under or near the posts and converted by Jack Lowe. Bishop was dismissed, along with his opposite number Geoff Higgins, in the 65th minute, and had he remained until the end there was little doubt Northern would have conceded even more points. Only recent signings Robbins and Holland could have been satisfied with their efforts in a woeful team performance.

This pitiful display coincided with Bradford Park Avenue's signing of Newcastle United's Jimmy Scoular as player-manager. They won 1–0 against Aldershot, in front of a crowd of 12,718, and moved into fourth place in the Fourth Division, in what became a promotion season.

Rochdale Hornets had lost 14 of their previous 16 games and were third from bottom of the table, when Northern visited the Athletic Grounds in search of their first double of the season. After being level 3–3 at half-time, thanks to a first-class try from Brook, Northern went down 14–6. The forwards' hard work was squandered by the lack of a ball-playing schemer. Hornets' hooker Platt was sent off near end for a challenge on Kosanovic, who was admitted to Halifax Infirmary with damage to nerves in his neck.

Alan Dawes was meant to play at loose-forward, but prop George McLean was a late emergency replacement. Underbank Rangers junior Alan Sutcliffe had a promising trial at stand-off, but Northern were later fined £10 for playing him before the correct registration form had reached the RFL's headquarters. He was recommended to Northern by

Halifax coach Albert Fearnley, after playing trials at Thrum Hall. As one of Northern's best prospects, he made many impressive performances with the 'A' team as an amateur and represented Yorkshire juniors in March. He signed as a professional for the start of the following season.

This defeat unfortunately marked the end of Geoff Higgins's first team career. A sound defender and intelligent attacker, who had played many outstanding games in his 67 appearances, he lost interest and left the game. He later attempted a comeback with the reserves in 1962–63, before being transfer-listed at £500. A self-employed slater and plasterer, in 1989, at the early age of 49, Geoff sadly collapsed and died following one of his early morning runs near his home in Pellon.

The fixture on 28 January against Wakefield Trinity was cancelled due to snow at Odsal. Then, having earlier made a vain bid for Hull KR's county centre Bill Riley, who had previously played for Batley and Halifax, before the Cup register closed, Northern loaned Alan Lancaster to Huddersfield, for whom he later signed. The club did secure two players on trial from Castleford; 23-year-old reserve full-back Arthur Hattee, a former Heworth junior, and sturdy centre Robert (Bob) Taylor.

In the league, Northern faced a stiff task at York without four regulars, but with the score 0–0 at half-time the game could easily have gone either way. Scrum-half Broadbent made a try for Doran in a 7–3 defeat, but Northern could also have scored near the end with better finishing. Welsh was prominent in the loose in a hardworking pack, but Northern had no one to match Jeff Stevenson's speed of thought.

Kosanovic returned for the first round Challenge Cup tie at Mount Pleasant, where, with a near full-strength side available, Northern faced a Batley side which had won only one of their last 10 games. Arthur Hattee made his debut and was seen as the possible answer to Northern's woeful goalkicking. The team had managed only one goal in the previous seven games. Trailing only 6–0 at half-time in heavy conditions, with the slope and wind at their backs in the second-half, Northern were favourites to win. However, although they hammered away at the Batley line, they had neither the speed nor craft to finish the job. They failed to make use of the wind, as full-back Jimmy

Lawton had done in the first-half with his 50-yard touch finders, and even conceded a try up the slope to lose 9–0.

Northern's hopes of a lucrative Cup run had thus ended at the first hurdle. On the same day, Leeds and Wigan drew 5–5 at Headingley before a crowd of 32,757, who paid £4,629, with another big gate to come at Central Park for the replay.

Kosanovic had received a severe knock at Batley and Welsh again deputised at Hull, where he more than held his own in the scrums against Tommy Harris. In the latter stages Hull's pack gained full superiority in The Boulevard mud against full-blooded opponents, but the final score of 24–0 did Northern no justice. The club then managed their first win of the year, 5–2, at the Barley Mow. Hattee landed Northern's first goal in eight matches and recent signing from Castleford, Bob Taylor, in for the dropped Penketh, made several clear breaks on his debut. One of these led to a try by Terry Robbins, who, along with Dave Horn, was sent off in the second-half.

On 2 March the former international full-back, Jimmy Ledgard, was appointed as coach on a three year contract. He also took over as stadium manager from Dai Rees before the latter moved to Halifax as a director. His first taste of rugby league, after playing rugby union with Sandal and Wakefield, was with Leeds during the war. He joined Dewsbury in 1944 and was signed by Leigh for a rugby league record transfer fee of £2,650 in January 1948. In January 1959 he returned to Dewsbury on a free transfer, but by December he was being offered on loan. Northern's bid to also sign him as a player fell below Dewsbury's £500 valuation.

Derek Davies had his best game of the season and scored two tries at Odsal as Northern led Workington Town 8–6 at the interval. But for defensive lapses and missed goalkicks Northern would have pushed Town even closer, but their half-backs, John Roper and 1958 tourist Harry Archer, dictated play in the final half-hour. Test forwards Brian Edgar and Norman Herbert were outstanding in the visitors' 25–13 victory. Unfortunately, Kosanovic retired injured in what proved to be his last game for Northern, having made 143 appearances. The attendance of 1,850 was about the season's average, but over 6,000 turned up at Odsal the following day to see Tommy Steele and a Show Biz XI play Yorkshire Cricket Club in a charity football match.

Five men were sent off in Northern's encouraging 15–9 win over Doncaster at Tattersfield. Matters boiled over in the 65th minute when centre Bob Taylor was ordered off for a foul on full-back Colin Price. For protesting Taylor's innocence, Holland was also dismissed and referee Eric Lawrenson attempted to calm the situation by also giving marching orders to Terry Robbins, along with Doncaster's Bernard Asquith and Kevin Doyle. All three Northern players were later suspended: Holland for four matches, Robbins for two matches and Taylor for one.

After two months spent recovering from a leg injury sustained against Leeds, Gray Robbins returned for Northern's visit to Parkside. Welsh won the scrums and Derek Davies was again back to his best form. But over-elaboration cost Northern several scores in an 18–9 defeat. Arthur Sharkey made his only appearance in the second-row in a disappointing Northern pack, but Hunslet's forwards missed the skills of Brian Shaw and Harry Poole, after their big money transfers to Leeds and Hull KR respectively.

The form of scrum-half Broadbent was Northern's only bright spot in a poor 26–0 defeat by Wakefield Trinity at Belle Vue. Referee Thomas lectured all the players before dismissing Gray Robbins in the closing minutes, following an incident with Trinity's hooker Geoff Oakes. Around this time prop Peter Marsden was loaned to Castleford until the end of the season, but he returned to Odsal the following term.

On Easter Saturday at Odsal, Doran's early try gave Northern the lead against Hull, who eventually ran out comfortable 27–6 winners. Missing four regular forwards, Northern were no match for the fearsome Hull pack, and it was one-way traffic in the second-half, despite Brian Smith keeping a close eye on their leading try-scorer, Terry Hollindrake, who had recently been transferred from Keighley for £6,000. On Easter Monday, Northern gave a vastly improved display in a 15–13 home defeat to Huddersfield. Their policy of playing open rugby, with tries from Smith, who notched two, and Welsh, nearly brought them a late victory. Unfortunately, hopes of a quick revenge were ruled out. The return game at Fartown the following day was postponed due to a blizzard.

Northern's early work against Dewsbury suggested a big win against a side which had not won away all season. However, after leading 8–0 at the break they were hard pressed to win a scrappy game 13–7.

Former Dewsbury centre Bob Taylor made some superb breaks, from one of which Penketh scored a try. With the return of Terry Robbins after his suspension, Northern fully merited their 13–5 home win over Barrow, their third double of the season. Broadbent again impressed with his touch-finding. He also scored a neat try and laid on another for Doran in a game which marked Norman Feather's last senior appearance. He was transfer-listed at £1,000, subsequently reduced to £500, before being crossed off the playing register in November 1962. There were many complaints from the supporters at hard-up Northern's decision to sell the original match programme for this rearranged game. There were over 20 team changes and the notes were months out of date.

Odsal then hosted the Challenge Cup semi-final when a crowd of 42,935 saw St Helens run out 26–9 winners over Hull, who were aiming for their third successive final. Only a brilliant try from Tom van Vollenhoven separated the sides at the interval, 5–4, but the eventual Cup winners changed their tactics in the second-half and their skilful play resulted in five more tries. Their winger Mick Sullivan insisted on returning to play after a head wound which later needed six stitches.

Ralph Winnard played at blind-side prop due to Holland's late arrival at Fartown. In a 27–13 defeat, Huddersfield's international scrum-half Tommy Smales scored two tries against Northern's shaky over-worked defence. On the same day, Bradford referee Jack Senior, who was a touch-judge in the opening World Cup game at Odsal, sent off six players in the Doncaster versus Wakefield Trinity game.

Wakefield Trinity had the slender hope of moving into a top-four play-off position when they visited Odsal for the penultimate game of the season. Although skipper Holland returned to bring the pack up to near full-strength, Northern were hit by 10 points in the first four minutes and Trinity had complete mastery in winning 34–11. Their brilliant passing brought them eight tries, including a hat-trick for the game's all-time leading points scorer, Neil Fox. The attendance of 3,800 paled in comparison to the earlier Thursday evening crowd of 20,461 at Park Avenue, against Peterborough United, as Avenue headed for promotion.

Although Northern led 11–7 at half-time in the final game of the season, they were no match for the Hull KR forwards led by Harry Poole. Just after the restart Poole himself crossed for a try and on the

70th minute Cyril Kellett won the game, 12–11, with his 100th goal of the season. Unfortunately, this proved to be Gray Robbins's last senior game, after making only 38 appearances. Back trouble sidelined him until Christmas, although he subsequently returned to play in the 'A' team, before being crossed off the register in 1962–63.

Match programmes were given away following the complaints after the Barrow game, but a new record low crowd of 500 showed the Bradford public's apathy towards affairs at Odsal, where the average attendance for the season had dropped to 1,864. In contrast, a crowd of 12,339 watched Avenue clinch promotion to the Third Division with a 2–1 win over Millwall, at a time when both Northern and relegated Bradford City were in dire financial trouble and fighting to survive.

To add to Northern's woes, Milan Kosanovic announced he had left the club, having been overlooked for the Easter games after he returned from injury. As previously mentioned, he had been unsettled for several seasons and was finally listed at £4,000 in January 1960, when he turned down a move to Barrow. One of Northern's greatest ever characters – in my mind's eye he can be seen openly admonishing his colleagues for missing tackles – he was signed by Wakefield Trinity in June 1961 for the giveaway fee of £2,000. This move saw him win both a Challenge Cup and Championship winner's medal, as well as appearing, with the rest of the Trinity team, in the film *This Sporting Life*, starring Richard Harris. He was also a member of the Featherstone Rovers Wembley squad in 1967.

In the pre-match carnival atmosphere at the Championship final, one supporter climbed onto the crossbar at the scoreboard end and had to be coaxed down by the police. Then, a sun-drenched Odsal crowd of 52,177 witnessed league leaders Leeds crowned champions for the first time in their history following their 25–10 defeat of Warrington. The maestro Lewis Jones, scorer of a brilliant solo try and five goals, lifted the trophy after masterminding a comprehensive win.

1960 –61 Summary
Position in league: 24th of 30 Played 36 W 10 L 24 D 2 – Pts 312–580
Yorkshire Cup: First round. Challenge Cup: First round.
Average attendance: 1,864 (1,869 league games only)

9. 1961–62: 73–5 humiliation
Bottom of the league

During the close season two 19-year-olds were signed from junior rugby: Alan Wigglesworth, a hooker who had played for Yorkshire Schools and been reserve for England under-19s; and the aforementioned Alan Sutcliffe, a nippy half-back, formerly of Underbank Rangers, who played half his games at centre in his first season as a professional.

Due to the success of the pools, Northern's chairman Jackie Barritt later boasted that £20,000 was available for new players. He and Cyril Bunney visited South Wales in August but returned empty handed. They had apparently offered £5,000 each to a Welsh international forward, Abertillery's Alun Pask, and Neath's forward Alun Dix. They had also been rejected by Cardiff's Welsh trialist forward, Dai Hayward. Northern's scouting in Wales later bore fruit, albeit on a smaller scale.

George McLean was still serving a three-match ban from the previous season with the 'A' team, but Trevor Jones returned for the first game, having been out since Christmas. Without having played a pre-season game, Northern kicked off with a 14–7 home loss to Keighley, having led 3–2 at half-time through a try by Doran. The game was played woefully slowly, lifted only by a 10 minute spell in the second-half by the visitors.

The following Monday, away to Hull KR, Northern never recovered from conceding 12 points in the first eight minutes. Despite producing some entertaining moves and centre Alan Sutcliffe's first-class service to Doran, Northern went down 29–8 to an impressive Rovers side. This game saw the final senior appearance for both David Walton, who crushed his feet when a car jack gave way at work, and Brian Smith, who scored 26 tries in 60 appearances.

Club captain Terry Robbins sustained a rib injury in the above game and missed the visit to Widnes, where Northern deserved their 10–7 interval lead. But shortly after the break, they lost centre Bob Taylor with a broken leg and Winnard's withdrawal from the forwards saw 12-man Northern struggle for possession. It proved to be Doug Holland's final game for the club. Widnes won 37–10, but Northern's performance suggested future success. Unfortunately, such optimism was misplaced.

Leeds were far the better side in winning 32–16 at Odsal on the following Wednesday evening. However, Northern were twice in front and scored 12 points in seven minutes in the second-half before needlessly conceding 10 points near the end. The Hattee brothers played against each other, with Arthur kicking five goals for Northern while centre Vince contributed a try and two goals to the Leeds total.

Northern then travelled to Belle Vue for the first round of the Yorkshire Cup to meet a star-studded Wakefield Trinity side, minus Neil Fox, who had been dropped due to a perceived loss of form. As referred to earlier, in the previous 12 months Trinity had paid out a rugby league record amount on new players, with a blend of formidable rugby league forwards, including, of course, former Northern favourite Milan Kosanovic, and a contingent of former South African rugby union backs. The outcome on that gloriously sunny Saturday afternoon, 2 September 1961, was a 73–5 humiliating defeat – 32–0 at half-time. Trinity ran in 17 tries including four from Harold Poynton and hat-tricks by Fred Smith and Alan Skene while full-back Gerry Round matched Trinity's club record with 11 goals. As if to rub salt into the wounds, from one of these kicks Round managed to send the ball through the perforated steelwork of the Agbrigg Road stand, which earned him a special round of applause. Northern's only consolation was a share of the gate from the crowd of 10,942.

On this energy-sapping day few sides would have lived with Trinity, who went on to retain the trophy against Leeds at Odsal. Their forwards, led by Don Vines, Brian Briggs and Derek Turner, were in devastating form and their backs handled at a bewildering pace. But some of Northern's tackling, particularly from the backs, was feeble and at least five tries were gifts because the men in red, amber and black capitulated long before the final whistle. Loose-forward Ralph Winnard was easily Northern's best player. The game highlighted the gulf in class between the top and bottom sides and helped make the case, yet again, for the need for two divisions.

As if to emphasise this latter point, the team that lost 10–0 to Batley on the following Tuesday, in an attractive, competitive game, showed only two changes from that against Trinity. Unfortunately, although

Northern had first use of the Mount Pleasant slope, poor handling nullified much of their good work.

As an experiment, Northern brought forward their game against Castleford, which marked the debut of hooker Wigglesworth, to the Friday night. But a crowd of only 1,470 were drawn to Odsal to see Northern's uninspiring 8–0 victory as Hattee's four goals saw off his former club. Northern supporters waited another five months for any further success. During this period there were 15 successive defeats, including a first round exit from the Challenge Cup against the men from Wheldon Road.

Northern had defeated Liverpool City on each of their eight previous meetings, but on their visit to Knotty Ash, where Eddie Trumble was City's full-back, they were deservedly beaten 23–12 after trailing only 13–10 at half-time. Young centre Alan Sutcliffe was one of the game's outstanding players, and went close after a 65-yard run. But there was little support from a well-beaten pack, who had kept the ball tight against a shaky defence. This was prop George McLean's final first team game. He joined Batley on a three month trial and was struck off Northern's register in February 1962. He became a director of new Northern in the mid–1970s.

Northern then gave Hunslet's former Dewsbury winger, Horace Grainger, a similar trial period. He had played association football professionally for Burnley and Chesterfield and was the brother of former international outside-left, Colin Grainger, who was at Leeds United. He made his debut in a 33–2 home loss to Widnes. Against a side which had played Wigan only two days earlier in the Lancashire Cup and were lacking four regulars, Northern played feebly before a crowd of 1,306.

Grainger scored two tries in a 24–20 defeat to York at Clarence Street, despite receiving poor service, and Northern later signed him from Hunslet for less than the £750 transfer-list price. This was a vastly improved display by Northern. Two-try Terry Robbins led a dominant pack, in which Peter Marston made his last senior appearance before being listed at £200. On his debut, trialist second-rower Alan Dickinson also impressed against his own club, but only played one more first team game and was not retained.

That was on 7 October at Salford, where 32-year-old open-side prop Don Hatfield made his debut after signing from Hunslet at a "reasonable fee". The former Dewsbury and Halifax player had been recommended by Terry Robbins in the hope of solving the ongoing scrummaging problems and to provide coaching to the forwards. After only six minutes play Northern took a 7–0 lead thanks to a well-taken try by Doran and Hattee's two goals, but they faded badly as Salford ran out 35–7 winners. Northern were then third from the bottom of the table, with only Doncaster and Blackpool Borough below them.

League leaders Wakefield Trinity had scored 347 points, including 81 tries, in the 12 league games before their visit to Odsal on 14 October – and after a gripping first quarter it was all one-way traffic against a hapless Northern defence. South African winger Jan Prinsloo's electrifying running was the highlight of Trinity's emphatic 38–7 win, watched by the highest home crowd of the season, 5,636. He scored the first of his six tries in the first minute. Although a brilliant break by Davies produced an equalising try for Broadbent, Northern were blitzed up to the interval, 25–5, when handicapped through Robbins's injury.

After a week's break due to the test match at Odsal, when Great Britain beat New Zealand 23–10 before a crowd of 19,989, league activities resumed on 28 October. Steve Hey, who had missed all the previous season due to cartilage trouble and work commitments, made a welcome return in a 9–0 home defeat against Halifax. On the hour, Seddon, in his first game of the season following illness, clashed with prop forward Frank Fox, which resulted in a mass brawl, the dismissal of both players and a rare two-match ban for the popular New Zealander. Halifax dominated possession, but Northern's defence held out until the 78th minute when Bernard Scott went over.

Derek Davies, Steve Hey and Terry Robbins – the latter of whom had withdrawn his transfer request in September after being persuaded by the directors that they had several irons in the fire and plenty of funds available for recruitment – were disillusioned with the team's performances; the £4 losing pay, which was a poor incentive when the 'A' team's winning pay was also £4; and the lack of any new quality signings. There seemed to be a consensus among supporters that trying to sign established rugby league players was a better policy than the signing of untried rugby union men. But when they did attempt to sign players of any note they found it difficult to persuade them to move to a bottom-of-the-table club. In fact, holding onto their better players was proving to be as great a task and before the Challenge Cup transfer deadline Northern had effectively lost the services of their best three players.

Northern had been negotiating with Oldham over the possible signing of former international full-back Bernard Ganley as an on-field organiser. He was on the list at £500 and was due to train at Odsal to see if he could regain his match fitness. Although nothing came of this move it was an indication that team manager Jimmy Ledgard's position was under threat.

On 4 November Tom Whitaker, an 'A' team trialist who was once on Batley's books, made his debut at stand-off in a 33–7 defeat at Hunslet, but spent almost the entire game on the left-wing due to an ear injury. Little was seen of him because not once did Northern make a worthwhile attack. This game also marked Derek Davies's last appearance for the club. The 25-year-old had finally been granted his wish for a transfer and Leeds beat Hull for his signature at slightly less than the £6,000 asking price. He had scored 36 tries in 139 appearances, but made countless other try-scoring opportunities for his colleagues in a career restrained by National Service. At Headingley his pace was utilised mostly on the wing. Around this time Northern also listed Tony Beevers at £500.

On their first return to Belle Vue following the Yorkshire Cup debacle in September, second-from-bottom Northern gave a surprisingly spirited display in the league encounter against Wakefield Trinity. After Northern conceded 15 early points, it was only in the last few minutes that Trinity scored their two second-half tries to cancel out scores by Hemingway and Grainger. The most pleasing feature in the 33–12 defeat was the manner in which the forwards stood up to the opposition's renowned pack; Steve Hey's direct runs up the middle frequently troubled the home defence.

Off the field there was some pleasing news. It was announced at the AGM on 8 November that Northern had made a profit of £5,004, on the year ending June 1961, which reduced the deficit to £1,471. Net receipts had been £8,675; players wages and expenses £6,700; staff wages £4,085; ground maintenance £1,372; and transfer fees, less those received, came to £1,720. The year's profit was due almost entirely to the success of the pools under their organiser Malcolm Davies. At the meeting Jackie Barritt made the claim that £20,000 was available to spend on new players and later that month their efforts in South Wales finally brought results with an outlay of almost £5,000.

The first signing, for about £2,000, was that of 22-year-old bricklayer, John Hardcastle, a prop from Maesteg. He had been a Welsh schoolboy and youth rugby union international and had represented Glamorgan. Two weeks later, Northern also signed 21-year-old colliery mechanic, Lance Davies, a highly-rated centre from Neath. He had been a reserve for that year's Welsh rugby union international trials. Northern had also wanted to sign his younger brother, Beverley, but he preferred to concentrate on his studies. Their father was former Rochdale Hornets player, Phil Davies.

Hardcastle produced plenty of 'fire' on his debut in a 21–0 home defeat to Hunslet on 25 November, but missed the following game due to a badly bruised shoulder. Despite their margin of victory, Hunslet still managed to squander numerous chances created by their elusive stand-off Brian Gabbitas and rampaging forwards Geoff Gunney and Billy Baldwinson. Referee G. Davies was the busiest man on the field and finally dismissed the hookers, Welsh, who got a two-match suspension, and Bernard Prior, for persistent scrum offences.

At Thrum Hall on 2 December, sleet made handling difficult. Northern held the advantage for long periods before losing 9–3 to Halifax, who were then ninth in the table. Seddon gave Northern the lead after 13 minutes when he dodged over, and Halifax's reply before half-time came from two goals by full-back Ronnie James, who, like Hardcastle, hailed from Maesteg. The game, which was watched by only 2,322, will perhaps be best remembered for the mass brawl in front of the main stand, which resulted in both Alan Sutcliffe and Colin Dixon being dismissed in the 72nd minute.

This dour contest also marked the last senior game for both former captain Trevor Jones – whose £250 signing from Batley had proved to be one of Northern's shrewdest buys – and the unsettled Steve Hey. Once described as a "rare and useful forward", Hey had been watched by Wigan in 1959, and, after an earlier transfer request had been refused, the 25-year-old was finally listed at £6,000. This was subsequently reduced to £4,000 on appeal. Since he had recovered from a groin injury Hey had appeared to be nearing his best form, and there were high hopes that his presence as a ball distributor would help the pack. Unfortunately, he was demoted to the 'A' team as a disciplinary measure after missing training and continued to stay away from Odsal. He later helped out his former junior club, Stanningley, and had trials with Bramley in 1964.

Lance Davies was down to play against Featherstone Rovers on 9 December, but the game was cancelled because of deep snow at Odsal. He finally made his debut the following Saturday against Doncaster, whose first win of the season against Dewsbury had put Northern at the bottom of the league table. Unfortunately, the game at Odsal had to be abandoned due to heavy fog after only 12 minutes play, when the visitors led by a Kevin Doyle drop-goal. The attendance of 405 was then the lowest ever at Odsal for a first team match, and the paying spectators, myself included, went away disgruntled because there was no refund. Our only consolation was that, again because of fog, the crowd of 6,305 at Park Avenue only watched eight minutes play against Southend United.

Both Sutcliffe and Welsh, who later announced his hasty retirement, were still suspended for the visit to Castleford, where a 34–10 defeat did Northern little justice. Trailing by 10 points in the first five minutes and 15–5 at half-time, Northern played their part in an action packed match. Lance Davies had an impressive first full game in his new code – his speed and direct play made two tries for his winger Doran.

There was a complete freeze out of the rugby league programme on Christmas Day, including Northern's fixture against Bramley at the Barley Mow. And on Saturday 30 December York's visit to Odsal was also postponed due to snow. With temperatures on New Year's Day at minus six degrees, the RFL faced the problem of rearranging 75 games, but rejected calls to extend the season.

On 6 January, Hull inflicted Northern's 14th consecutive defeat at The Boulevard, where they had last won in 1947. Hull were odds-on to extend Northern's dismal record because on the wings they had the flying dentist, Wilf Rosenberg, their recent £5,000 signing from Leeds, and their "sensational discovery", Clive Sullivan, in only his third senior game. The sinewy 18-year-old Welshman was then serving in the Army at Catterick Camp and had been rejected by Northern after playing a trial game a few weeks earlier – a decision they seriously lived to regret. One of the touch-judges in that game apparently recommended the future Great Britain captain to Hull, who immediately snapped him up after he had scored a hat-trick of tries in his trial game with them.

119

Northern only trailed 8–6 at half-time but, as so often was the case that season, they threw in the towel in the second-half to lose 30–6. Due to cartilage problems, this was loose-forward Ralph Winnard's last senior appearance until November.

In a 19–8 home defeat to Liverpool City, Hull's reserve winger, John Coggle, whose chances at The Boulevard were now limited with the arrival of Rosenberg and Sullivan, scored on his debut. During his month's trial he also impressed with his defensive work and was later signed at an undisclosed fee. The only other time that Northern troubled City was when Tom Whitaker intercepted and raced 80 yards for a spectacular touchdown. In a well-beaten pack, Terry Griffett made his one and only appearance of the season, after being discharged from the Army, and Alan Sutcliffe returned at scrum-half after suspension.

This game, watched by a crowd of only 563, was a sad ending to captain Terry Robbins' brief Northern career. The club's most outstanding attacking forward was finally granted his wish for a move before the Challenge Cup transfer deadline. Listed at £6,000, he moved to Bramley for a "very substantial fee" and in part-exchange for second-rower Tony Marker, who had been unable to command a regular first team place.

The disappointment of losing Terry Robbins came during the week when there was anxiety in the city due to the outbreak of smallpox, and on Monday 15 January I queued outside St George's Hall, along with thousands of other Bradfordians, in order to be vaccinated. On the advice of the Bradford Medical Officer of Health, Dr John Douglas, Northern's home game on the next Saturday against Hull KR was called off, but the trip to Barrow on 3 February went ahead after Northern's squad had been inoculated against the potentially fatal disease.

As the Challenge Cup transfer deadline approached, Northern found that most rugby league players with any ambition preferred to sign for stronger clubs, who could offer better playing terms and the prospect of more regular winning pay. Consequently, they were unsuccessful in their attempt to sign as player-coach 29-year-old Jeff Stevenson, the former Leeds and international scrum-half, who had been listed by York at £9,000. He later moved to Hunslet. Northern were also ignored by Dennis Goodwin, the former Barrow international and Leeds second-rower, who was then listed at £1,250 and preferred to move to York.

Northern versus Keighley at Odsal on 19 August 1961. Back: Trevor Jones, Doran, Crabtree, Arthur Hattee, Hemingway, Brian Smith, Holland; front: Welsh, Derek Davies, Terry Robbins, Broadbent, Sutcliffe, Penketh. (Courtesy Bradford Bulls Foundation RL Heritage Project)

Against Doncaster, Seddon makes the tackle, with Welsh (9), Crabtree (left), Abed and Hatfield (right) in attendance. (Courtesy *Rugby League Journal*).

Leeds prop or second-rower, Colin Tomlinson, was another player who rejected a move to Odsal. The club were also interested in Hull centre, Brian Saville, who was then on the list at £4,000, and Brian Shacklady, Huddersfield's Wigan-based second-rower, but both attempts failed. Northern were also apparently rejected by Cardiff's 24-year-old centre Meirion Roberts, who had been named as a replacement for Malcolm Thomas, who had been signed by Oldham, in the Welsh union side to face Scotland.

However, before the transfer deadline Northern did manage to secure the services of Hunslet scrum-half Dennis Tate for less than the listed price of £2,500, and back-rower Colin Taylor, the brother of Northern centre Bob Taylor, from Castleford for about £2,000. Tate had been with Hunslet since the age of 16 and had considerable first team experience, but had been listed following the arrival of Jeff Stevenson. Colin Taylor later took over as Northern's captain and was good enough to be in the Hunslet and Featherstone Rovers Wembley squads in 1965 and 1967, respectively.

The new recruits, who included Tony Marker, made their debuts in a 14–2 defeat at Barrow, where Doran continued his 'A' team experiment of playing in the second-row. Hailed as Northern's best defensive winger for some time, Coggle gave Barrow's dangerman Bill Burgess a torrid time, while Taylor's intelligent play at loose-forward marked him out as a potential pack leader. The new look side so impressed the directors that it was retained for the first round Challenge Cup tie at Wheldon Road.

Although Northern lost 12–0, their 300 or so supporters came away from Wheldon Road well satisfied with their team's performance. Castleford, whose only home defeat so far that season had been against the mighty Wakefield Trinity, could hardly have anticipated such a stern tussle. Colin Taylor went close in the opening minutes after intercepting against his former club, and Coggle was only prevented from scoring by a desperate tackle from full-back Albert Lunn. In a tight, thrilling game, Lunn's two penalty goals were all that separated the sides until the hour mark, when tries from Geoff Ward and Peter Small sealed Castleford's place in the second round. Marker sprained his right hand 10 minutes from the end, but managed to finish the game.

In their 23rd completed game of the season, Northern picked up winning pay for only the second time, with a 3–0 win over Dewsbury at Odsal, where there were home debuts for Marker, Tate, Taylor and Trevor Schofield, a former Shaw Cross junior. Dewsbury, who were only three places above Northern, but had beaten Halifax in the Cup the previous week, dominated possession. However, their heavy forwards played into the hands of Northern's improved defence, until Lance Davies crowned a fine performance with the only score after a fine run from Grainger. This ended Northern's 15-match losing run.

Keighley had won only one of their previous nine games before Northern's visit to Lawkholme Lane, but were on top for most of the game despite losing scrum-half Syd Hebden in the opening minutes. A snap try by Grainger just after half-time, when Keighley led 8–2, brought Northern's forwards to life and Schofield crossed in the 76th minute to give Northern a fortunate 10–10 draw. The home fixtures, against York – rearranged from the Christmas period – and Featherstone Rovers on Saturday 3 March and Wednesday 7 March respectively, were both postponed due to snow and ice and the frozen state of the Odsal pitch.

Northern then gave a trial to Goeli Abed, a 22-year-old South African centre of Malayan descent, who had also had trials with Leeds and Hunslet since being brought to England by Leeds bookmaker Jim Windsor. He made his Northern debut at Headingley, where the Loiners were still smarting from their 17–16 home defeat to Leigh in a Challenge Cup replay the previous Monday afternoon – a game which I was privileged to have watched, in a crowd of 32,000, from near to where Leigh prop Stan Owen controversially hoodwinked the Leeds defence.

Against Northern, only Lewis Jones's effortless goalkicking divided the sides at half-time – 14–8 – with Abed having had a hand in both Northern's first-half tries by wingmen Coggle and Grainger. In heavy conditions, the game became a test of strength between the packs, before Leeds came out on top, 20–8. After excellent cover defence from Northern, Leeds scored late tries from Australian full-back Ken Thornett and teenage left-winger, Geoff Wriglesworth. It was worth the occasional trek to Headingley to see this exciting prospect, who toured with the Lions in 1966 and later joined new Northern. A former Heworth junior, he was one of the few farmers then playing the game.

The following week the directors caused some bemusement with the arrival at Odsal of Jock McAvoy who was then a free agent. The Scottish former Warrington, Hull KR and Whitehaven utility back, returned to his original club, Workington Town, and played full-back in the 1958 Challenge Cup final. Having coached Dewsbury earlier in the season, McAvoy appeared to take charge against Salford at Odsal on 17 March, apparently without the prior knowledge of the team manager, Jimmy Ledgard. In one of the dreariest games of the season, Northern lapsed into their lethargic ways after conceding two early tries and Salford easily won 20–6 in front of a crowd of 1,323.

There then followed a hectic week at the end of March, when Northern conceded their first ever double to fellow strugglers Doncaster. The 16–2 defeat in the rearranged home game virtually guaranteed that they would finish at the bottom of the league. Northern, who were handicapped when Doran broke his nose, were easily beaten by the Dons, who belied their lowly position with slick handling and strong backing up.

Praise was then heaped on the reserves who played against Featherstone Rovers at Odsal the following Monday, when an injury-hit Northern gave debuts to J. Bentley at hooker and Peter Smith in the second-row. As well as scoring a try, Lance Davies made a success of his move to stand-off by speeding up the back play as Northern recovered from an early 10 point deficit to trail only 13–12 at half-time. However, for the first 20 minutes of the second-half, Northern never touched the ball and Rovers, who fielded three 19-year-olds in Arnold Morgan, Tony Lynch and Carl Dooler, finished 34–12 winners. Second-rower Terry Clawson scored five goals and two tries.

A weary Northern then had little to offer in the return game at Tattersfield, where their 25–5 defeat against Doncaster was the home side's biggest win in six years. After earlier announcing his retirement, hooker Gerald Welsh made a comeback in this game. After the game Goeli Abed was signed after a successful five-match trial. He had shown some neat touches and impressed with his goalkicking and touch-finding.

Due to postponements, Northern then had to play their last nine games in 30 days, during which time 'player-coach', a term the directors insisted the press should not use to describe him, Jock McAvoy played at full-back, centre and finally loose-forward. He made his debut at centre in the 28–2 home defeat to Bramley on Wednesday 4 April, when, in appalling conditions, their Maori full-back Johnny Wilson's eight goals took his total to 100 for the season, and, their prop, Dave Horn, was again sent off.

Northern's home game against Barrow on Saturday 7 April was called off due to a waterlogged pitch, but the first of Odsal's two Challenge Cup semi-finals, when Wakefield Trinity beat Featherstone Rovers 9–0 before a crowd of 43,627, went ahead on Wednesday 11 April. Both Trinity and Rovers had objected to the midweek early evening kick-off due to the inconvenience for their supporters. On the following Saturday, Huddersfield booked their place at Wembley with a 6–0 defeat of Hull KR, in front of a crowd of 31,423, which was modest by Odsal's standards.

On the same day Northern travelled to Post Office Road, where Featherstone Rovers, perhaps still feeling the effects of their encounter with Trinity, waltzed into a 16 point lead before the top-four contenders became apathetic. Trailing 19–8 at the interval, Northern took full advantage of Rovers' indifference and the rare feat of scoring a fourth try put them within a point. Only great tackles by full-back Jack Anderson prevented Taylor and Grainger adding further Northern tries, before a Terry Clawson penalty in the 75th minute eased Rovers to an unconvincing 21–18 victory. Half-backs Trevor Schofield and Len Haley outplayed Don Fox and Terry Mullaney, while Bill Seddon was inspirational at centre, and former Halifax junior, R. Radonic, impressed on his debut in the second-row.

Bramley's 18–5 win over Northern at the Barley Mow clinched their place in the following season's First Division – two divisions having finally been agreed for the 1962–63 season. Despite another spirited display, in which they restricted the Villagers to 2–2 at half-time, Northern were extremely limited on attack. Their only try, by Colin Taylor, came from a speculative up-and-under from Seddon.

Hull had won only one of their previous 11 games when they visited a near-waterlogged Odsal on 21 April; and, before a crowd of only 483, Northern took an early lead through a try from Schofield. The sides were level 5–5 at the interval. Northern had been the better side up to half-time, but Hull then scored four unanswered tries, including Wilf Rosenberg's third, to run out easy 25–5 winners.

There was no joy for Northern over the Easter period with a 20–12 defeat at Dewsbury on Easter Monday and a 24–12 loss to York at Odsal the following day. At Crown Flatt they conceded three first-half tries and trailed 11–5 at the break; their points came from a converted try to Coggle. With Dewsbury handicapped by an injury to centre Don Lockwood, Northern managed to recover to 14–12 when Welsh went over and Abed landed his third goal. However, Dewsbury's elusive scrum-half, Johnny Bullock, settled the issue with two late well-taken tries. Playing in his first game since he broke his nose against Doncaster, try-scorer Jack Doran was later found to have broken his wrist in the York game.

Remarkably, after the trials and tribulations of their worst ever season, Northern then ended the campaign on a high note. Jock McAvoy had seen the need for an experienced forward leader and although he had no previous experience of the position, volunteered to move to loose-forward to replace the injured Taylor. Under his inspired promptings, and using his experience as a former half-back, Northern recorded three successive home victories in the space of six days.

Batley had lost all but one of their previous 16 games before the fixture at Odsal on Saturday 28 April. McAvoy was an immediate success in his new position and scored two tries in an 18–11 victory. On the following Monday, Hull KR sent a strong side to Odsal, but, after losing centre Alan Burwell in the 15th minute with a shoulder injury, never looked like holding a reinvigorated Northern. Moving with rare speed and purpose, Northern fully merited their shock 9–3 win. Their points came from three superb tries from Seddon, Grainger and Sutcliffe. In the final game of the season, before a crowd of 842, Northern then earned a special bonus for completing an unexpected hat-trick of wins when they were fortunate to beat Barrow 16–14. Barrow scored four tries and were the more polished attacking force, but Northern had the more reliable goalkicker in Abed, who kicked his fifth goal in converting Northern's second try, by Hatfield, which had come from an up-and-under by Seddon.

Despite these welcome end-of-season victories, Northern's hopes of a continued revival were clearly out of the question until they could curb their tendency to sign players who were mostly other clubs' cast-offs. The response that McAvoy – a stop-gap number 13 – had been able get from his forwards proved how much Northern so badly needed a class addition to their pack, where Hardcastle, Marker and Taylor were considered useful signings. Of the backs, Abed was still a raw recruit from rugby union, Tate was always likely to pose a threat and Lance Davies had by far the most potential. Unfortunately, due to the pack's general shortcomings, in a season when Northern finished at the bottom of the league for the first time since the 1931–32 season, the backs had been asked to do far too much tackling.

In the Championship final Wakefield Trinity were seeking to become only the fourth club in the game's history to win All Four Cups, having beaten Huddersfield at Wembley the previous Saturday. The usual 50,000-plus crowd was expected, but heavy rain helped reduce the attendance to 37,451. Most of us were soaked to the skin when Tommy Smales's try in the closing minutes caused a mini crowd invasion at the scoreboard end as the Fartowners gained a 14–5 surprise revenge victory.

1961–62 Summary
Position in league: 30th of 30 P 36 W 5 L 30 D 1 – Pts 288–766
Challenge Cup: First round. Yorkshire Cup: First Round.
Average attendance: 1,495

Chairman Jackie Barritt welcomes South African Rudi Hasse, pictured
in his blazer and cravat, to Odsal.

10. 1962–63: More South Africans
The great freeze causes fixture congestion

Before the start of the new season, 37-year-old Frank Moore, the former Leigh, Hull KR, York, Featherstone Rovers and Wakefield Trinity forward, was signed as a forward coaching assistant to Jimmy Ledgard. The campaign started on Friday 10 August with a 22–8 defeat at Keighley in the Lazenby Cup. Northern's captain, Len Haley, who was then in his benefit season, and Jack Doran, who broke a rib, sustained injuries which caused the second-rower to miss the first seven games.

Further early season signings were A.M. Poxton, a Featherstone junior introduced by Frank Moore, who made his debut in the second-row in the Lazenby Cup game; Featherstone Rovers' 22-year-old scrum-half, Mick Reynolds, who was signed at an undisclosed fee after completing an impressive month's trial; and 21-year-old policeman Alan Martin. The latter was a useful goalkicking loose-forward, who was signed from Halifax for £600, in face of competition from Doncaster. Unfortunately, Tony Marker announced his retirement because of being promoted at work, but he did return to make four appearances late in the season

In the close season, while on holiday in South Africa, Jackie Barritt signed former South African rugby union second-row forward Rudi Hasse. The 25-year-old, who was six feet four inches tall, had been recommended by former Hunslet winger Ronnie Colin, who was then playing in one of the new rugby league teams in South Africa. After being joined by his wife and two young children, Hasse sat out the first four games to gain experience from the touchline before his baptism in his new code.

With the introduction of two divisions, August and September was taken up by the new Eastern Divisional Championship. The idea was that the Second Division sides would retain some of their traditionally lucrative derby games. However, playing the top four Yorkshire sides from the previous season meant that Northern, like other lower clubs, were in for some heavy beatings early in the season, which, it was felt, could dampen enthusiasm before the start of the Second Division campaign. Consequently, Northern finished 14th of 16 clubs in the Eastern Divisional Championship, but caused a major shock by winning their final game, admittedly when the top-four play-off places had already been decided. Financially, the new competition was a complete disaster for Northern.

A scoring flourish of 13 points in the last seven minutes gave Leeds a flattering 27–5 victory in the opening, Friday night, game at Headingley. With Hardcastle outstanding in an enthusiastic pack, Northern trailed only 14–5 up to the 73rd minute, after which Leeds crossed for three tries, including one to stand-off Derek Davies. Despite limited opportunities, Lance Davies impressed at centre and scored Northern's only try shortly after half-time. The Leeds display would have been very ordinary but for the skilful handling of Fred Pickup at loose-forward and, in the words of Alfred Drewry of the *Yorkshire Post,* "the almost casual brilliance of the inimitable (Lewis) Jones".

On the following Wednesday, at Odsal, Northern were no match for Huddersfield's rampaging forwards, led by Ken Bowman and Austin Kilroy, or the brilliance of scrum-half Tommy Smales. The reigning league champions ran out easy 31–5 victors. Loose-forward Alan Redfearn, who could not command a place in either Huddersfield's 1962 Wembley or Championship final sides, scored a hat-trick of tries in the second-half. Northern's only try came in the 75th minute from a Seddon up-and-under, which bounced off the cross bar for Welsh to touch down.

For the visit of the Challenge Cup holders, Wakefield Trinity, on the Saturday, Northern dropped four players, including Don Hatfield, who, having made 28 appearances, failed to regain his place and later decided to retire. They gave debuts to Moore, Hasse and trialist Mick Reynolds. Lacking many of their regulars, Trinity rarely moved in their usual precision-like style and were shaken by Northern's magnificent late rally, in which Tate and Reynolds scored tries to take the score to 13–10. Leading 13–2 at half-time, Trinity only made sure of their 19–10 victory through Northern presenting them with two late tries. Colin Taylor, who unfortunately injured his back, was among Northern's better performers, and Hasse made a commendable debut after an earlier run out with the 'A' team.

On the following Wednesday and Friday Northern travelled to Featherstone Rovers and Huddersfield, where they were totally outclassed on each occasion, 43–16 and 37–0, respectively. At Post Office Road there was a first appearance for Alan Martin in Northern's reshuffled pack, in which Wigglesworth failed to gain much possession. Consequently, Rovers, who were led brilliantly by four-try man Don Fox, ran riot in the second-half. It was the same story at Fartown where third-choice hooker Bentley fared no better and Northern, trailing 12–0 at half-time, caved in after the break. Full-back Frank Dyson scored a hat-trick of tries to add to his eight goals. This was Poxton's fifth and final game, following a pulled leg muscle.

Northern went down 11–5 to Bramley in the Yorkshire Cup at Odsal after dominating possession and leading 5–3 at half-time through a solo try from Martin, converted by Seddon. They missed their opportunity to build a substantial interval lead against the out-of-form First Division side and thereby earn the £17 winning pay that was on offer. Bramley were only assured of victory when full-back Johnny Wilson kicked a 75th minute penalty, variously described as "from 10 yards inside his own half" and "from 60 yards". The most impressive back on the field was Mick Reynolds, who moved from the right-wing to stand-off after Tate injured his hand.

Due to bruising a shoulder in the above cup tie, Len Haley missed his benefit game at Odsal in the Eastern Championship. Derek Davies played on the left-wing for Leeds, who won 21–18. In an exhilarating contest, in which the lead changed hands five times, the out-of-form visitors were relieved to hear the final whistle as 12-man Northern battered their line. Martin retired injured after 20 minutes with a broken finger and Hardcastle, Taylor and Hasse worked tirelessly. The South African also impressed with his speed and willingness to 'mix it' against seasoned league campaigner Jack Fairbank, who, along with Ken Thornett, was cautioned for rough play in a robust struggle. On this form, Northern looked capable of mounting a formidable challenge in the Second Division. However, the attendance of 2,781 was well down on previous visits by Leeds; the receipts of £308, after expenses, went to Len Haley's benefit fund.

Sadly for Northern, Wakefield Trinity were able to include all their five 1962 tourists – Neil Fox, Round, Wilkinson, Poynton and Turner – for the first time that season, when Northern visited Belle Vue the following Saturday. Trinity's improved form was directly traceable to the return of Derek Turner, who repeatedly sliced through Northern's thin defence. Trinity lost Ian Brooke with concussion after 18 minutes, but still led 22–11 at half-time and cruised to a 45–11 victory. Prop

Jack Wilkinson scored two of Trinity's 11 tries. Unfortunately, due to cartilage trouble, this proved to be captain Colin Taylor's last game until May.

Following on from this blow, Northern then produced one of the shocks of the season by thrashing the previously unbeaten Featherstone Rovers in the final game of the Eastern Championship. Playing some scintillating rugby, Northern led 18–2 at half-time and finished worthy 21–13 winners. Rovers' solitary try came in the last minute. Moore, Hardcastle, Hasse and Martin, with a try and three goals, were dominant figures in the pack, while Penketh was their star back, and had a hand in three of Northern's five tries. Even allowing for the fact that Rovers had already booked their place in the divisional play-offs, this was a remarkable 80 minute performance from Northern, from the moment that Alan Sutcliffe scored after a 40-yard diagonal dart to the clubhouse corner. It led us all to believe that, on this form, no Second Division side could possibly live with them.

The new regional championship was a complete flop as far as attendances were concerned: only a total of 8,832 had watched the four home games, when the previous season the league fixtures against Leeds and Wakefield Trinity alone had brought nearly 10,000 to Odsal. The whole structure of the competition was so unbalanced, with the top four clubs playing the bottom four, that the interest in these previously attractive games was lost on the paying public. For example, takings at the Featherstone game were only £150, yet £180 was paid out in winning pay.

Seddon replaced the injured Abed at full-back for the opening game in the Second Division. Northern, despite having won only one point in their previous 30 away games, were expected to account for a weak Liverpool City side at Knotty Ash. After leading 7–4 at half-time, Northern were level until shortly before the end when defensive lapses resulted in two City tries and a 17–9 defeat. Nonetheless, it was a satisfactory performance. Martin, who scored all Northern's points, was again outstanding.

In a scrappy game, Northern then opened the home league campaign with an unconvincing 12–10 win over Dewsbury. The visitors, who had conceded an average 37 points in their previous away games that season, led 10–7 at the interval, mostly thanks to dominating possession. After earlier scoring a fine solo try, stand-off Alan Sutcliffe produced another of his breathtaking bursts to lay on the match winner for John Coggle. After their recent performances, there was an encouraging attendance of 1,700.

They then had a golden opportunity of improving on their dismal away record at Salford. Their hosts had won only once that season and conceded an average of 35 points per game. But, after leading 5–3 at the interval from a Hasse try created by Sutcliffe, Northern were again handicapped by a lack of possession and lost 16–5. An all-in brawl in the 75th minute resulted in the dismissal of Penketh for the first time in his career, for which he received a two-match suspension. Moore's injury caused him to miss only one game. But, with the surprising return of veteran Wynne Jones on a free transfer from Featherstone Rovers, supporters wondered whether Northern would have benefitted more from signing a 'runner' rather than another old head. They missed Colin Taylor's skill and dash.

Particularly in view of the improved work of their backs, one of Northern's major worries was the lack of scrum possession. They made numerous attempts in October and November to rectify the weakness, but were disappointed when two proposed deals both fell through. First, Salford's Batley-based hooker George Harwood decided to concentrate on his decorating business, and then Keighley's young hooker, Eric Redman, who was listed at £1,000, withdrew his transfer request after the clubs had agreed a swap for stay-away Gerald Welsh, who was then listed at £400. Welsh later moved to Lawkholme Lane following a month's trial, despite having been sent off in his first 'A' team game. Northern's search for a replacement continued however, after dropping their interest in Leigh's county hooker Walt Tabern, who was on the list at £1,250.

As Wigglesworth, who had occupied the hooking spot in the previous six games, did not appear to be the answer, Northern reverted to former Wyke junior, J. Bentley, who had impressed in the loose earlier in the season and received good reports for his work in the 'A' team. But Northern continued to struggle for a fair share of the ball until they signed George Gomersal from Hunslet in late December.

The visit of Rochdale Hornets on 27 October produced one of Odsal's most entertaining games for a long time. The Hornets' wildly enthusiastic supporters made up at least a quarter of the crowd of 2,027. The visitors were by far the better side in terms of speed, backing-up and ideas, but it was not until the closing stages that the visitors wore down a fine Northern defence to win 22–7. One of the highlights of the afternoon was the manner in which the colossal Fijian second-rower, Laitia Ravouvou, scattered Northern defenders in his many runs up the middle.

After several weeks' negotiations, Northern announced the signings of two South African rugby union players from Western Province, 22-year-old half-back Vernon Peterson and 23-year-old second-rower Enslin Dlambulo. No signing fee was agreed, but Northern paid their expenses and employed them on the groundstaff. They initially stayed with Goeli Abed.

Both Peterson and Dlambulo arrived in England in time to witness Northern's away game against bottom club Doncaster on 3 November, when 24-year-old Henry Sharratt, who only that week had been listed by Dewsbury at £750, made his debut in the second-row. The South Africans could not have been too impressed with their first view of British rugby league or the club, as they watched Northern lose 34–4. It was the first time in their history that Doncaster had topped 30 points, which included a hat-trick of tries from former Leeds utility back Eric Horsman. Northern conceded five tries in 32 minutes, despite some great tackling from Tate. They then totally lost control after 65 minutes when Martin went off with a leg injury, which caused him to miss the next two games.

In one of the most depressing games seen at Odsal for some time, Liverpool City maintained their position of second in the league behind leaders Keighley with a 7–2 victory over a disjointed Northern side. It was a messy struggle between two mediocre sides watched by a crowd of 631. Northern's pack grafted individually, but they had no set plan, and with many dropped passes the game was punctuated with numerous scrums. With Peter Nunns down in Staffordshire on a three week course, there was an opportunity for reserve winger, Derek Foster, who made the first of only four first team appearances on the left-wing. After recovering from a cartilage operation, loose-forward Ralph Winnard made his first team comeback, but the following week's game proved to be his swansong.

This was at Crown Flatt, where Dewsbury deserved their 15–10 victory after clinging on following the loss of hooker John Kelly after 65 minutes. Trailing 15–0 at the interval, Northern came back into the game shortly after half-time with a converted try by their half-back, Mick Reynolds, and a late try to Ralph Winnard, who therefore had the distinction of scoring both on his debut and in his final senior game. On the day, along with Hasse and Sharratt, he was among Northern's better forwards. He retired in the 1963–64 season, after 161 first team appearances.

When Salford visited Odsal on 24 November they had already conceded 40 or more points on five occasions, including a 43–0 loss at Batley. However, they were far superior to Northern in every department in the first-half and led 8–5 at the interval. Once Northern drew level, however, following a converted try by the forceful Martin, the visitors could not cope with the determined runs of Hasse and Sharratt, or the fluid handling of Northern's backs, of whom Penketh was by far the most dangerous. Northern's enterprising play produced a 20–13 victory. Unfortunately, with the 'A' team also winning, the club were out of pocket on the day. The receipts were only £65 from a crowd of 744, while the wage bill alone was £245.

Northern fielded an unchanged side for their visit to Rochdale, where they conceded four tries in the first 20 minutes and finally lost 23–7. Hornets, whose Fijian winger Joe Levula scored two of their seven tries, played some attractive rugby. But Northern's defence was atrocious, and with limited possession they showed little imagination in attack. This was Frank Moore's 15th and final game for Northern before he retired. To replace him they had targeted Leeds's former international, Abe Terry, but the deal fell through with the player after the clubs had agreed terms.

Around the time of Doncaster's visit to Odsal on 8 December, when the Dons triumphed 10–3, some people in Bradford had been issued with smog masks because of the dangerous levels of sulphur dioxide in the air. However, it was thick mud that the players had to contend with because the Odsal pitch was a quagmire following early morning rain. Despite the conditions, both sides handled surprisingly well in the early stages and Northern opened the scoring with a fine try from Doran. Unfortunately, they again paid the price for their inability to gain scrum possession, and Doncaster got a special bonus in their winning pay of £12/10 for their third successive win. Alan Hepworth had another great game against Northern, including a 40-yard run after he caught the ball from the first kick-off.

Keighley, who later won promotion after finishing behind Hunslet, moved to the top of the Second Division table as a result of their easy 30–2 win over Northern at Lawkholme Lane. Despite being reduced to 12-men in the 37th minute with the loss of young loose-forward Albert Eyre, they still managed to end their fourth successive game without conceding a try. Northern gave an outing to 'A' team prop John Reynolds, the brother of stand-off Mick Reynolds, who received two cautions for his over-aggressive play on his only first team appearance. He had arrived at Odsal as a free agent having been crossed off the Featherstone Rovers register. Stand-off Alan Sutcliffe broke a finger in this game and failed to regain a place until the next season.

Thick fog in the surrounding area delayed Barrow's arrival at Odsal and the game kicked-off 25 minutes late. Mick Reynolds was unable to reach the ground because of the fog, and in the rearranged backs Fred White, a free transfer signing from Hunslet, made his debut on the right-wing in place of Doran, who moved to centre. Policeman Rodney Thomas came in at number eight for his first appearance of the season. Despite missing Bill Burgess, Barrow were in a different class to Northern and ran out 36–5 winners. Their prop, Don Wilson, was the best player on the field and he moved like a winger over 20 yards to round Abed for Barrow's sixth try. Northern's only try, from Davies, came in the dying minutes, when the Odsal track lights were used on the instructions of referee Charlie Appleton.

Northern's only consolation was that hooker George Gomersal had won an equal share of possession, following his signing from Hunslet on a month's trial. A product of Hunslet Intermediates, he had represented Yorkshire Under–19s in 1958 and had been understudy to Bernard Prior, the Yorkshire county hooker, and former international Sam Smith.

At Northern's AGM on 5 December the eight shareholders present re-elected Messrs Barritt, Bunney, Harry Hornby Junior and Dr Harry Fidler, and approved the accounts for the year ended 30 June 1962, which showed a loss of £864 and a deficit of £2,411. Net receipts were £8,210; players' wages and expenses came to £7,531 and staff wages £4,084; while ground maintenance amounted to £2,463. After spending £12,562 on new players, there was a loss on transfer fees of £6,063. Answering critics of the club's recruitment efforts, Mr Bunney admitted they had made a few mistakes, but thought certain players had now grown in value. Jackie Barritt spoke about the problems they were facing to rebuild the team, but said: "There was no question of making special concessions to players as an inducement to join us".

The loss would have been much greater but for the pools, and it was therefore unfortunate that at the same meeting the directors had to announce that the pools organiser, Malcolm Davies, had resigned. He had to give six months' notice to terminate his contract with effect from 20 May and later joined Keighley in a similar capacity. In his two and half years in charge, he built up the membership from about 2,000 to the maximum 15,000, which made it one of the most successful in the league. In his time the pools income was £32,000; over £18,000 was spent on new players.

Many of the pools agents, however, were highly critical of the directors for not spending more of this income on signing top quality players. The result was the formation of a new supporters' club, whose sole purpose was to raise funds to buy players. There was then conflict with the club's own scheme, membership of which dropped to 9,000 members – a loss of £100 a week to the club – at a time when Northern had no other income because of the big freeze which wiped out virtually all rugby league from the end of December to the end of February. A solution was agreed at a meeting in January, when the supporters' club agreed to suspend their fundraising until the membership in the official pool reached the maximum number, in return for regular reports of how the pools money was being spent. In view of Northern's dire financial position, it was a compromise that was long overdue and the two pools were later merged.

Hailed as one of their best moves for some considerable time, on 2 January 1963 Northern announced the appointment of 54-year-old Harry Beverley as team manager and coach. The previous season he had steered Bramley into the First Division, but had left the club following a disagreement with the directors over team selection. He had previously coached Halifax and Wakefield Trinity and had a reputation as a straight talker and strict disciplinarian. His appointment resulted in Jimmy Ledgard being sacked and he sought legal advice after being told this at the previous night's training session.

As a 17-year-old, Beverley joined Hunslet as a centre or winger, but later became a dynamic loose-forward. He was in the Hunslet side which won the Challenge Cup in 1934, and among his six test appearances against Australia he was in the pack that tamed the Kangaroos in Sydney and Brisbane on the 1936 tour. In 1937 he moved to Halifax and won another Challenge Cup winner's medal in 1939. Since retiring from the game he had worked for a Bradford brewery. He ordered all the players to attend a Saturday afternoon training session, but his work was hampered by the big freeze which started with the cancellation of a trip to York on 29 December, shortly before he arrived at Odsal.

Apart from the pools, the £55 receipts from the Barrow game were Northern's only income for the next 10 weeks. They did not play from 22 December until 23 February, during which time seven league games and the Challenge Cup tie against Wakefield Trinity were cancelled due to snow and ice. In the 69 day cold spell up to 2 March 1963 only seven games, including Northern's at Whitehaven, were completed in the entire rugby league programme. The RFL decided that the season must end on 30 May, regardless of the weather. Northern eventually played seven times in May.

Prior to Beverley's arrival, Northern had used 18 forwards in their efforts to find an effective combination, and the pack continued to be a major problem. Although the backs had some glaring faults, it was mainly due to them having to do too much of the forwards' work in defence that they were proving to be ineffective. The lack of a consistent share of possession had also hampered the team's chances, and fitness was also an issue.

The selectors' determination to find a solution was shown when they dropped Alan Martin and Rudi Hasse for the cancelled game against York. Apart from Colin Taylor, that season Martin had been by far Northern's most intelligent attacking forward. But his recent form had suffered due to a lack of support. The game against Barrow proved to be his 15th, and last, for the club. It was a pity that more was not seen of his combination with Colin Taylor, who was back in light training after a cartilage operation; they had combined well in the two games they played together.

In the league's worst side and without talented colleagues to lead them, few former rugby union forwards could have had such a difficult baptism as Hardcastle and Hasse. Despite showing early promise, Hasse was still finding it difficult to adjust to rugby league and his omission for the cancelled game at York was no surprise. Hardcastle had quickly earned a reputation as the club's hardest working forward. His consistency was rewarded with his selection as travelling reserve for the Welsh side, which included Terry Robbins, which lost to France 23–3 in Toulouse on 17 February.

Unfortunately, the hardest part of the league programme was still to come because Barrow, York, Hunslet, Leigh, Blackpool Borough and Whitehaven all had a chance of promotion. For their first game after the freeze Northern travelled to Whitehaven on 23 February, where they were totally outclassed 34–8 by a faster and fitter side. Although declared fit, the ground was still rock hard near the edges and some players were reluctant to tackle, which resulted in several of Whitehaven's 10 tries. The Cumbrians were well led by Scottish scrum-half Brian Shillinglaw. Their right-winger Les Lowther scored five tries, which equalled their club record.

On his return Tony Marker suffered a knee injury in the first few minutes, but the captain was still Northern's best forward, scored a try and helped 'nurse' Enslin Dlambulo through his first senior game. For a recent convert from rugby union, the mobile, slightly-built South African showed impressive ball skills and defended better than most of the team. There were also debuts for former Featherstone junior, E. Flynn, at full-back and policeman Brian Monaghan, who made his only first team appearance on the left-wing. On the other flank, Fred White scored Northern's other try, in his second and final first team game.

On 9 March, Northern travelled to Hilton Park, for a rearranged game from January, to meet the Second Division's 'glamour' side. Leigh had been favourites to win promotion after some big money signings, but they were then languishing fourth from the bottom of the league. However, they were barely out of Northern's half and won 33–2. Former England and British Lions rugby union international Bev Risman played brilliantly at full-back and scored two tries and six goals. Mick Martyn, the game's most prolific try-scoring forward, also crossed twice. Northern's forward deficiencies were again evident; only Hardcastle and Gomersal made any impression. However, Peter Nunns's robust centre play almost blotted Leigh's star centre Ken Large out of the game.

Despite strenuous efforts to clear the frozen Odsal pitch of snow and ice, Northern's first round Challenge Cup tie against Wakefield Trinity had been called off three times, on the 9, 13 and 28 February,

139

before it was finally played on Monday 11 March at 4.15pm. The Cup holders were confident that the game would be played at Belle Vue, following an RFL directive that the venue could be switched if a home ground remained unplayable. But an amazing thaw set in at Odsal on Wednesday 6 March and before the weekend the ground was declared fit for the following Monday. Because of the delay, the second round draw had already been made. The winners would meet Liverpool City at home.

For the long awaited visit of Trinity, Northern made only two changes – Abed replacing Flynn on the right-wing, and Dlambulo replacing the injured Marker in the second-row – from the side that had crashed only two days before at Leigh. Yet the transformation in their play was remarkable, and before losing 15–3 to the Cup holders, a determined Northern side had shaken Trinity with an unbelievably tenacious defence. Northern's much criticised pack refused to take a backward step, and at centre Nunns and Penketh gave their opposite numbers Colin Greenwood and Neil Fox punishing games. In a great team effort, prop forward Rodney Thomas helped Gomersal win plenty of possession and was useful in the loose, while Sharratt had his best game so far.

Dlambulo loses the ball in a double-tackle in the cup tie against Wakefield Trinity, watched by Sharratt and Hasse and Trinity's Jack Wilkinson and Geoff Oakes. (Courtesy Robert Gate).

140

Although lacking Trinity's finesse, Northern took the lead in the opening minutes with a try by Abed and it was not until the 32nd minute that Trinity drew level. It was a tough, bitter slog on a quagmire of a pitch and it was only in the closing stages that Trinity took control. Keith Holliday, Ken Hirst, Milan Kosanovic, Neil Fox and Bob Haigh scored tries for Trinity, while Fox and Round missed 10 kicks at goal. However, the crowd was a disappointing 2,069.

Because the 'A' team were already scheduled to play at Odsal on 16 March, Northern were unable to rearrange their game against Keighley, although both clubs were free to play after going out of the Cup. Northern thus had another two week break before their visit to Parkside, where Hunslet, under player-coach Fred Ward, stepped up their promotion challenge with a convincing 38–15 win. Northern twice levelled the scores in the first-half with tries from Penketh and Reynolds, and trailed only 15–10 at the interval. But Hunslet's superiority was such that, after pulling a thigh muscle in the opening minutes and retiring to the wing, centre Geoff Shelton still managed to score two tries. Top honours went to his centre partner Alan Preece, who collected a hat-trick of tries in a 22 minute spell in the second-half. The robust Peter Nunns provided one of the highlights of an entertaining game with a try after racing 80-yards towards the railway end of the ground. Seddon had a painkilling injection at half-time, after an early knock to his ribs, but played courageously to the end.

In the 'A' team game against Hunslet at Odsal on the same day there were injuries to Sutcliffe, who broke a wrist; Taylor who broke his jaw; and Doran with a broken nose. More bad news was that Marker faced suspension after being sent-off. However, Dennis Tate was back in training after a four month absence following a short-lived retirement.

Northern kept the same side for the visit of promotion candidates Whitehaven, and managed a shock 7–7 draw. It seemed that Harry Beverley might be able to steer them away from the bottom spot. With steadier finishing, they could easily have built on their 7–2 interval lead, but a bad defensive lapse in the 77th minute, which allowed Harry Hughes to cross, cost them winning pay. Northern's improved attacking work was credited to hooker Gomersal, who had been signed after his month's trial. As well as being a constructive support player he continued to win a fair share of possession. This had benefitted the backs, and Penketh and Nunns were hailed as Northern's best centre partnership for some time. Unfortunately, the crowd was only 543 with receipts of about £50. Recent gates had been insufficient to pay the players' wages and the club was almost totally dependent on income from the pools.

Northern's revival was short-lived, and in their last 10 games they scored only 45 points and conceded 288, including 63 tries. In their last four away games they failed to score a single point. In this spell, along with serious injuries to Reynolds and Coggle, Northern also lost Bill Seddon with a fractured cheek bone. In this, his 11th, season, the stalwart New Zealander had decided to retire after making 283 appearances, excluding Lazenby Cup games, scoring 307 goals and 46 tries. Yet he made a surprising comeback in the 'A' team in 1963–64, before he finally hung up his boots and returned to New Zealand.

At Odsal, Blackpool Borough were without their stand-off Syd Fenton for the last 45 minutes with a suspected broken jaw, but still won 23–7. Playing opposite the legendary Brian Bevan, Coggle went near after a 50-yard sprint just before half-time, but, apart from a try by Reynolds in the 64th minute, this was one of Northern's few attacks. Reynolds injured his arm while scoring and missed the game at Batley the following Monday, when stand-off Dennis Tate did not turn up.

Consequently, Northern had to urgently reshuffle their backs. Penketh and Lance Davies, at scrum-half, formed a new half-back pairing, and the inexperienced Flynn came in at right centre. Although Marker was sent-off, there could be no excuses as Batley, for whom Brian Ward scored a hat-trick of tries, easily won 31–0. In his final senior appearance, Bill Seddon missed half the game due to the previously mentioned fractured cheekbone. Hasse, who hurt his back, and Coggle, with a broken nose, also suffered injuries. This was Marker's last senior game because, having served a one-match suspension, he suffered from a recurring knee injury.

Yet another fixture was postponed due to the weather when, on Wednesday 17 April, Northern's game against Leigh was called off because of a waterlogged pitch. The decision was made by referee Davies only 30 minutes before kick-off with about 200 fans present.

There was then another blank Saturday due to the Challenge Cup semi-final at Headingley, where the crowd of 21,479 was some 10,000 below the average at Odsal since 1955. There were also only 15,566 at the other semi-final at Swinton's Station Road. Odsal was no longer regarded as the premier ground in Yorkshire, but, despite the dangerous condition of much of the wooden terracing, it was still the chosen venue if a Challenge Cup final replay was required. Then came the welcome news that the Corporation were planning to spend £50,000 on new concrete terracing at the Rooley Avenue end to accommodate 20,000 fans – the work was to start in December.

Northern then had the misfortune to play third-placed York in consecutive games. They lost 31–7 at Odsal on Wednesday 24 April and 38–0 at Clarence Street on 4 May. Since losing Jeff Stevenson to Hunslet, York had built a mobile pack around Albert Firth, Geoff Steel, both former Trinity players, David Lamming, previously with Featherstone Rovers, and Dennis Goodwin, who had played for Leeds. They handled brilliantly at times in both games. At Odsal, their full-back Willie Hargreaves celebrated his 400th appearance with one of the game's best tries, and Geoff Smith's hat-trick took him close to their club record of 31 tries in a season.

In contrast to York's team building efforts, there was criticism that Northern were relying on other clubs' cast-offs when three Doncaster 'A' teamers were taken on trial. Forward Rodney Sharpe never did make the first team, but both open-side prop Bernard Robinson and winger David Horton, a former Bradford junior who previously played for Huddersfield, went straight into the side at York. Although Mick Reynolds was limping throughout most of the second-half, Northern's willingness to play open rugby earned them admiration from the 3,895 crowd. Although the whitewash at Clarence Street was Horton's only first team opportunity, during his extended trial until the end of the season Robinson did enough to impress Northern, who were desperate for an open-side prop, but they were unable to agree terms with Doncaster for a permanent transfer.

Northern's only consolation for a dismal end to the season was the return after injury of captain Colin Taylor and the fine performances of both Tony Beevers, whose fine tackling helped cement his place at full-back, and Vernon Peterson, who made the first of only six appearances for the first team in a plucky 22–6 home defeat to Hunslet. Peterson's duel with county stand-off Brian Gabbitas was an outstanding feature of the game, which Hunslet's mobile pack dominated. Much was

143

expected of him, but, unfortunately, he later returned home to South Africa permanently due to domestic problems.

Northern's four South Africans played together for the first time in the club's history on Wednesday, 15 May, when Northern lost 30–0 at Blackpool, where Mick Reynolds dislocated an elbow. On the following Saturday, through two tries from Colin Taylor, Northern held a 6–0 lead over visitors Leigh until the 25th minute, when, unfortunately, they lost stand-off Len Haley. Leigh then took full control and ran out 31–16 winners – their fastidious full-back, Colin Tyrer, accounted for 16 of their points. Excluding the abandoned game against Doncaster in December 1961, the crowd of 435 was a new low.

In a 17–3 home defeat to Batley on the following Wednesday evening, Northern had enough possession and chances to have won, but were too orthodox against a speedier Batley side, who were reduced to 12-men with a dismissal in the 65th minute. Unfortunately, Coggle injured his knee and missed the rest of the season.

Northern's resistance lasted only eight minutes at Barrow, then Bill Burgess scored the first of his four tries in a 39–0 defeat. Despite being down to 12-men for all the second-half, Barrow still managed to score 23 points. Stand-off Les Woolveridge created havoc and full-back Tommy Dawes finished with two tries and six goals.

A 25–6 defeat to already promoted Keighley at Odsal on Wednesday 29 May brought the curtain down on another disastrous season for bottom-placed Northern. For the Lawkholmers, Roy Sabine scored a hat-trick of tries, while Welsh full-back Garfield Owen just fell short of breaking the club's points in a season record by managing only five goals from 11 kicks. Northern's points came from two tries by centre George Penketh, who earlier in the month had seen his transfer fee cut from £4,000 to £2,500. In May Northern also listed, at £750, loose-forward Alan Martin, who had not trained since December. He later had a trial at Bramley in 1963–64, when there were hopes of an exchange deal, but he was not signed by Bramley and stayed away from Odsal until the end.

1962 –63 Summary
Eastern Division: 14th of 16 P 8 W 1 L 7 – Pts 86–236
Second Division: 14th of 14 P 26 W 2 L 23 D 1 – Pts 163–632
Yorkshire Cup: First round. Challenge Cup: First round.
Average attendance: 1,257

11. 1963–64: The loyal 324
The end of the road for Northern

In August First Division neighbours Halifax had been able to splash out £10,500 on stand-off Alan Kellett from Oldham and Ken Roberts from Swinton. Northern's only signings of the summer were former Castleford and Huddersfield winger, Doug Iredale, who was taken on trial from Blackpool Borough, and former Doncaster full-back and free agent, Jack Appleyard, neither of whom made the first team. However, Northern also gave an 'A' team trial to 17-year-old Clayton forward, Stan Fearnley, the son of the Halifax coach, Albert Fearnley, both of whom, along with Kellett and Roberts, later served new Northern with some distinction.

After a number of threats of strike action by players on both sides of the Pennines, as the new season approached the so-called 'Big Five' – Wigan, St Helens, Leeds, Widnes and Wakefield Trinity – finally agreed to pay £16 and £20 respectively for home and away wins and £10 for a loss. Huddersfield called a meeting of the remaining clubs to discuss the implications of these terms, but Featherstone Rovers had already settled on £15 for a win and £8 for a defeat against the 'Big Five'. In contrast, Bramley's rates were £10 winning pay and £6 for a loss. Six of their players, including former Northern captain Terry Robbins, held out for more. Northern's terms were said to be £8 for a win and £4 for a defeat. In mid-November, the Rugby League Council, who also looked into bonus payments to players, decided that winning pay could not be more than twice losing pay. All of which, of course, was largely academic for Northern because they managed to win just once in their final, curtailed season.

In the opening game at Odsal, before a crowd of 953, Dewsbury led 15–3 at half-time, but last season's next-to-bottom club were mostly confined to their own '25' in the second-half because Northern staged a thrilling comeback, and scored three unanswered tries. Unfortunately, try-scorer Abed missed all his seven attempts at goal, which cost Northern a deserved victory. Without Hasse, who had seriously injured his finger at work in the close season, the lightweight Dlambulo was the pick of the pack. However, his second-row partner, Trevor Brewer, injured his hip and missed the rest of this shortened campaign.

145

Brian Smith covers as Featherstone Rovers' Ken Greatorex and Don Fox fail to execute a move during the Yorkshire Cup tie at Odsal. (Courtesy Ron Bailey).

The last-known team photograph of the old Northern side (neatly attired) taken before the game against Batley at Odsal on 12 October. Back: Abed, Doran, Hardcastle, Crabtree, Wigglesworth, Gomersal, Hume; front: Lance Davies, Reynolds, Len Haley, Beevers, Carr, Coggle.
(Courtesy John Hamer).

Whitehaven had still not resolved their pay dispute with their players. Their opening game against Northern the following Wednesday evening was postponed and was never played. Spared this long midweek journey to Cumberland, Northern were then full of enterprise at Barrow on the Saturday and scored three tries, from Coggle, Abed and Davies, before a crowd of 4,132. They were badly hit by injuries and lost 29–9 after being level 3–3 at half-time. Full-back Beevers was a virtual passenger throughout the game with an ankle injury and winger Schofield had to quit just after the break, when Barrow scored 18 points in a 17 minute spell.

At times against Barrow, Northern's pack held up fairly well under pressure, but the urgent need for forward strengthening was highlighted on the following Wednesday evening at Odsal, when they were totally outclassed by Doncaster's pack. Northern's support play was almost non-existent; only try-scorers Wigglesworth and Penketh emerged with any credit in a 16–8 defeat. It was unfortunate that full-back Flynn broke his arm in his final first team appearance.

And yet, on the following Saturday at Odsal, apart from Abed returning at full-back, the same side gave a fine display against Featherstone Rovers in the Yorkshire Cup. Rovers led 12–5 at the interval, but only managed to score four tries to Northern's two, which included an obstruction try to Coggle. There was little to choose between the sides until the last quarter, but Don Fox kicked six goals in the final score of 24–10. Penketh was again Northern's best back as they handled with surprising speed in this department. The greatly improved defence owed much to the work of John Hardcastle, who had his best game since joining the club.

Enigmatic Northern were making a habit of saving their best form for the top clubs. This was also the case on the following Monday at Odsal, in the first of the Eastern Division fixtures, when an unchanged side gave Wakefield Trinity a good game before losing 25–14. Northern trailed 16–4 at the break, but staged a great second-half rally and kept the subdued visitors on their toes until the end. Unfortunately, after this game Northern lost their best back with the transfer of George Penketh – the scorer of 32 tries in 130 appearances – to Featherstone Rovers for close to the £2,500 asking price. He had wanted a move for several months. After his departure both Colin Taylor and Lance Davies had their transfer requests granted, and were listed at £2,000 and £3,000 respectively.

As a result of their negotiations with Rovers, Northern were able to take their reserve prop Derek (Rodney) Carr on trial. He had made only a handful of first team appearances since signing for Rovers in 1958, but he went straight into Northern's side that thrashed Salford 27–6 at Odsal and was later signed for £500. In the reshuffle, Crabtree moved into the second-row and Dlambulo played on the right-wing. Northern led only 7–3 at half-time, but in the last 10 minutes their backs scored three tries after some fine handling. Goeli Abed contributed six goals and a try. It was Northern's first win since November 1962, against the same opposition, and their highest score since the 1959–60 season.

Along with a loan signing, Leeds reserve forward, Ian Hume, Bill Seddon made a surprise appearance in the 'A' team against Batley at Odsal on 21 September. That day Northern's unchanged side travelled to Knotty Ash, and confidently expected a rare away win. Unfortunately, they gave one of their worst displays for some time, and lost 17–7 to Liverpool City in an atrocious game. Coggle revealed some first-class touches when he moved to stand-off after Sutcliffe broke his thumb, an injury that meant he missed the rest of the season. Northern's passing was laboured and only Carr and try-scorer Wigglesworth made any impact in a cumbersome pack.

The following Saturday matters only got worse. Northern were thrashed 43–0 at promotion contenders Leigh. Against a side that earlier in the season had beaten Wigan at Central Park in the Lancashire Cup, Northern were 22 points down when they lost centre Schofield with a serious ankle injury just before half-time. It was their worst display since the trouncing at Belle Vue in 1961; several of the nine tries were conceded through abysmal defence.

There was no respite for this beleaguered Northern side, because the following Saturday at Odsal a full-strength, but disappointing, Huddersfield beat them 30–7 in the Eastern Division. Northern were handicapped from the 15th minute through the loss of their captain, Colin Taylor, with a leg injury. After further injuries to Hardcastle, in the 60th minute, and Nunns, with just five minutes left, they finished with only 10 men. Young giant prop, Ian van Bellen, marked his senior debut for the Fartowners with two of their six tries, and second-rower Ken Bowman, after being named in the Great Britain side to face

148

Australia at Wembley in the first test, also celebrated with a brace. It was another miserable experience for Northern before their highest home crowd of the season, 1,742.

It was a mystery how Northern then managed to lose 12–9 to Batley in the league game at Odsal. The visitors included their left-winger, Norman Field, who risked possible injury ahead of playing for Great Britain against Australia in the first test on the following Wednesday night. After trailing by 10 points in the first 20 minutes, Northern's second-half performance belied their lowly position. However, with Lawton limping on the wing, Batley stoutly defended their 10–2 interval lead and denied Northern four or five almost certain tries. Trialist Ian Hume made his debut at loose-forward, but this game was captain-for-the-day Len Haley's finale in senior rugby. The last player at the club to have been in the 1952 championship leading side, excluding Lazenby Cup games, he made 285 first team appearances, at full-back, centre, stand-off and scrum-half. His well-deserved retirement was delayed because of the demands made for his services with the 'A' team and to help the club deal with the growing crisis.

Despite losing 25–3, Northern were not disgraced at Tattersfield, where Doncaster were then a difficult team to beat. In an open game Northern defended well after conceding nine early points and opened out play whenever they had the opportunity. Although Rudi Hasse made a welcome return to the pack, Northern were again overwhelmed in the scrums. They missed Gomersal. Also absent were Lance Davies and Goeli Abed who, that afternoon, were groom and best man, respectively.

Northern did most of the attacking in a dour return against Liverpool City, but still lost 6–2, mostly due to poor finishing. With no funds available to sign experienced players, Northern gave two juniors a chance. The debutants were right-winger Stewart Wilkinson from Dewsbury, and former Wyke scrum-half Malcolm Thornton. The latter's skilful passing, shrewd kicking game and enthusiasm in defence won him a lot of respect.

The visit of Rochdale Hornets then provided Odsal with 80 minutes of first-class entertainment. After trailing 13–0 at one stage, Northern set the game alight by taking a 17–16 lead before Hornets finally rallied to win the most thrilling game of the season 27–17. Hornets' Fijian hooker Voate Drui was sent off near the end of a game that finished seven tries to three. Northern's scorers were Coggle, Reynolds and Dlambulo. But this was three more than Hornets had conceded in all their Division Two games so far that season. The only pity was that it was witnessed by a crowd of only 934, many of whom had travelled from Rochdale, on the day that Australia's 50–12 mauling of Great Britain at Swinton was televised live.

On the eve of Northern's 26–10 defeat at Batley on 16 November, it was announced that Harry Beverley had resigned as coach. He ended his duties after the game at Mount Pleasant, where quick thinking by Thornton produced early tries for Doran and Coggle. Northern got to within a point of their opponents in the second-half. Unfortunately, they faded badly and were no match for the enterprising home backs, who scored five of their six tries, much to the home crowd's delight. For a change, thanks to Gomersal's hooking, Northern were not short of possession. He was one of their most consistent and hardworking players in the loose.

Beverley had only been able to introduce juniors, trialists, and loan signings because of the club's dire financial situation. For the last few months he had worked voluntarily because it could no longer afford to pay him. He later said that his resignation had not been over money and he was sad to see a once great club in such a lowly position. Loyal clubman Len Haley and captain Colin Taylor took over the coaching on the same unpaid basis, and were well aware of the club's serious financial difficulties. But even they could not have envisaged to what depths Northern were to sink before the inevitable end came.

On Saturday, 23 November 1963, when Northern lost 29–0 to Barrow before the lowest crowd in their history, the *Telegraph & Argus* gave full coverage of the assassination of John F. Kennedy in Dallas the day before. Unfortunately, due to bowing to female pressure, I cannot claim to have been at Odsal with those 324 hardy souls who braved foul torrential rain, which helped produce some of the lowest crowds of the season for the West Riding's association football and rugby league clubs. For example, Halifax, with 3,352, Hunslet, who drew 2,700, Dewsbury with 1,300 and Bramley, with 800, all suffered badly at the gate. In football only 4,541 spectators cheered Bradford Park Avenue to a 4–1 victory over Darlington.

The severe weather must have been fairly widespread, because Bradford City's away game – ironically, at Barrow – was abandoned after 29 minutes due to a waterlogged pitch. Therefore, it is unlikely that many Barrow supporters would have made the trek to a desolate Odsal to see their team, under player-coach Jim Challinor and including Bill Burgess and full-back Eddie Tees, totally outclass Northern. It was described as a black day for the club with no encouraging features in the side's performance. Abed had the misfortune to crack a rib, and it was also a sad end to Jack Doran's senior career, after 130 appearances and 42 tries.

In contrast to this sporting malaise, for the following Sunday all police leave was cancelled, in order for them to control the anticipated queues at the Gaumont box office for the Beatles concert on 21 December. With the opening of the £300,000 Excel Bowl, adjacent to Park Avenue, it was obvious that a bleak Odsal Stadium and third-rate rugby league had a problem trying to compete with such modern entertainment. Harry Beverley had come up with the idea of giving out free season tickets to schoolboys, but Northern needed to put something extra special in the shop window if the club was to regain the wider public's support.

The scheduled Eastern Division game at Wakefield on 30 November was postponed because of the third test against Australia at Headingley, so Northern had a week's rest before their next home fixture. But they were again no match for the star-studded Leigh side, who the previous week had thrashed Wigan in the Western Division. Northern took an early 5–0 lead through a try from Dlambulo, converted by Beevers, but their fast moving opponents ran out 33–5 winners. Two of Leigh's nine tries were scored by Mick Martyn, who took his total for the club to 162, and thus broke the club record held by Bill Kindon. It was estimated that over half the crowd of 841 were Leigh supporters. The team that day, when I can truly make the claim, "I was there", was as follows: Beevers, Dlambulo, Nunns, L. Davies, Coggle, Thornton, M. Reynolds, Hardcastle, Trevor Whitaker, Wigglesworth, Hasse, Yeoman, Taylor (c).

Following his loan transfer from Bramley, second-rower J.E. Yeoman had the dubious distinction of having made his debut and only appearance in old Northern's last game; but equally this was also the case for hooker Trevor Whitaker who had been signed only two days before the game.

151

BRADFORD NORTHERN 5

1 Beevers

2 Dlambulo   3 Nunns   4 Davies   5 Coggle

6 Thornton   7 Reynolds

8 Hardcastle 9 Whittaker 10 Wigglesworth 11 Hasse 12 Yeoman 14 Taylor

Referee:
R. L. THOMAS
(Oldham)

Touch Judges:
G. T. L. SMITHSON
S. ROBSON

Arr. 824

14 Hurt 12 Martyn 11 Murphy 10 Owen 9 Lewis, J. 8 Bishop/

7 Entwistle   6 Rhodes

5 Leadbetter   4 Collins   3 Lewis, G.   2 Large

1 Grainey

LEIGH   33

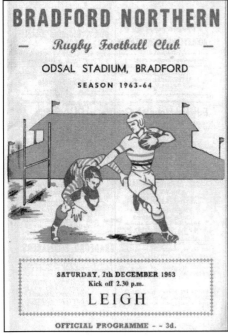

The team line-ups and front cover from the final match programme.

On the following Wednesday, 11 December 1963, the dramatic news broke in the *Telegraph & Argus* that it was the "End of the road for Northern". The previous evening, Jackie Barritt had informed Oldham's secretary, Bert Summerscales, that the club could not fulfil their fixture on the following Saturday, and the 'A' team game at Odsal against Dewsbury was also cancelled. Jackie Barritt and other directors visited the RFL headquarters that evening and Bill Fallowfield, the RFL secretary, held a press conference on the Friday. Len Haley said that he felt the club could not have continued as it was, but felt confident it would resume. But it was a worrying time for Enslin Dlambulo, who had only just been joined from South Africa by his wife and young family. He now faced the prospect of losing his job as Odsal's groundsman.

Ironically, the news came at a time when the Corporation's £50,000 scheme to install concrete terracing at the Rooley Avenue end of Odsal had just started. There had been an apology to supporters in the Leigh match programme for the inconvenience this caused. However, the pools were now bringing in only £23 a week and the club had lost an estimated £400 in the week of the Barrow game, when the receipts were only £30.

Odsal's new terracing taking shape at the time of the club's demise.
(C.H. Wood)

Only 11 shareholders attended the AGM held on 30 December, where Northern reported a loss of £1,664, for the year ending 30 June 1963. The deficit balance was £4,413, with total liabilities of £8,099. Net receipts were only £4,155 while players' wages and expenses came to £7,677. Jackie Barritt said that the big freeze and having to play two or three games a week at the end of the season had seriously affected the gates, which averaged only 1,257. The shareholders made it clear that they wanted the present directors to stand down and were in favour of going into liquidation, but legally this course of action could not be taken immediately. Cyril Bunney said they were willing to resign if a new group was prepared to take over the current liabilities, which by then were around £10,000.

In mid-January the RFL management committee decided that Northern's membership was terminated from the time that they indicated they could no longer fulfil their fixtures. The players were given free agent status, on the understanding that they could be retransferred to any new club that may be formed in Bradford. In a letter to the *Telegraph & Argus*, while on a tour of North Africa, Harry Hornby considered that this was a sound decision and fair to the players. The club contested this decision, however, until it was finally verified by the Rugby League Council on 18 March, after which Northern went into liquidation. This allowed a new company to be formed free of all debts. Northern's record had been expunged and the league table changed on 14 February, by which time, fortunately for those of us whose second home had been Odsal, tentative plans had been made to form a new club.

1963–64 Summary
Eastern Division: P 2 W 0 L 2 D 0 – Pts 21– 55 (record expunged)
Second Division: P 13 W 1 L 12 D 0 – Pts 109–284 (record expunged)
Yorkshire Cup: First round.
Average attendance: 1,021

12. 1964–65: Men of vision
A new Northern is formed

Following Northern's demise Trevor Foster co-ordinated efforts to form a new club. On 12 February, 1964 a working committee, made up of businessmen and former players, was formed at the Bay Horse Hotel, Dudley Hill. After their chairman, Joe Phillips, had negotiated with Bradford Corporation for a new lease on Odsal Stadium, were a new club to be formed, the consortium submitted their application for membership of the Rugby Football League on 23 March.

The litmus test came three weeks later at the stirring public meeting on 14 April at St George's Hall. Over 1,500 people attended, including officials from the Rugby League and former Northern greats, to hear the proposals and to give their support. Ernest Ward made a short impromptu speech from the balcony in which he supported the new venture, but he was critical of the RFL's offer to buy a maximum £500 shares. He compared this with the thousands of pounds the RFL had spent on trying unsuccessfully to establish the game in Italy. A collection and pledges on the night raised almost £1,000 and £1 shares were quickly bought up by the public and other rugby league clubs. The new company, Bradford Northern (1964) Ltd, was formed on 20 April and officially registered on 27 July with nominal capital of £10,000 in £1 shares.

Joe Phillips addresses the meeting at St George's Hall in April 1964, watched by RFL officials and Trevor Foster.

The first directors were Joe Phillips; John Cameron, area manager of an oil company; Philip J. Lloyd, licensee of the Bay Horse Hotel; George Brown, an optician; Ronald L. Johnson, managing director of Alfresco (Garage) Ltd; Frank Hillam, motor dealer; J. W. Peel, sub-postmaster; Geoffrey Cooper, an accountant; with the company secretary, Geoffrey W. Turton. In early July, two former Halifax directors, Harry Womersley, a licensee, and Jack Fricker, a wool merchant, joined the board. The Thrum Hall connection was further increased with the appointment of Ken Dean, a former international half-back and member of Halifax's 1954 and 1956 Challenge Cup final sides, as reserve team coach.

With a dozen supporters' clubs having been formed around the city and a new pools' promoter appointed, there was around £7,000 in the kitty by mid-June. Hardly a day went by without news of Northern's interest in signing new players as they set about recruiting before pre-season training started. This was on 7 July, when 20 players from the old club were joined at Odsal by 33-year-old, former international prop, Jack Wilkinson, who Wakefield Trinity generously agreed to release on a free transfer as player-coach, and the first six new recruits. A tourist in 1954 and 1962, he had represented Great Britain in World Cup and test matches against Australia and New Zealand, and also played in four Wembley finals, with Halifax, his home town club, in 1954 and 1956, and Trinity in 1960 and 1962.

Once the new club looked certain to be established, the RFL had agreed to them re-signing players, who were on the old Northern books before the crisis. The Corporation also helped by granting Northern a one year lease on Odsal at a peppercorn rent, while, at the same time, refused a speedway promoter use of the stadium.

The new Northern were admitted back into the Rugby Football League on 22 May, when the clubs also agreed to return to one division, with a top-16 play-off. Another change was the use of two substitutes before the start of the second-half, for injured players. Both proposals were ratified by the RFL's AGM in June.

Thanks to the support of the Bradford public and the goodwill of other clubs, the new directors put together a completely new squad of first team players for around £15,000. Remarkably, this was less than the amount the old club had received from the sale of Jack Scroby, Terry Robbins and Derek Davies.

The new recruits were Albert Tonkinson, Castleford's 27-year-old Yorkshire county and Great Britain 'shadow' squad prop; Willie Walker, Hunslet's 27-year-old centre, who played at Odsal in the 1959 Championship Final against St Helens and was in the Great Britain 'shadow' squad in 1962; Mike Brown, Halifax's fearless South African winger; Halifax based centre Brian Todd, who had moved from Keighley to St Helens in January for £2,000; Bryn Jones, Halifax's 31-year-old former Fylde rugby union and Lancashire scrum-half, who had been at Thrum Hall since 1957; and Wakefield Trinity's 27-year-old reserve hooker David Wakefield, whose knee injury at work later compelled Northern to sign Workington Town's 23-year-old Terry Ackerley as a replacement.

As their future full-back, Northern signed Huddersfield's 26-year-old Keith Williams, who kicked over 100 goals for Halifax in 1963–64 before moving to Fartown. A speedster in his younger days, who could play at stand-off or on the wing, he scored 44 tries in the 1959–60 season for Halifax and held the club record of eight tries in a game against Dewsbury. Northern then signed three forwards; Leeds's promising 23-year-old reserve Gil Ashton; Oldham's 22-year-old loose-forward Johnny Rae, then the fastest forward in the game, who had represented Cumberland and could also kick goals; and Warrington's Welsh international Idwal Fisher. Oldham's 26-year-old centre Brian Lord became Northern's 12th new player; and they completed the proposed first team by signing Wakefield's highly-rated 21-year-old centre or stand-off, Ian Brooke, for only £2,750. He had played in the 1963 Challenge Cup Final and more than fulfilled his potential – including touring with the Lions in 1966 – before Trinity bought him back for £8,000. The old club lost Milan Kosanovic at a giveaway price, but the new Northern benefitted from Trinity's largesse.

Although there was the boost of surprisingly winning the pre-season Headingley Sevens, Northern unfortunately lost Mike Brown with a fractured cheekbone. This resulted in the signing of Rochdale Hornets' 16 stones Fijian winger Joe Levula. In his youth he had clocked 9.7 seconds for the 100 yards in the Empire Games and in 1951 and 1952 was a sensation when he toured New Zealand and Australia with the Fijian rugby union side. He arrived in Rochdale in 1961 and made 80 first team appearances for Hornets. Although well past his peak when he joined Northern, perhaps nearer 33-years-old rather than 29 as publicised, he was still one of the game's top personalities and accomplished finishers. He could also kick goals, even in his bare feet.

Levula's signature brought Northern's total spending on the opening squad to around £15,000, as follows: Williams £1,500, Wakefield – estimated £750, Lord £2,150, Todd £1,200, Walker £750, Brown £750, Brooke £2,750, Jones £250, Wilkinson free, Ackerley £750, Tonkinson £600, Ashton £500, Fisher £1,500, Rae £1,250 and Levula £300.[1]

Joe Phillips made the bold prediction that, with the right strength of support, the new club would win a major trophy within three years. None of the former club's players were really considered capable of holding down a regular first team place if the new organisation's hopes were to be met, and the Bradford public certainly demanded new faces. But there was not quite the wholesale clear out that has previously been specified. A few moved permanently to other clubs and several re-signed under the RFL's ruling after playing for other clubs as free agents up to the end of the 1963–64 season. Of the 20 players who returned to training in July, nine were later given free transfers. Mick Reynolds and Dennis Tate were not at pre-season training, and trialists Ian Hume and Yeoman returned to Leeds and Bramley, respectively.

Wakefield Trinity took over the contract of Rudi Hasse, but he did not make his first team debut until September, in a 45–5 home win over Keighley. In November he was granted a free transfer with the proviso that any future club would have to pay his fares back to South Africa on his retirement. Enslin Dlambulo moved to Keighley, where he played out the rest of his career; John Coggle, who at the time of Northern's collapse was well up the league's try-scoring chart with 10 in 16 appearances, signed for Hull KR on 10 January after a short trial at Batley; while the last captain, Colin Taylor, initially joined Castleford but later moved to Hunslet, where he played against new Northern in their second game. He was a non-playing member of Hunslet's 1965 Wembley squad and was also in Featherstone Rovers' Wembley squad in 1967, after playing in the second round against Castleford.

Eleven players returned to the new set-up, after playing with or interesting other clubs. In January Tom Whitaker signed for Dewsbury, while John Hardcastle and J. Bentley both went to Keighley. Alan Sutcliffe, Derek Carr, and Alan Wigglesworth joined Oldham, Batley and

---

[1] *Telegraph & Argus* 7 September 1964

York, respectively. Goeli Abed and Lance Davies both failed to impress St Helens in the week or so that they spent at Knowsley Road, and were both struck off their register in the first week of February. Davies later went on trial to Leeds. Malcolm Thornton and Peter Nunns both moved to Huddersfield, but were struck off their register in June. George Gomersal was the last player in the League to be registered before the Cup deadline on 2 February, and was due to play for Batley against Leigh on 22 February.

Of the players who were in dispute with the old club, loose-forward Steve Hey, who had helped out his former club, Stanningley, over the two years since he last played for Northern, signed up for trials with Bramley and scored a try in the victory on 15 February. Alan Martin signed for Huddersfield and scored in his only first team appearance, at Doncaster on 28 March, before being crossed off their list.

The new management started a youth policy for the 'A' team, and had signed three promising forwards; the previously mentioned 17-year-old, Stan Fearnley, the son of Northern's future coach, Albert; 19-year-old Ian Crawshaw from Greetland; and 18-year-old Ian Potter from Siddal. And, having built a new first team squad, at the end of July they earmarked players who were considered first team material.

Accordingly, free transfers were granted to the following nine players who did not fit the above criteria. Apart from the former Doncaster forward John Yemm, all had previous first team experience with the defunct club, namely Tony Beevers, J. Bentley, Trevor Brewer, Phil Crabtree, E. Flynn, Walter Hemingway, Peter Nunns and Alan Wigglesworth. Tony Beevers, who had scored old Northern's last points, later had spells at Keighley, Batley and Dewsbury. On retiring from the game he took up refereeing before becoming a director at several clubs, including new Northern.

By this time, Goeli Abed, Derek Carr, Lance Davies, John Hardcastle, Alan Sutcliffe, and Malcolm Thornton had all returned to Odsal. But in this first season George Gomersal, Trevor Schofield, Henry Sharratt, Tom Whitaker, and 21-year-old, former Keighley scrum-half, Terry Albone, only a reserve with old Northern, who had moved to Batley in March as a free agent, also made first team appearances. Added to which, Jack Doran and Terry Griffett were down to play in the 'A' team on the opening day against Batley, while winger or centre David Horton later played in the 'A' team, along with Len Haley. At least 15 players from the old club were on the new club's playing register in 1964–65, and of the 39 players who made the first team in that first season, 11 (see below) were from the defunct club.

1964 –65	App	G	T	Pts	1965 –66 App
Goeli Abed	7	4	1	11	
Terry Albone	1				
R (Derek) Carr	12		1	3	
Lance Davies	8(1)		3	9	
George Gomersal	2				
John Hardcastle	9		1	3	
Trevor Schofield	1				
Henry Sharratt	2				
Alan Sutcliffe	6(1)				9(1)
Malcolm Thornton	3(1)				
Tom Whitaker	3				

Apart from the transfer-listed Lance Davies, only Derek Carr, John Hardcastle, and Alan Sutcliffe were retained for the second season, when only Sutcliffe managed to secure a first team place. He made his last appearance at Castleford in November 1965. He later moved to Huddersfield on a free transfer, made his debut on 11 March 1967 at Oldham, and was crossed off the Fartown register in January, 1968

George Gomersal was transfer-listed at £500 in January 1965, which was later reduced to £250. He and Trevor Schofield were crossed off the Northern register before the end of the first season. At that time Henry Sharratt, Tom Whitaker and Malcolm Thornton were each listed at £250, before being granted free transfers before the start of the 1965–66 campaign. Subsequently, scrum-half Thornton went on trial to Bramley, and made his first appearance in a pre-season charity game against Keighley. He was soon joined at the Barley Mow by Lance Davies, who, having been named as substitute for Northern's pre-season friendly against Blackpool Borough, was transferred for about £500. The centre's fee had been reduced from £1,750 to £750 and Northern had earlier refused Dewsbury's offer of a reserve hooker in part-exchange. Goeli Abed, who had been transfer-listed at £500, moved to Batley. He made several telling breaks and kicked three goals on his debut against Whitehaven during August 1965. He was later joined at Mount Pleasant by Henry Sharratt.

For the opening game against Hull KR on 22 August, Odsal presented a wonderful spectacle with the new concrete terracing mostly finished. A crowd of 13,542 enjoyed a fine exhibition of open rugby. It was a baptism of fire for the new side against the 1964 Challenge Cup runners-up, but they led 10–7 at half-time and 13–7 after 45 minutes. But in the final quarter their cover defence was exposed and Rovers won deservedly 34–20. The only blot on the afternoon was referee Eric Clay's dismissal of centre Brian Todd and Rovers' hooker Alan Holdstock after a second half skirmish.

On the following Monday evening at Hunslet, Northern might so easily have beaten the Yorkshire Cup holders had they not wasted three clear cut chances and presented the Parksiders with two first-half tries in an 18–13 defeat. After 15 minutes try-scorer Lance Davies replaced Levula, who retired due to a pulled thigh muscle. Due to such leg injuries, he soon lost his first team place, but still entertained fans in the 'A' team's Saturday morning fixtures at Odsal, which invariably attracted bigger crowds than had previously watched many of the old club's first team games.

Due to Todd's two-match suspension and the spate of injuries Northern had to turn to old Northern players Abed, Carr, Davies, Sharratt and Thornton, who was on the bench, for the Saturday evening visit to Post Office Road. They held the lead until the 78th minute with a try from Abed and five goals from full-back Keith Williams. Rovers then snatched a dramatic 15–13 victory through a late conversion from the touchline by Terry Clawson. If this was not sickening enough for the travelling fans, and there were certainly more than 324, prop Albert Tonkinson was harshly dismissed near the end and received a three-match ban.

Aware of the need to strengthen the pack, Northern had signed 23-year-old second-rower Keith Ashcroft from St Helens for £1,250. He made his debut at Odsal on Wednesday 2 September, when a crowd of 10,002 saw Northern beat Salford 20–12. But it was only when Johnny Rae went up the middle for a typical 50-yard solo try in the 78th minute that Northern were assured of their first league victory, in which Abed kicked four goals. To put this win into perspective, the previous September the old Northern had beaten the same opposition far more convincingly.

Against Salford the forwards had been ineffective as a unit; and in the first round of the Yorkshire Cup – minus Ashcroft, who was ineligible, and Tonkinson, who was suspended – their individual efforts were unable to break down Huddersfield's renowned dour defence. The Fartowners' international scrum-half, Tommy Smales, masterminded Northern's 17–6 defeat. Brian Todd had returned after his suspension and the following Wednesday played for Yorkshire against Cumberland at Whitehaven. He kept his place in a 33–10 win over Lancashire at Hull, when Yorkshire, captained by Tommy Smales, clinched the championship.

Following the defeat to Huddersfield, the directors issued an ultimatum to the players that unless matters improved within two weeks further new signings would be made. High on their 'wanted' list was Bradford born Ron Morgan, Swinton's Welsh second-rower. He had played in the second test against Australia in 1963 and was on offer at £7,500. But, within weeks of Northern's interest, he signed for Leeds for about £4,750. Northern's next signing was Jack Scattergood, a 24-year-old rugby union centre from Old Brodleians. He failed to make the first team this season, but won a Yorkshire Cup winners' medal in 1965 with a gutsy display at full-back.

Although Walker was fit to resume, Abed's outstanding form meant he kept the left-wing spot for Batley's visit. Northern made hard work of their 18–5 victory. Their four tries came from individual efforts. Peter Fox, a future Northern coach, was a great pack leader for Batley and helped frustrate a Northern side that was clearly in need of a general.

In these opening games, the backs had proved their strike potential and it was hoped that the new team would begin to gel once the forwards had ironed out their flaws with more match practice. But there was also a lack of cohesion at half-back, and Northern managed to win only two of their first 14 league games up to mid-November. They languished, like their predecessors, near the foot of the table with ever-diminishing support.

The season was only rescued following appointment of all-time great Gus Risman as team manager and the introduction of more new blood. The most notable signings were Tommy Smales, Terry Clawson and Alan Hepworth, all of whom had tormented Northern in the past few years – and young Queenslanders, Errol Stock and Garth Budge.

Northern produced pathetic displays in losing 16–7 at Doncaster and 12–10 to lowly Liverpool City at Odsal. In the latter game there were immediate debuts for 23-year-old former Cleckheaton rugby union winger David Metcalfe, in place of the injured Abed, and 32-year-old

Stan Moyser, who made a comeback after retiring in 1962. The former Dewsbury, Halifax, Featherstone Rovers, Batley, and Hunslet hooker or blind-side prop scored a try in a woefully disjointed team performance. Williams had a nightmare game with costly goalkicking misses. Individually, Northern looked impressive; the highlight was Brian Lord's amazing 100-yard cross field try-scoring run. But overall they lacked any method, and with an attendance of only 4,929, the 'new' club had lost over half of its original support.

Following this setback Northern announced that Gus Risman had been appointed as the new team manager. He had been approached by Joe Phillips for the advertised post. A former Great Britain captain and tourist in 1932, 1936 and 1946, he had played as a guest with Northern in the Second World War and managed Workington Town, Oldham and Salford, after a distinguished playing career. He had represented Great Britain in 15 tests and played 17 times for Wales. The owner of a driving school in Manchester, he had been out of the game for the previous two years and content to watch his son Bev play for Leigh. He was given a one-year contract of £1,000 to work alongside coaches Wilkinson and Dean.

Risman's first game in charge was a 16–9 defeat at the Barley Mow, where the forwards were tame in comparison to the Bramley six, who included former Northern captain, Terry Robbins. Levula landed three goals, having taken over the kicking duties from Williams, in what was the captain and full-back's last senior game. Northern's directors must have been worried because harder fixtures were about to start.

In a thrilling 7–5 home defeat to Castleford, in which Johnny Rae raced 75-yards for one of his trademark touchdowns, Northern experimented with Todd at full-back, reserve Tom Whitaker at stand-off and Ian Brooke in his rightful position at centre. In the end it was poor goalkicking that cost Northern the game because they only landed one, by Todd, from eight attempts. Nothing had changed in that respect from the old days.

Fielding four former 'old' Northern players in Trevor Schofield, Goeli Abed, Tom Whitaker and George Gomersal, the team then conceded six tries in a 24–3 loss to Halifax at Thrum Hall. Playing against his old colleagues, Mike Brown had an excellent debut and kept the number two place until the end of the season. But the side's performance was the worst of the season so far. There were clear weaknesses at half-back and in the pack.

With the international transfer ban having been relaxed, Northern then signed two 22-year-olds from the Rockhampton North club in Queensland on transfer free, one-year contracts. Stand-off Garth Budge and full-back Errol Stock helped resolve two problem positions. After making his debut at Odsal against Whitehaven, Budge quickly developed into one of the league's best defensive players and made the stand-off spot his own until his return home. With reserve scrum-half Tom Whitaker partnering Budge, and their backs, Brown, Lord, Todd, and two-try Walker, producing their best rugby of the season, Northern led 8–5 at half-time. Unfortunately, Northern's forwards were again the problem and the Cumbrians, brilliantly led by second-row forward Bill Holliday, finally coasted to a 26–10 victory.

Earlier the club had made what turned out to be one of their shrewdest signings when they secured the signature of 21-year-old second-row forward Tony Fisher, a former Welsh youth international who had represented the RAF and Combined Services at rugby union. The future Great Britain hooker, who played in the 'A' team in his first season with Northern, was then based at Darlington and was due to leave the RAF in three weeks. Northern had paid for his early release after seeing him play three outstanding 'A' team trials. Ironically, having been dropped after the Whitehaven game, his elder brother, Idwal, refused to play in the 'A' team and was transfer-listed at £2,500. He joined Bramley the following season.

After recovering from an injury, Errol Stock then became Northern's fourth full-back in as many games. This pocket dynamo made a great impression in an 8–0 defeat at Hull. His opposite number, Arthur Keegan, prevented three certain tries before winger Brian Sullivan – his brother Clive was on the other wing – scored in the dying minutes.

The following day Northern arranged for a team of trialists to play the Bradford League open age side at Odsal. This led to the signing of 18-year-old Queensbury prop forward David Hill. He made his debut in the 1965 Yorkshire Cup semi-final replay against Huddersfield and later became a fixture in Northern's pack. He won county honours in 1967 when Yorkshire and Australia inaugurated Belle Vue's floodlights – a night when, unfortunately, he suffered severe concussion after an unsavoury incident with a member of the Australian front-row.

1964–65: New Northern against Huddersfield in the Yorkshire Cup. Back:
Ashton, Fisher, Rae, Levula, Ackerley, Carr, Lord; front: Brooke, Williams,
Wilkinson, Abed, Jones, Todd. (Courtesy Robert Gate).

Lord scores in the first match against Hull KR. (Courtesy *Rugby League Journal*)

New coach Gus Risman with Tonkinson, Ashton, Williams and Ackerley.
(Courtesy *Rugby League Journal*).

Yorkshire county centre Brian Todd fractured his cheekbone in a 12–2 revenge defeat by Salford at the Willows. After this he was listed at £5,000 after a disagreement on playing matters. Almost immediately, Huddersfield turned down a straight swop for test second-rower Ken Bowman. Todd eventually joined Halifax in exchange for two former rugby union men, stand-off David Stockwell, and centre or full-back, Alan Rhodes.

Despite major repair work, there were still problems with Odsal's drainage and until the end of the season there was not a blade of grass on the pitch. These conditions appeared to suit the Northern forwards because they adapted to larking about in the mud. Malcolm Thornton stepped in successfully at scrum-half for Northern's two successive home wins over York and Wakefield Trinity. He then lost his place due to the signing of the mercurial Tommy Smales in the last week of November.

Earlier in the season, the 30-year-old Huddersfield and Yorkshire skipper had upset his club officials by publicly expressing his dissatisfaction over so-called 'broken-time' payments having been stopped. Halifax had been fined £500 for making illegal payments to winger Johnny Freeman, so other clubs were clearly anxious and temporarily put a stop to such backhanders. This resulted in the former Great Britain scrum-half being transfer-listed at £8,000, which was later reduced to £6,500. But Northern secured his signature for nearer £3,000. The former Glasshoughton junior had joined Featherstone Rovers in 1952 and moved to Fartown in December 1955. As previously mentioned, he led Huddersfield at Wembley and in the Championship final in 1962. After playing twice against France in 1962, he captained Great Britain against Australia in 1963.

With his first team opportunities now limited, scrum-half Bryn Jones was transfer-listed at his own request at £500. He was exchanged in January for Keighley's 24-year-old winger Mel Smith, who had earlier announced his retirement from rugby league after an incident at Lawkholme Lane which upset him. The former junior AAA champion sprinter had scored 59 tries in his 107 appearances.

Ian Crawshaw made his debut in a 14–2 win over York, in which Lance Davies returned at centre and scored one of Northern's two tries. The other went to Stock, who was proving to be a real personality with his sure tackling and enthusiasm for joining the attack. Johnny Rae, who was soon to benefit from Tommy Smales's wizardry around the scrum, showed his versatility by landing four goals.

Smales's debut was delayed due to a thigh injury, but without him Northern revelled in the mud and beat Wakefield Trinity 3–0 in a thriller at Odsal. Mike Brown took one of the game's few chances to dive in at the corner in the closing minutes. Northern's forwards rose to the occasion against more polished opponents in what was a long, hard slog of tackling. Although the conditions may well have worked in Northern's favour, the result was greeted with tremendous applause from the crowd of 7,658.

Tommy Smales then skilfully guided Northern to a 2–0 win over Dewsbury at Odsal; Johnny Rae's first-half penalty settled matters. Northern had scored only 11 tries in the previous 11 games. The enterprising backs were restricted because of the forwards' tendency to die with the ball. The modest attendance of 4,761 was still the second highest of the afternoon, almost a year to the day of old Northern's final game.

Ambitious Northern had earlier offered both Keith Williams and George Gomersal in part-exchange for Doncaster's outstanding 23-year-old second-rower, Alan Hepworth, who was then listed at £4,000. However, the hooker scuppered the original move. The final deal, which involved Williams and a slight cash adjustment on Northern's part, was delayed until after Christmas. Hepworth made his debut, along with centre Alan Rhodes, in squelching mud and rain at Whitehaven, where Tommy Smales's surprise first-minute try earned Northern a 3–3 draw. Deputising for the injured Ackerley, Gomersal made his last appearance before being transfer-listed at £500, along with Lance Davies at £1,750.

Northern's 8–3 victory over Leeds at Odsal was their first in 11 seasons against the Loiners and, but for a lack of scrum possession, the margin of their fourth successive home win would have been much greater. For what was once a lucrative derby, the crowd was only 4,238, one of eight league games in that first season which fell below the 5,000 mark, and a far cry from the early season support. Despite the poor conditions, Northern responded well to the leadership of man-of-the-match Smales. He engineered both tries from centres Rhodes and in-form Ian Brooke. With their recent acquisitions Northern were on the fringe of developing into a leading side, but the directors wanted to sign both Huddersfield's Ken Bowman and Featherstone Rovers' Terry Clawson before the Cup deadline. This would have cost in the region of £5,000, money which, like most clubs, they did not have readily available.

Apart from keen interest in the Challenge Cup, during the depths of winter most clubs were under great financial strain from falling attendances. For example, because of incessant rain, on the same day in West Yorkshire the following attendances were recorded: Keighley 400 – their lowest post-war crowd, Batley 500, Halifax 2,847, Wakefield Trinity 4,378, and Huddersfield 2,567. In December the Leeds players, who were among the best paid in the league, volunteered to take a £2 cut in winning pay because of poor attendances at Headingley. The Featherstone Rovers players even agreed to play one match in January for no wages because of the state of the club's finances. To ease their own financial problems, Hunslet proposed a merger of Batley and Dewsbury and for them to share the Parkside ground. After Northern's game at Wakefield on 23 January was postponed due to snow and ice,

Northern submitted an unsuccessful plan, similar to Lance Todd's proposals in the 1930s, for a summer season from March to October to be played in the evenings with 'A' team games as curtain-raisers. They were 30 years ahead of their time.

Northern had made tentative enquiries about signing 24-year-old Terry Clawson in September, when he was then in dispute with his club. He had been at Post Office Road for eight years and after several requests for a transfer had been turned down, the Great Britain international was finally listed in November at £8,000. This was later reduced to £6,000. Rovers had already named him in their team for the visit to Odsal on 30 January, but Northern secured his signature for £3,000 in time for him to make his debut in a tense 11–5 defeat. He converted Willie Walker's try as Northern trailed 7–5 at half-time. Former Northern centre George Penketh unfortunately broke his leg and the game could have swung either way. However, Rovers dominated the second-half possession and were faster and better drilled. Their forwards Les Tonks, Mal Dixon who scored a try, and Arnold Morgan, were well led by Don Fox, who kicked four goals.

Playing at prop, Clawson proved his worth in the first round Challenge Cup tie at Hilton Park, where Northern's large away following were well-rewarded with a pulsating 7–6 victory over in-form Leigh. Smales prompted his side in masterly fashion and the forwards hammered Leigh's powerful pack into submission. Clawson had given Northern a 2–0 interval lead with a sixth minute penalty. Leigh drew level following a Bev Risman penalty, but Northern struck in the 65th minute when Ian Brooke won an electrifying chase for the loose ball after Brown had cross-kicked. Clawson converted and then Northern had to defend grimly in the tense final 15 minutes. Risman landed two late penalties before his last minute attempt drifted wide. The manner in which they achieved this outstanding result meant Northern were once again a serious power in the game.

They had conceded only three tries in 10 matches before their clash at Odsal with Wakefield Trinity in the second round. The Cup favourites had not conceded a try in their previous eight games. Due to the closeness of the scores, the crowd of 19,905, who paid £3,692, Northern's highest since the Cup tie against Featherstone Rovers in 1955, was treated to a thrilling contest. However, Northern looked overawed by the occasion and stodgy compared to a still below-par

Trinity, who fully merited their 10–7 victory because they were superior in all departments. However, the game could so easily have swung Northern's way, had they been awarded a penalty try following an incident when they only trailed by the half-time score of 5–2. After looking a certain try-scorer, Ian Brooke was blatantly tripped by Trinity's South African winger, Gert Coetzer. However, the first-half try-scorer only conceded a penalty following his dismissal. Twelve-man Trinity still managed a match-clinching try by speedster Berwyn Jones before Ian Brooke raced in against his old side. It was the first try conceded by Trinity in over 700 minutes of rugby.

Back to the bread and butter of the league, Northern needed to rise five places if they were to qualify for the inaugural end-of-season top-16 Championship play-offs. It was no easy task, particularly because, due to the play-off deadline and the backlog of fixtures, seven games were crammed into April.

Northern made heavy weather of their 8–0 win over Bramley at a snow-covered Odsal, before they travelled to Craven Park for one of the most entertaining games in years. Hull KR, who had splashed out £14,000 on star Cumbrian forwards Bill Holliday and Frank Foster, led 17–0 at half-time, but Northern played some brilliant rugby in the second-half before losing 22–17. Their performance won them many friends on that side of the Humber when there was a genuine rapport between two enterprising clubs and their supporters. Northern then produced a commanding display in the driving snow and slush at Odsal to beat Hunslet far more convincingly than the 16–10 result. Smales was again inspirational and Hardcastle's inclusion at prop gave Northern a rare pull in the scrums. The only disappointment was the crowd of 2,252, Northern's lowest of the season.

Northern failed to keep 'Classy Cas' half-backs Keith Hepworth and Alan Hardisty in check at Wheldon Road and trailed 22–0 at half-time. However, they fought back fiercely to finish 22–10 down at the close. Tonkinson's season ended when he was sent-off near the end against his former colleagues. He was subsequently given a six-match ban. Northern then conceded the double to Halifax in a disappointing derby at Odsal, where both sides seemed more intent on settling old scores than playing rugby in ideal conditions. In a 9–7 defeat, Rhodes's clear cut try came from one of Smales's many inspired moves around the scrum base. However, Northern had no forward to match either Terry Fogerty or Colin Dixon.

Northern met Wakefield at Belle Vue on the Monday after Trinity's defeat to Hunslet in the Challenge Cup semi-final. A 12–0 half-time lead flattered Trinity and Northern had enough possession to have won. They fought back to 12–7, but the forwards struggled to provide openings for their gifted backs. Stock's try came after an 80-yard sprint by Brooke. This was the first of six games in nine days, including four in five days over Easter.

The glut of fixtures allowed me to visit Fartown on the Wednesday afternoon before Northern's evening game at Odsal against Keighley. Standing at pitch-side shortly before kick-off, I remember quizzing Keighley's prop, Dave Worthy, about the prospects of the game going ahead, because the pitch then resembled a paddy field. Despite the conditions, Northern's pack was the most mobile for many weeks and Clawson displayed his leadership qualities, as well as scoring a try and three goals, in a 15–0 victory. Garfield Owen failed to score for the first time since early April 1964. Alan Sutcliffe successfully deputised for the injured Tommy Smales. He played at half-back in four of the final five games Northern won in that inaugural season.

In achieving the double over Leeds for the first time since 1952–53, Northern were never in any great danger of losing at Headingley, before a crowd of only 4,300. In fact they should have won by more than the final score of 7–2. On Easter Monday at Odsal, Northern then beat Hull 15–9 in try-scorer Errol Stock's and Garth Budge's last game of the season before they returned to Australia. Both players were given a tremendous send-off at the end of the game and at a social event in the clubhouse.

The next day at Odsal, 21-year-old stand-off Dave Stockwell made an impressive debut in a 23–9 win against Doncaster. He had a hand in three of the five tries, one of which was scored by Lance Davies in his final first team appearance. It was Northern's fourth win in seven days, and the crowd of 5,005 brought the season's aggregate home attendances to just short of 130,000. The average league attendance was 5,812 and the overall average 6,834, similar to the 1955–56 figures. Northern ended the league season with a comfortable 10–0 win over a disjointed Liverpool side at Knotty Ash. So, despite winning their last five league games, and nine of their last 13, Northern finished in

17th place, a position the old Northern last occupied in 1954–55. So affairs at Odsal had come full circle.

Having missed out on the top 16, Northern therefore competed in the incredibly named Bottom 14 Competition, which Bramley, Dewsbury and Salford elected to boycott. In an experiment with the laws, the players were allowed to play-the-ball only once and, if the same side were then caught in possession, they had to release the ball using the rugby union method. Following their 15–9 defeat at Widnes opinion was divided on the play-the-ball experiment. The worry was that the game would soon resemble touch-and-pass and that top-class forwards would be stopped from using ball-handling skills, which were such a feature of rugby league.

Further tinkering with the rules resulted, of course, in first the four-tackle and later the six-tackle rule, which, together with two substitutes being allowed for any reason, immeasurably altered the game. But rugby league was still played mostly on winter Saturday afternoons, there were still contested scrums and the forwards tried hard not get in the way of the backs. Although the game was still only part-time, there were plenty of first-class athletes and characters at each of the 30 professional clubs to brighten up the rugby league supporter's week.

In those days, people still went to a game in anticipation of clever scrum-half play, blind-side moves, classy centre and wing partnerships, and to see the ball moved to the wing for an overlap. And there was always intelligent banter with opposition supporters and the chance to learn more about their players. In that respect, little had changed from when I first set foot inside Odsal as an inquisitive eight-year-old.

The following season, with thousands of Bradfordians travelling to away games and being proud to be seen as club supporters, Joe Phillips's prophecy came true when the Yorkshire Cup was won. And there were more heady days to come, which were all the more glorious due to having endured many of old Northern's lowest moments.

1964–65 Summary
Position in league: 17th of 30 Played 34 W 15 L 18 D 1 – Pts 345–347
Challenge Cup: Second round. Yorkshire Cup: First Round
Average attendance: 6,834 (5,812 league only)

13. What caused Northern's demise?

So how did such a great club, which played in three successive Challenge Cup finals from 1947 to 1949, were top of the league table in 1952 and Yorkshire Cup winners in 1953, fall so quickly from the heights? True, Cardiff in 1952, and Belle Vue Rangers in 1955, had both fallen by the wayside since the Second World War, but in 1963 Northern became the first club to fail to finish their fixtures in professional rugby league since Streatham & Mitcham in 1937.

Little wonder that Northern's collapse sent shock waves throughout the game, when many other clubs were struggling to keep their heads above water, and attendances generally, after the post-war boom years, were on the decline. In part this was caused by the RFL's own policy of agreeing to the live televising of test matches on a Saturday afternoon, in direct competition to league games. But other factors, such as increased car ownership and competition from association football, also played a part.

Being in the West Yorkshire conurbation, as well as benefitting from the away support of local rivals, Northern had always had to compete with other neighbouring rugby league clubs, as well as two Football League sides in Bradford City and Bradford Park Avenue. In 1960-61 Avenue gained promotion to the Third Division with an average home crowd of over 9,200, during which season nine of Avenue's home games were in direct competition with Northern's, and they also managed to average over 7,500 in 1962–63, even as they faced relegation.

Whereas Avenue could advertise the fact that they had standing room for over 14,000 under cover in the heights of winter, all the standing room at Odsal was exposed to the elements. The vast stadium was seen at its best in the warmer weather, in the early part of the season or at the Challenge Cup semi-finals and Championship finals. In the depths of winter, with only a few thousand or hundreds in the ground, it could be a forbidding place with a climate all of its own. As an incentive for supporters to make the trek to Odsal top in bad weather, Northern did open up the New Stand free of charge at some of their games, but by that time the club was on its last legs.

From around the 1956–57 season, Northern were a side very much in transition, with replacements urgently needed to fill the void left by the loss of so many world class players from those halcyon days. To find a centre successor to the great Ernest Ward and a reliable goalkicker to take over from Joe Phillips would have been difficult enough. Northern's goalkicking was generally lamentable following the New Zealander's departure, and there were only a couple of games which Northern won due to their better marksmanship in the seasons up to 1963. Also, winning enough scrum possession was always a major problem in those declining years.

Such playing matters were, of course, vitally important, but there were several other factors, which helped sow the seeds of the club's demise and which the hapless directors found difficult to address.

With few, if any, schools playing the game there was no great tradition of producing home-grown talent in Bradford. For example, in the 1952 Championship leading squad only Norman Haley was a local junior, and only a handful of players recruited from the Bradford Amateur League managed to play in the first team from 1954 to 1963. In fact, there were almost as many South Africans turning out for the club in the latter days, than locally born players.

In the past Northern had relied heavily on recruitment from Welsh rugby union, but a continuation of this policy meant the risk of substantial sums of money on untried talent. In any case, it seemed the well had finally run dry, for the time being at least. From 1954, despite the many scouting trips to South Wales, try as they may, Northern only managed to persuade two players – John Hardcastle and Lance Davies – to sign directly from Welsh rugby union clubs. In fact, fewer Welsh players came north in the 1950s than many other periods in the twentieth century, to the extent that the Welsh international side had to be disbanded

With the retirement of Trevor Foster and the loss of Ken Traill, Northern's situation cried out for the signing of a couple of major, established rugby league players, who could then have brought out the best in the talented youngsters, who were then emerging. And in 1958–59, when Northern climbed to 10th in the league, the opportunity was again missed to sign a player of some note. In fact, the upkeep of Odsal, and its notoriously muddy pitch, was a major drain on resources, so the onus had been on selling, resulting in the departure

174

of Milan Kosanovic, Jack Scroby, Terry Robbins and Derek Davies, who could well have laid the foundation for another era of success.

As they progressively dropped to the bottom of the league, Northern had found it difficult enough to hold on to these better players, while, with the possible exception of Colin Taylor, no above-average rugby league man, with any real ambition, would touch them. They therefore continued to rely on trying to unearth new young talent from other local leagues in West Yorkshire, and by the end they were almost dependent on the signing of veterans of the game, trialists and players on free transfers.

Northern's decline coincided with Wakefield Trinity's rise as a major force in the game. Trinity's success was built, not only on a strong local youth setup, but on home and international signings of a scale not previously seen in the game. The recruitment by Trinity's ambitious chairman, Stuart Hadfield, of several South Africans was reminiscent of Harry Hornby splashing out a small fortune to bring over the five New Zealanders in 1950. When Northern's visionary chairman announced his retirement on health grounds in February 1957, the club missed his business acumen and zeal as much as the loss of any of their great players. The later departure of footballing directors Trevor Foster and Dai Rees further weakened the board, but perhaps just as significant was the decline in Northern's pools income following the termination of the contract of its organiser, Malcolm Davies.

The Welsh flier had proved to be one of Northern's shrewdest buys, but his contribution off the field has perhaps been underestimated. Most clubs in those days were heavily dependent on their network of pools agents, and once he left to join Keighley in a similar capacity Northern's pools income totally collapsed. Furthermore, his parting in 1962–63 unfortunately coincided with the Big Freeze, when Northern took only £55 in gate receipts in a 10 week spell and were relying almost exclusively on their meagre pools income.

The 1962–63 season also saw the introduction of two divisions, which also contributed to Northern's demise. Because of the game's unique one division structure, in both 1957–58 and 1958–59, Northern had been deprived of a potentially five figure gate, when, as the leading Yorkshire side from the previous season, Leeds had to join the Lancashire League.

Two divisions was meant to overcome the anomaly of such a situation and provide more competitive rugby, while the previously lucrative derby matches against the top sides were to be retained by the introduction of an early season Divisional Championship. Unfortunately, in that season of snow and ice, Northern not only had additional travelling expenses, and played more Lancashire than Yorkshire opponents, but the Divisional Championships never captured the imagination of the public and were financially disastrous.

As the appendix shows, up to their demise Northern's decline in attendances was quiet dramatic, but who is to say where those previously ardent supporters went on a Saturday afternoon? How many were attracted by the entertainment on offer across the city at Park Avenue or down the road at Fartown, Thrum Hall, Lawkholme Lane or Headingley? How many simply drifted away until the time came that Northern could put something in the shop window? The photograph of the meeting at St George's Hall in April 1964 shows an audience made up mostly of middle-aged and older men, with hardly anyone under the age of 50 and only a handful of women. The reborn Northern not only won back those supporters who had despaired of the club, but also attracted a new generation of younger followers – significantly, of both sexes. Suddenly, it was cool to be seen at Odsal.

Tommy Smales, seen here leading Huddersfield to their Championship final success over Wakefield Trinity. His signing by new Northern in November 1964 helped rescue the club's first season.

However, as we have seen, success was not immediate, because the original squad of players was not quite good enough, and the new enterprise attracted many casual supporters. The first directors had to show plenty of initiative, in order to rescue what could have been a disastrous first season, and to lay the foundations for the club's future security. Under further new management, in the 1970s and 1980s Northern won the First Division Championship and the Premiership title, and when the sport entered a new era in 1996 the renamed Bradford Bulls were at the forefront of the change to summer rugby.

The problem of Odsal has never been satisfactorily resolved, however. At the start of 2012, the RFL purchased the lease for the stadium from Bradford Council to save it from the possible threat of housing development, and ensured that this famous ground was not lost to the sport. Finally, this millstone was removed from around the club's neck. Ironically, this caused a cash flow crisis for the club, which had to appeal to its supporters for £500,000 to survive. Unfortunately, at the time of writing, the Bulls have entered into administration, staff cuts have been implemented, and a new buyer is being sought.

Whatever the future holds, as this book hopefully records, some of my most abiding memories are of Odsal in the mid-1950s and early 1960s and the game's involving the old Northern. I have therefore taken up Len Haley's challenge to name a side to oppose his selection mentioned in the Foreword. Len has deprived me of some obvious candidates in the backs but left me with an abundance of choice in the forwards. My team would be: Goeli Abed, Brian Smith, Lance Davies, Alan Sutcliffe, John Coggle, Derek Davies, Geoff Higgins, George McLean, Milan Kosanovic, Brian Hambling, Terry Robbins, Jack Scroby, Steve Hey. Perhaps the only certainty, given Northern's goalkicking record from 1956 onwards, is that this imaginary game would have been decided by tries.

Appendix 1: Results, scorers and attendances

Home matches: opponents in CAPITALS
Results and scorers 1954—55

		F	A	Scorers	Att
14 Aug	DONCASTER	35	16	T: Smith 2, Knopf, Carter, W. Jones, Jenkins, Foster, L. Haley, H. Griffett. G: Phillips 4.	6,500
18 Aug	Castleford	8	4	G: Phillips 4.	2,500
21 Aug	Widnes	15	12	T: Jenkins, Smith, L. Haley. G: Phillips 3.	4,687
25 Aug	WIGAN	11	0	T: Mageen. G: Phillips 4.	15,000
28 Aug	BRAMLEY	21	7	T: Mageen, Jenkins, Storey, Knopf, Phillips. G: Phillips 3.	8,500
4 Sept	Dewsbury	18	11	T: Mageen 2, McLean, Traill. G: Phillips 3.	5,000
11 Sept	Castleford YC1	13	10	T: H. Griffett. G: Phillips 5.	8,168
18 Sept	WHITEHAVEN	24	18	T: Knopf 2, Wilson, Radford. G: Phillips 6.	8,500
21 Sept	HUNSLET YC2	5	3	T: W. Jones. G: Phillips.	8,105
25 Sept	Wigan	11	20	T: Radford. G: Jenkins 4.	18,319
30 Sept	Hull YCSF	5	10	T: Traill. G: Jenkins.	17,000
2 Oct	HALIFAX	7	13	T: Traill. G: Jenkins 2.	16,000
9 Oct	Hunslet	9	16	T: Phillips. G: Phillips 3.	15,600
16 Oct	FEATHERSTONE R	7	14	T: Seddon. G: Jenkins 2.	8,000
23 Oct	Warrington	10	15	T: Smith, Mageen. G: Phillips 2.	10,180
30 Oct	HULL	10	10	T: Knopf, Smith. G: Phillips 2.	7,000
6 Nov	Halifax	14	13	T: Mageen 2. G: Phillips 4.	9,719
13 Nov	Batley	11	4	T: Storey, Smith, Knopf. G: Phillips.	3,000
19 Nov	WAKEFIELD TRINITY	9	3	T: Smith. G: Phillips 3.	6,500
27 Nov	Featherstone R	22	15	T: Smith 3, L. Haley. G: Jenkins 4, Phillips.	4,500
4 Dec	WIDNES	2	10	*Abandoned 77 mins. Result stood.* G: Phillips.	2,000
11 Dec	Huddersfield	10	22	T: Knopf, G. Jones. G: Phillips 2.	10,955
18 Dec	LEEDS	3	12	T: L. Haley.	8,500
25 Dec	KEIGHLEY	9	18	T: McLean. G: Phillips 3.	7,000
27 Dec	Keighley	5	6	T: Seddon. G: Phillips.	7,400
1 Jan	York	11	17	T: Knopf 2, Phillips. G: Phillips.	6,726
8 Jan	YORK	5	15	T: Foster. G: Phillips.	5,500
29 Jan	Bramley	12	9	T: L. Haley, McLean. G: Phillips 3.	4,026
5 Feb	HUDDERSFIELD	10	8	T: L. Haley, McLean. G: Seddon 2.	8,500
12 Feb	WARRINGTON CC1	9	4	T: L. Haley. G: Seddon 3.	14,302
19 Feb	Hull	0	24		8,500
5 Mar	FEATHERSTONE R CC2	2	7	G: Phillips.	20,575
12 Mar	CASTLEFORD	23	23	T: McLean 3, Smith, Radford. G: Phillips 4.	4,500
16 Mar	BATLEY	26	4	T: McLean 2, Smith, Winnard. G: Phillips 6, Seddon,	3,500
26 Mar	Leeds	15	17	T: Phillips, Seddon, L. Haley. G: Phillips 3.	8,000
30 Mar	DEWSBURY	27	3	T: McLean 2, Seddon, Smith, Phillips. G: Phillips 6.	3,500
2 Apr	Doncaster	22	15	T: McLean 2, Traill 2, Seddon, Radford. G: Phillips 2.	1,000
9 Apr	WARRINGTON	8	13	T: Radford, Traill. G: Seddon.	10,000
11 Apr	Whitehaven	4	12	G: Seddon 2.	5,566
16 Apr	HUNSLET	30	25	T: L. Haley 2, Smith 2, Knopf, McLean, Foster, Seddon. G: Seddon 3.	8,000
20 Apr	Wakefield Trinity	12	31	T: McLean 2. G: Jenkins 3.	2,817

Results and scorers 1955—56

		F	A	Scorers	Att
15 Aug	*KEIGHLEY LC*	*23*	*22*	*T: Knopf 2 Hamilton, Jones, McLean. G: Phillips 3, Seddon.*	*5,727*
20 Aug	Liverpool City	23	8	T: McLean 2, Mageen, Knopf, Storey. G: Phillips 4.	1,653
24 Aug	BRAMLEY	40	14	T: McLean 4, Hambling, Knopf, Phillips, Traill, Mageen, Mackie. G: Phillips 4, Seddon.	5,000

178

Date	Opponent	F	A	Scorers	Att
27 Aug	HUNSLET YC1	27	23	T: McLean 2, Seddon 2, L. Haley, Knopf, Phillips. G: Phillips 3.	8,939
3 Sept	Leeds	12	24	T: Seddon, Knopf. G: Phillips 3.	15,000
9 Sept	Bramley YC2	12	5	T: McLean, L. Haley. G: Phillips 3.	3,855
10 Sept	BATLEY	31	13	T: McLean 4, Sutton, Smith, Scroby. G: Phillips 3, Seddon 2.	5,500
14 Sept	Hunslet	3	16	T: McLean.	7,800
17 Sept	Hull KR	15	8	T: Phillips, Seddon, Sutton. G: Phillips 3.	4,769
20 Sept	Hull YCSF	16	23	T: Jenkins, Seddon. G: Phillips 5.	16,000
24 Sept	LEIGH	35	16	T: Jenkins 2, McLean 2, Hambling, Seddon, H. Griffett. G: Phillips 4, Jenkins 2, Seddon.	10,500
1 Oct	Swinton	6	10	G: Phillips 3.	6,000
8 Oct	WORKINGTON TOWN	29	19	T: Smith 3, McLean 2, Phillips, Jenkins. G: Phillips 4.	8,000
15 Oct	Doncaster	20	10	T: McLean 3, Smith. G: Phillips 4.	1,500
22 Oct	CASTLEFORD	34	20	T: Seddon 2, Carter, Smith, Phillips, Jenkins, Mageen, McLean. G: Phillips 5.	7,000
29 Oct	HUDDERSFIELD	14	2	T: Phillips, Radford. G: Phillips 4.	12,000
5 Nov	FEATHERSTONE R	8	21	T: McLean 2. G: Phillips.	9,500
19 Nov	Castleford	19	17	T: McLean, Jenkins, L. Haley. G: Phillips 5.	3,266
23 Nov	NEW ZEALAND	6	11	G: Jenkins 3.	5,271
26 Nov	HULL	14	6	T: McLean 2, Smith, Sutton. G: Phillips.	6,000
3 Dec	HULL KR	31	13	T: McLean 3, Phillips 2, Jenkins, Seddon. G: Phillips 5.	6,000
10 Dec	LIVERPOOL CITY	27	0	T: McLean 3, Oddy, Radford. G: Phillips 6.	2,400
17 Dec	Workington Town	8	26	G: Phillips 4.	4,542
26 Dec	KEIGHLEY	16	5	T: McLean 2, Seddon, Sutton. G: Phillips 2.	6,000
27 Dec	Keighley	17	2	T: McLean, Radford, W. Jones. G: Phillips 4.	4,000
31 Dec	Hull	4	28	G: Phillips 2.	10,780
7 Jan	WAKEFIELD TRINITY	34	10	T: Oddy 2, McLean 2, Hambling, W. Jones, Jenkins, Glynn. G: Phillips 5.	6,000
14 Jan	Batley	15	5	T: McLean 2, Seddon. G: Phillips 3.	1,500
21 Jan	HUNSLET	18	3	T: McLean, Sutton, L. Haley, Jenkins. G: Phillips 3. *Abandoned 69 min, result stood*	4,500
28 Jan	Bramley	26	7	T: McLean 3, Jenkins, H. Griffett, Seddon. G: Phillips 4.	5,615
4 Feb	Halifax	12	17	T: Mageen 2. G: Phillips 3.	11,028
11 Feb	Hunslet CC1	10	9	T: McLean, Jenkins. G: Phillips 2.	11,591
3 Mar	Rochdale H CC2	5	2	T: McLean. G: Phillips.	12,364
7 Mar	Leigh	2	7	G: Phillips.	5,846
10 Mar	Wakefield Trinity	10	11	T: Scroby, Smith. G: Phillips 2.	8,701
14 Mar	LEEDS	5	17	T: Mageen. G: Phillips.	10,000
19 Mar	YORK	9	4	T: McLean 3.	4,500
24 Mar	St Helens CC3	6	53	G: Phillips 3.	22,485
27 Mar	HALIFAX	12	12	T: McLean 2. G: Phillips 3.	9,000
31 Mar	Featherstone R	12	26	T: McLean, Lancaster, Smith.	6,500
2 Apr	DONCASTER	17	17	T: Scroby, Seddon, D. Davies, G: Jenkins 3, Seddon.	5,500
7 Apr	Huddersfield	11	7	T: McLean 2, Lancaster. G: Phillips.	6,655
14 Apr	SWINTON	27	13	T: McLean 5, Smith, Scroby. G: Phillips 2 Seddon.	6,000
20 Apr	York	6	21	G: Phillips 3.	4,002

Results and scorers 1956–57

Date	Opponent	F	A	Scorers	Att
14 Aug	*Keighley LC*	*13*	*19*	*T: T. Jones, Seddon 2. G: Seddon 2.*	*4,800*
18 Aug	Wakefield Trinity	7	10	T: Smith. G: Seddon 2.	2,789
22 Aug	LEEDS	14	40	T: M. Davies, D. Davies. G: Seddon 4.	10,500
25 Aug	ST HELENS	7	34	T: D. Davies. G: Seddon 2.	5,500
29 Aug	Huddersfield	10	45	T: M. Davies, Radford. G: Seddon 2.	6,286
1 Sept	Castleford YC1	17	23	T: M. Davies 4, Seddon. G: Seddon.	3,037
3 Sept	*ALBI (Friendly)*	*20*	*8*	*T: Rodwell 4. G: Lee 3, Jenkins.*	*1,400*

179

Date	Opponent	F	A	Scorers	Att
5 Sept	YORK	5	17	T: Jenkins. G: Lee.	4,000
8 Sept	BARROW	16	41	T: M. Davies 2, T. Jones, Rodwell. G: Lee 2.	4,000
15 Sept	Doncaster	19	7	T: M. Davies 2, L. Haley. G: Seddon 5.	1,400
22 Sept	Featherstone R	18	21	T: M. Davies 3, Rodwell. G: Seddon 3.	5,500
6 Oct	Hull KR	22	10	T: Seddon, Maclean, Lancaster, Radford. G: Seddon 5.	4,544
8 Oct	*HUDDERSFIELD**	*14*	*6*	*T: D. Maclean, M. Davies. G: Seddon 4.*	*1,084*
13 Oct	WARRINGTON	11	16	T: Lee, Glynn, Radford. G: Seddon.	6,000
24 Oct	AUSTRALIA	11	23	T: M Davies 3. G: Seddon.	3,000
27 Oct	HALIFAX	17	11	T: Scroby, T. Jones, Lancaster. G: Seddon 4.	10,000
3 Nov	Batley	12	9	T: M. Davies 2. G: Seddon 3.	5,500
10 Nov	HUNSLET	7	18	T: T. Jones. G: Seddon 2.	6,000
17 Nov	Bramley	24	14	T: Smith 2, M. Davies, Radford. G: Seddon 6.	4,484
24 Nov	CASTLEFORD	24	14	T: M Davies 3, T. Jones 2, Scroby. G: Seddon 3.	4,500
8 Dec	York	5	17	T: Smith. G: Seddon.	4,477
15 Dec	HULL	10	17	T: Smith 2. G: Seddon 2.	3,000
22 Dec	Leeds	0	5	*Abandoned 24 mins. Result did not stand.*	*4,000*
5 Jan	FEATHERSTONE R	15	7	T: Lancaster 2, Radford. G: Seddon 3.	2,500
12 Jan	Castleford	0	13		2,603
19 Jan	DEWSBURY	23	10	Rodwell 2, Maclean, Seddon, Scroby, Hopkins, Winnard. G: Jones.	1,700
26 Jan	BRAMLEY	11	0	T: Maclean, L. Haley, Rodwell. G: Seddon.	3,000
2 Feb	Barrow	2	7	G: Seddon.	7,416
9 Feb	DEWSBURY CC1	20	7	T: Rodwell 2, Winnard, Radford. G: Jenkins 3, Seddon.	6,646
16 Feb	WIGAN	14	5	T: Rodwell, Radford, Hopkins, Winnard. G: Seddon.	6,000
27 Feb	WIDNES CC2	8	10	T: Rodwell, Maclean. G: Seddon.	6,959
2 Mar	Hunslet	12	19	T: Maclean, Rodwell. G: Best 3.	7,000
9 Mar	DONCASTER	9	3	T: Sutton, Rodwell, Hopkins.	3,500
16 Mar	St Helens	6	23	T: Maclean 2.	12,500
20 Mar	Leeds	15	25	T: Winnard, Maclean, Scroby. G: G. Haley 3.	9,126
23 Mar	Dewsbury	14	13	T: Radford, Sutton, Seddon, G. Haley. G: Seddon.	4,000
25 Mar	KEIGHLEY	3	18	T: Sutton.	5,000
3 Apr	Wigan	5	38	T: Sutton. G: Seddon.	12,107
6 Apr	Warrington	18	17	T: Maclean, Smith, Seddon, Sutton. G: G. Haley 3.	7,220
10 Apr	WAKEFIELD TRINITY	9	23	T: Sutton. G: G. Haley 2, Seddon.	3,200
13 Apr	Hull	3	23	T: Seddon.	10,000
15 Apr	HUDDERSFIELD	7	26	T: D. Davies, G: G. Haley, Beevers.	3,500
20 Apr	Halifax	18	15	T: Hopkins, Jenkins, Winnard, Smith. G: Beevers 3.	9,504
22 Apr	HULL KR	22	18	T: Smith 2, Jenkins, Seddon, Beevers, Hopkins. G: Beevers 2.	2,700
27 Apr	Keighley	23	16	T: Scroby 2, G. Haley, Smith, Winnard. G: Jenkins 2, Beevers 2.	5,500
1 May	BATLEY	22	12	T: Smith 2, Jenkins, Winnard. G: Jenkins 4, Beevers.	2,000

* Experimental rules

Results and scorers 1957–58

Date	Opponent	F	A	Scorers	Att
12 Aug	*KEIGHLEY LC*	*19*	*31*	*T: Winnard, Smith, Hambling, Scroby, Radford. G: Beevers 2.*	*6,200*
17 Aug	Huddersfield	15	33	T: Smith 2, Carter, Seddon, Radford.	8,407
21 Aug	SWINTON	5	20	T: Smith. G: Beevers.	4,100
24 Aug	WORKINGTON TOWN	13	3	T: Oddy 2, D. Davies, G: Beevers, Jenkins.	3,000
26 Aug	Castleford	19	5	T: Jenkins 2, Rodwell 2, Carter. G: Beevers 2.	4,282

Date	Opponent	F	A	Scorers	Att
31 Aug	Dewsbury YC1	28	12	T: Smith 3, Jenkins 2, Rodwell, Radford, Daniels. G: Jenkins, Jones.	5,033
7 Sept	DEWSBURY	36	22	T: M. Davies 4, Radford 2. Scroby, Jenkins, Beevers, Smith. G: Jones 3.	3,700
14 Sept	LEIGH	37	7	T: D. Davies 2, Scroby 2, M. Davies, Daniels, Oddy, Smith, Jones. G: Jenkins 5.	4,500
17 Sept	FEATHERSTONE YC2	5	2	T: M. Davies. G: Jenkins.	5,776
21 Sept	Warrington	8	16	T: M. Davies, Jenkins. G: Jenkins.	8,534
28 Sept	WHITEHAVEN	28	16	T: Radford, Jenkins, Kosanovic, Smith. G: Jenkins 8.	4,000
30 Sept	YORK YCSF	2	2	G: Jenkins.	10,794
2 Oct	York YCSFR	8	14	T: Jenkins, G. Haley. G:Carter.	9,019
5 Oct	Swinton	20	20	T: M. Davies 2, Scroby 2, Daniels, Smith. G: Jenkins.	5,000
12 Oct	Dewsbury	17	17	T: Daniels 3, M. Davies, Kosanovic. G: Beevers	4,000
19 Oct	WAKEFIELD TRINITY	11	10	T: M. Davies 2, Winnard. G: Scroby.	10,000
26 Oct	Halifax	8	16	T: M. Davies, G. McLean. G: Jenkins.	13,153
2 Nov	HUNSLET	3	12	T: M. Davies.	7,000
9 Nov	Wakefield Trinity	6	37	T: Daniels, M. Davies.	8,909
16 Nov	HULL	15	12	T: Smith 2, L. Haley. G: Jenkins 3.	3,500
23 Nov	Bramley	15	24	T: M. Davies 2, Daniels. G: Jenkins 3.	4,000
30 Nov	FEATHERSTONE R	2	20	G: Jenkins.	4,000
7 Dec	Hull K R	3	7	T: M. Davies.	3,000
14 Dec	Whitehaven	19	24	T: Daniels 2, G. Haley, Smith, M. Davies. G: Jenkins 2.	3,703
21 Dec	DONCASTER	31	5	T: M. Davies 3, D. Davies 2, Daniels 2, G. McLean, Radford. G: L. Haley 2.	2,300
25 Dec	KEIGHLEY	0	10		4,500
26 Dec	Keighley	21	19	T: M. Davies 3, Winnard 2. G: Jenkins 3.	7,000
28 Dec	CASTLEFORD	35	12	T: M. Davies 5, Jenkins 2, Radford 2, L. Haley, Hemingway. G: Jenkins.	3,500
4 Jan	Leigh	13	4	T: D. Maclean, Feather, G. Haley. G: Beevers 2.	6,000
11 Jan	YORK	11	13	T: M. Davies, L. Haley, Radford. G: Beevers.	4,000
18 Jan	Doncaster	18	3	T: Jenkins 2, D. Davies, Smith. G: Seddon 3.	600
1 Feb	Workington Town	0	9		5,720
12 Feb	Bramley CC1	15	9	T: Radford, M. Davies, G. Haley. G: Seddon 3.	2,344
15 Feb	HULL K R	8	6	T: Kosanovic, Jenkins. G: Seddon.	2,000
22 Feb	Rochdale H CC2	8	11	T: M. Davies, Jenkins. G: Jenkins.	9,317
1 Mar	Hunslet	7	10	T: Lancaster. G: Jenkins 2.	5,300
8 Mar	HALIFAX	4	5	G: Beevers 2.	6,000
15 Mar	WARRINGTON	5	19	T: M. Davies. G: Beevers.	4,500
29 Mar	Hull	11	28	T: M. Davies 2, D. Davies. G: Beevers.	8,000
7 Apr	Batley	21	6	T: M. Davies 3, Winnard, Smith. G: Beevers 3.	2,500
8 Apr	BATLEY	31	22	T: M. Davies 4, Winnard 3, Radford, A. Dawes. G: Beevers 2.	3,000
12 Apr	HUDDERSFIELD	21	24	T: Smith, Winnard, A. Dawes, M. Davies, D. Davies. G: Thompson 2, Jenkins.	5,000
19 Apr	York	13	26	T: Daniels, M. Davies, Smith. G: Thompson 2.	4,669
23 Apr	BRAMLEY	21	13	T: Hemingway, Daniels, Feather, Jenkins, Higgins. G: Jenkins 3.	2,500
30 Apr	Featherstone R	23	38	T: M. Davies, Daniels, Winnard. G: Jenkins 7.	2,600

Results and scorers 1958–59

Date	Opponent	F	A	Scorers	Att
12 Aug	Keighley LC	17	25	T: Daniels, Crabtree, M. Davies. G: Walshaw 3. DG: Daniels.	4,500
16 Aug	Salford	15	13	T: L. Haley 2, Radford. G: Walshaw 3.	6,000

181

Date	Opponent	F	A	Scorers	Att
20 Aug	LEIGH	15	7	T: M. Davies 2, Radford. G: Walshaw 3.	4,000
23 Aug	HULL	8	21	T: M. Davies, Handley. G: Walshaw.	6,000
26 Aug	Dewsbury	12	21	T: G. Haley, Daniels. G: Walshaw 3.	4,300
30 Aug	YORK YC1	23	31	T: Handley 2, Kosanovic, D. Davies, M. Davies. G: Walshaw 4.	5,168
6 Sept	Hull K R	14	19	T: Jenkins, G. Haley, D. Davies, Jones. G: Walshaw.	5,500
13 Sept	WARRINGTON	16	26	T: Jenkins, Daniels. G: Walshaw 5.	4,000
20 Sept	York	20	3	T: M. Davies 2, Daniels, Jones. G: Jenkins 4	4,926
27 Sept	DONCASTER	26	16	T: Jenkins 2, Winnard, Daniels. G: Jenkins 6, Beevers.	3,000
4 Oct	Batley	11	11	T: Jenkins, Beevers, M. Davies. G: Jenkins	4,000
11 Oct	HUNSLET	7	17	T: M. Davies. G: Walshaw 2.	5,000
18 Oct	Featherstone R	5	29	T: Jenkins. G: Walshaw.	3,700
25 Oct	HULL K R	17	20	T: M. Davies 2, Kosanovic, Higgins, Daniels. G: Walshaw.	3,000
1 Nov	Doncaster	17	15	T: G. Haley, Higgins, M. Davies. G: Jenkins 4.	900
8 Nov	DEWSBURY	38	13	T: M. Davies 3, D. Davies 3, Penketh 2, Daniels, Higgins. G: Jenkins 3, Seddon.	2,500
15 Nov	Wakefield Trinity	8	13	T: Daniels, M. Davies. G: Seddon.	6,000
22 Nov	YORK	16	12	T: Daniels 2. G: Seddon 5.	2,500
6 Dec	Halifax	23	18	T: M. Davies 2, Penketh, Jones, Daniels. G: Seddon 4.	6,401
13 Dec	WHITEHAVEN	27	12	T: Jones 2, L. Haley 2, Daniels, M. Davies Seddon. G: Jenkins 2, Seddon.	2,000
20 Dec	Leigh	9	31	T: Hey. G: Seddon 3.	5,000
25 Dec	BRAMLEY	36	16	T: M. Davies 2, Winnard, Daniels, Scroby, Kosanovic, Jones, Radford. G: Seddon 6	3,500
26 Dec	Bramley	17	9	T: M. Davies, Winnard, Higgins. G: Seddon 4.	3,500
27 Dec	Huddersfield	31	6	T: M. Davies 3, Jones, Higgins, Winnard, Daniels. G: Seddon 5.	5,171
3 Jan	SALFORD	9	15	T: G. McLean, M. Davies, Hemingway.	3,000
24 Jan	Whitehaven	3	15	T: M. Davies.	4,000
31 Jan	Hull	7	22	T: Radford. G: Seddon 2.	8,000
14 Feb	Widnes	10	14	T: M. Davies, Hey. G: Jenkins 2.	5,032
21 Feb	HUDDERSFIELD CC1	2	11	G: Jenkins.	6,470
28 Feb	BATLEY	29	15	T: Daniels 3, Higgins, Winnard, Penketh, Jones. G: Seddon 4.	2,000
7 Mar	KEIGHLEY	18	8	T: Penketh, M. Davies, Jones, Daniels. G: Seddon 3.	3,500
11 Mar	CASTLEFORD	9	23	T: Winnard, Daniels, Hey.	2,000
14 Mar	Castleford	12	11	T: Seddon, Daniels. G: Seddon 3.	2,000
16 Mar	HALIFAX	10	13	G: Seddon 5.	4,000
28 Mar	Hunslet	15	15	T: Doran, Penketh, Radford. G: Seddon 3.	6,400
30 Mar	HUDDERSFIELD	7	18	T: Daniels. G: Seddon 2.	3,500
31 Mar	Keighley	12	11	T: Penketh, D. Davies. G: Seddon 3.	5,500
4 Apr	WAKEFIELD TRINITY	12	9	T: Higgins, D. Davies. G: Seddon 3.	7,500
18 Apr	WIDNES	18	12	T: Penketh 2, Winnard, Jones. G: Seddon 3	3,000
25 Apr	Warrington	14	6	T: Higgins, Kosanovic. G: Seddon 4.	4,000
29 Apr	FEATHERSTONE R	20	8	T: Radford, Penketh, Seddon, Kosanovic. G: Seddon 4.	3,000

Results and scorers 1959–60

Date	Opponent	F	A	Scorers	Att
10 Aug	*Keighley LC*	*19*	*18*	*T: Winnard, Hemingway, M. Davies. G: Seddon 2, Jones 2, Beevers.*	*4,200*
15 Aug	WORKINGTON TOWN	20	15	T: Hey, Doran, Jones, Kosanovic, G: Seddon 4.	4,250
20 Aug	Doncaster	16	17	T: M. Davies, Penketh, Doran, Hey. G: Seddon 2.	1,000
22 Aug	Warrington	6	35	G: Seddon 3.	6,759
26 Aug	KEIGHLEY	13	11	T: Doran. G: Seddon 5.	4,250

182

Date	Opponent	F	A	Scorers	Att
29 Aug	HULL YC1	10	23	T: Jones, Winnard. G: Seddon 2.	4,376
5 Sept	WIDNES	12	10	T: Hey, Hemingway. G: Seddon 3.	2,500
12 Sept	Whitehaven	19	19	T: Brook, Radford, Hey. G: Seddon 5.	5,704
19 Sept	Leigh	10	19	G: Seddon 5.	5,098
26 Sept	HALIFAX	23	13	T: Doran 2, Penketh 2, Winnard.	
				G: Seddon 4.	5,000
3 Oct	Leeds	15	16	T: Hey, Higgins, Radford. G: Walshaw 3.	10,612
10 Oct	HUNSLET	6	30	T: Doran 2.	5,000
17 Oct	FEATHERSTONE R	8	29	T: Brook, Hey. G: Seddon.	2,750
24 Oct	Workington Town	14	19	T: Penketh 2, Walton, Doran. G: Seddon.	2,997
26 Oct	*KEIGHLEY*	*40*	*34*	*Radford/Jenkins/Ernest Redman Testimonial*	*1,500*
31 Oct	BATLEY	10	11	T: Penketh 2. G: Seddon 2.	3,000
4 Nov	AUSTRALIA	8	29	T: Penketh, Jones. G: Seddon.	4,126
7 Nov	Featherstone R	5	16	T: Winnard. G: Seddon	3,600
14 Nov	Hunslet	4	16	G: Seddon 2.	3,100
21 Nov	Hull K R	10	14	T: Smith, Doran. G: Seddon 2.	2,749
28 Nov	CASTLEFORD	19	8	T: Marston, Lancaster, Doran. G: Seddon 5.	1,500
5 Dec	Halifax	11	14	T: Lancaster. G: Jones 4.	6,176
12 Dec	Keighley	15	30	T: Smith, Seddon, Doran. G: Jones 3.	3,876
19 Dec	HUDDERSFIELD	10	18	T: Penketh, D. Davies. G: Jones 2.	1,100
25 Dec	Bramley	6	20	T: Hemingway, Smith.	1,138
26 Dec	BRAMLEY	33	2	T: H. Griffett 2, Doran 2, Hemingway,	
				Marston, Smith. G: Seddon 6.	1,500
2 Jan	Huddersfield	12	18	T: H Griffett, Feather. G: Seddon 3.	4,729
9 Jan	DONCASTER	13	7	T: A. Dawes, Winnard, D. Davies.	
				G: Seddon, Thompson.	1,000
23 Jan	YORK	5	9	T: Winnard. G: Seddon.	1,300
30 Jan	Hull (Abd 75 min.)	7	16	T: Winnard. G: Jones 2. *(Result stood)*	5,220
6 Feb	HULL	13	14	T: Smith, Higgins, Marston. G: Seddon 2.	2,000
13 Feb	Castleford CC1	8	4	T: Smith 2. G: Seddon.	3,725
20 Feb	Batley	9	9	T: Doran. G: Seddon 3.	2,500
27 Feb	Swinton CC2	9	13	T: Doran. G: Jones 2, Seddon.	8,189
5 Mar	HULL KR	2	14	G: Seddon.	2,000
19 Mar	WARRINGTON	5	5	T: Kosanovic. G: Seddon.	1,550
26 Mar	Widnes	15	11	T: Penketh, D. Davies, Smith. G: Seddon 3.	2,667
2 Apr	LEEDS	4	29	G: Seddon 2.	5,250
16 Apr	LEIGH	17	19	T: L. Haley, Higgins, D. Davies. G: Seddon 4.	1,750
18 Apr	York	3	10	T: Smith.	2,946
19 Apr	WAKEFIELD TRINITY	17	28	T: Seddon, L. Haley, Doran. G: Seddon 4.	7,500
23 Apr	WHITEHAVEN	29	20	T: Smith 2, D. Davies 2, L. Haley, Walton,	
				Hey. G: Seddon 4.	1,500
27 Apr	Wakefield T	5	28	T: Doran. G: Seddon.	8,463
30 Apr	Castleford	9	26	T: Lancaster. G: Walshaw 3.	2,700

Results and scorers 1960–61

Date	Opponent	F	A	Scorers	Att
9 Aug	*Keighley LC*	*5*	*29*	*T: Doran. G: Trumble*	2,500
13 Aug	Blackpool Borough	0	18		1,485
17 Aug	FEATHERSTONE R	5	27	T: Doran. G: Trumble.	3,100
20 Aug	BATLEY	7	14	T: Trumble. G: Trumble 2.	1,850
24 Aug	Hull KR	7	33	T: Davies. G: Walshaw 2.	4,873
27 Aug	CASTLEFORD YC1	7	25	T: Davies. G: Walshaw 2.	1,774
3 Sept	Barrow	18	5	T: G. Robbins, Doran, Trumble, Brook.	
				G: Walshaw 2, Jones.	2,421
10 Sept	ROCHDALE H	20	9	T: Smith 2, G. Robbins, Trumble.	
				G: Walshaw 4	1,600
17 Sept	LEEDS	7	16	T: Brook. G: Walshaw. DG: Broadbent.	5,500
19 Sept	Workington Town	2	28	G: Walshaw.	1,600
28 Sept	CASTLEFORD	17	18	T: Broadbent, Hemingway, Marston.	
				G: Walshaw 4	1,500
15 Oct	YORK	13	16	T: Smith 2, Doran. G: Walshaw 2.	1,350
22 Oct	Batley	15	7	T: Nunns, Doran, Smith.	
				G: Walshaw 2. DG: Broadbent.	3,350

Date	Team	F	A	Scorers	Att
29 Oct	KEIGHLEY	10	10	T: Nunns 2. G: Walshaw 2.	1,600
5 Nov	Featherstone R	4	23	G: Seddon 2.	2,800
12 Nov	HUNSLET	12	2	T: Smith, Nunns. G: Seddon 3.	2,400
19 Nov	Keighley	5	18	T: Kosanovic. G: Seddon.	2,200
3 Dec	Castleford	7	7	T: Nunns. G: Seddon. DG: Higgins.	1,000
10 Dec	Dewsbury	3	7	T: Smith.	1,400
17 Dec	DONCASTER	11	8	T: Doran 2, Smith. G: Jones.	950
26 Dec	BRAMLEY	9	8	T: T. Robbins, Kosanovic, Smith.	1,150
31 Dec	Leeds	3	19	T: Higgins.	11,981
14 Jan	BLACKPOOL B	6	35	T: Penketh, Brook.	1,100
21 Jan	Rochdale H	6	14	T: Brook, Davies.	940
4 Feb	York	3	7	T: Doran.	2,017
11 Feb	Batley CC1	0	9		2,225
18 Feb	Hull	0	24		7,500
25 Feb	Bramley	5	2	T: T. Robbins. G: Hattee.	670
4 Mar	WORKINGTON TOWN	13	25	T: Davies 2, Hemingway. G: Hattee 2.	1,850
11 Mar	Doncaster	15	9	T: Davies, Doran, Smith. G: Hattee 3.	650
18 Mar	Hunslet	9	18	T: Smith. G: Hattee 3.	2,400
25 Mar	Wakefield Trinity	0	26		7,728
1 Apr	HULL	6	27	T: Doran, Feather.	1,200
3 Apr	HUDDERSFIELD	13	15	T: Smith 2, Welsh. G: Hattee 2.	1,800
8 Apr	DEWSBURY	13	7	T: Penketh, Davies, Doran. G: Hattee 2.	1,400
12 Apr	BARROW	13	5	T: Doran 2, Broadbent. G: Hattee 2.	1,000
17 Apr	Huddersfield	13	27	T: Penketh 2, Davies. G: Hattee 2.	2,589
22 Apr	WAKEFIELD TRINITY	11	34	T: Smith, Penketh, Doran. G: Hattee.	3,800
25 Apr	HULL KR	11	12	T: Crabtree, Doran, Smith. G: Hattee.	500

Results and scorers 1961–62

Date	Team	F	A	Scorers	Att
19 Aug	KEIGHLEY	7	14	T: Doran. G: Hattee 2.	1,718
21 Aug	Hull KR	8	29	T: Nunns, Doran. G: Sutcliffe.	6,750
26 Aug	Widnes	10	37	T: D. Davies, Doran. G: Sutcliffe 2.	5,000
30 Aug	LEEDS	16	32	T: D. Davies, Marston. G: Hattee 5.	4,075
2 Sept	Wakefield T YC1	5	73	T: D. Davies. G: Hattee.	10,942
5 Sept	Batley	0	10		1,900
8 Sept	CASTLEFORD	8	0	G: Hattee 4.	1,470
16 Sept	Liverpool City	12	23	T: Broadbent, Hattee. G: Hattee 3	500
23 Sept	WIDNES	2	33	G: Hattee.	1,306
29 Sept	York	20	24	T: Grainger 2, T. Robbins 2. G: Hattee 4.	2,873
7 Oct	Salford	7	35	T: Doran. G: Hattee 2.	3,000
14 Oct	WAKEFIELD TRINITY	7	38	T: Broadbent. G: Hattee 2.	5,636
28 Oct	HALIFAX	0	9		2,322
4 Nov	Hunslet	7	33	T: Hemingway. G: Seddon 2.	1,500
18 Nov	Wakefield Trinity	12	33	T: Hemingway, Grainger. G: Hattee 3.	8,554
25 Nov	HUNSLET	0	21		1,493
2 Dec	Halifax	3	9	T: Seddon	2,370
16 Dec	DONCASTER	0	2	Abandoned 12 mins. Result did not stand.	405
23 Dec	Castleford	10	34	T: Doran 2. G: Seddon 2.	2,056
6 Jan	Hull	6	30	T: Grainger 2.	7,500
13 Jan	LIVERPOOL CITY	8	19	T: Whitaker, Coggle. G: Beevers.	563
3 Feb	Barrow	2	14	G: Seddon.	2,319
10 Feb	Castleford CC1	0	12		4,250
17 Feb	DEWSBURY	3	0	T: L. Davies	1,030
24 Feb	Keighley	10	10	T: Grainger, Schofield. G: Seddon 2.	1,600
10 Mar	Leeds	8	20	T: Coggle, Grainger. G: Seddon.	6,056
17 Mar	SALFORD	6	20	G: Seddon 2, Abed.	1,323
24 Mar	DONCASTER	2	16	G: Abed.	790
26 Mar	FEATHERSTONE R	12	34	T: L. Davies, Tate. G: Abed 3	904
31 Mar	Doncaster	5	25	T: Hemingway. G: Abed.	1,150
4 Apr	BRAMLEY	2	28	G: Beevers.	502
14 Apr	Featherstone R	18	21	T: C. Taylor, Grainger, Haley, Seddon. G: Seddon 2, McAvoy.	2,699
16 Apr	Bramley	5	18	T: C. Taylor. G: Seddon.	1,100

184

Date	Opponent	F	A	Scorers	Att
21 Apr	HULL	5	25	T: Schofield. G: Abed.	483
23 Apr	Dewsbury	12	20	T: Coggle, Welsh. G: Abed 3.	900
24 Apr	YORK	12	24	T: Doran, Sutcliffe. G: Abed 3.	1,001
28 Apr	BATLEY	18	11	T: McAvoy 2, Coggle, L. Davies. G: Abed 3.	738
30 Apr	HULL KR	9	3	T: Seddon, Grainger, Sutcliffe.	722
4 May	BARROW	16	14	T: Tate, Hatfield. G: Abed 5.	842

Results and scorers 1962–63

Date	Opponent	F	A	Scorers	Att
10 Aug	*Keighley LC*	*8*	*22*	*T: Coggle, Tate. G: Abed.*	*2,000*
17 Aug	Leeds ED	5	27	T: Davies. G: Seddon.	8,000
22 Aug	HUDDERSFIELD ED	5	31	T: Welsh. G: Seddon.	1,819
25 Aug	WAKEFIELD T ED	10	19	T: Tate, M. Reynolds. G: Seddon 2.	2,756
29 Aug	Featherstone R ED	16	43	T: Martin, M. Reynolds. G: Seddon 5.	4,013
31 Aug	Huddersfield ED	0	37		4,480
8 Sept	BRAMLEY YC1	5	11	T: Martin. G: Seddon.	1,262
15 Sept	LEEDS ED	18	21	T: Nunns, Sutcliffe, Coggle, Hardcastle. G: Seddon 3.	2,781
22 Sept	Wakefield T ED	11	45	T: Sutcliffe, Penketh, M. Reynolds. G: Seddon	6,741
29 Sept	FEATHERSTONE R ED	21	13	T: Sutcliffe, Martin, M. Reynolds, Nunns, Hardcastle. G: Martin 3.	1,476
6 Oct	Liverpool City	9	17	T: Martin. G: Martin 3.	453
13 Oct	DEWSBURY	12	10	T: Sutcliffe, Coggle. G: Martin 3.	1,700
20 Oct	Salford	5	16	T: Hasse. G: Martin.	3,000
27 Oct	ROCHDALE H	7	22	T: Sutcliffe. G: Martin, Seddon.	2,027
3 Nov	Doncaster	4	34	G: Martin, Seddon.	1,600
10 Nov	LIVERPOOL CITY	2	7	G: Seddon	631
17 Nov	Dewsbury	10	15	T: M. Reynolds, Winnard. G: Seddon 2.	607
24 Nov	SALFORD	20	13	T: Foster, Hasse, Bentley, Martin. G: Seddon 3, Martin.	744
1 Dec	Rochdale H	7	23	T: Penketh. G: Seddon 2.	3,079
8 Dec	DONCASTER	3	10	T: Doran.	525
15 Dec	Keighley	2	30	G: Seddon.	1,400
22 Dec	BARROW	5	36	T: Davies. G: Abed.	632
29 Dec to 13 Feb All matches postponed due to Big Freeze.					
23 Feb	Whitehaven	8	34	T: White, Marker. G: Abed.	1,992
9 Mar	Leigh	2	33	G: Seddon.	3,000
11 Mar	WAKEFIELD T CC1	3	15	T: Abed.	2,069
23 Mar	Hunslet	15	38	T: Penketh, Nunns, M. Reynolds, G: Seddon 3.	4,000
30 Mar	WHITEHAVEN	7	7	T: Coggle. G: Abed 2.	543
13 Apr	BLACKPOOL BOROUGH	7	23	T: M. Reynolds. G: Abed 2.	617
15 Apr	Batley	0	31		1,200
24 Apr	YORK	7	31	T: Penketh. G: Abed 2.	782
4 May	York	0	38		3,895
8 May	HUNSLET	6	22	G: Abed 3.	1,262
15 May	Blackpool Borough	0	30		1,000
18 May	LEIGH	16	31	T: Taylor 2, Doran, Brewer. G: Robinson 2.	435
22 May	BATLEY	3	17	T: Beevers.	703
24 May	Barrow	0	39		2,048
29 May	KEIGHLEY	6	25	T: Penketh 2	1,124

Results and scorers 1963–64

Date	Opponent	F	A	Scorers	Att
24 Aug	DEWSBURY	12	15	T: Coggle 2, Abed, Sutcliffe.	953
31 Aug	Barrow	9	29	T: Abed, Coggle, Davies.	4,132
4 Sept	DONCASTER	8	16	T: Wigglesworth, Penketh. G: Reynolds.	766
7 Sept	FEATHERSTONE YC1	10	24	T: Coggle, Davies. G: Abed 2.	1,005
9 Sept	WAKEFIELD T ED	14	25	T: Coggle, Reynolds. G: Abed 4.	1,686
14 Sept	SALFORD	27	6	T: Abed, Sutcliffe 2, Coggle, C. Taylor. G: Abed 6.	1,044
21 Sept	Liverpool City	7	17	T: Wigglesworth. G: Abed 2.	463

185

		F	A	Scorers	Att
28 Sept	Leigh	0	43		6,210
10 May	HUDDERSFIELD ED	7	30	T: Coggle. G: Abed 2.	1,742
10 Dec	BATLEY	9	12	T: Coggle. G: Abed 3.	1,235
19 Oct	Doncaster	3	25	T: Dlambulo.	1,400
11 Feb	LIVERPOOL CITY	2	6	G: Beevers.	699
9 Nov	ROCHDALE H	17	27	T: Coggle, Reynolds, Dlambulo. G: Beevers 4	934
16 Nov	Batley	10	26	T: Doran, Coggle. G: Beevers, Taylor.	1,089
23 Nov	BARROW	0	29		324
7 Dec	LEIGH	5	33	T: Dlambulo. G: Beevers.	841

Results and scorers 1964–65

		F	A	Scorers	Att
22 Aug	HULL KR	20	34	T: Levula, Lord 2, Brooke. G: Williams 4	13,542
24 Aug	Hunslet	13	18	T: Davies. G: Williams 5.	5,000
29 Aug	Featherstone R	13	15	T: Abed. G: Williams 5	3,000
2 Sept	SALFORD	20	12	T: Walker 2, Levula, Rae. G: Abed 4.	10,002
5 Sept	HUDDERSFIELD YC1	6	17	G: Williams 3.	11,140
12 Sept	York	4	14	G: Williams 2	3,500
19 Sept	BATLEY	18	5	T: Todd, Carr, Ashton, Rae. G: Williams 2, Todd.	5,583
26 Sept	Doncaster	7	16	T: Walker. G: Williams 2.	1,600
3 Oct	LIVERPOOL CITY	10	12	T: Moyser, Lord. G: Williams, Todd.	4,929
10 Oct	Bramley	9	16	T: Todd. G: Levula 3.	2,950
17 Oct	CASTLEFORD	5	7	T: Rae. G: Todd.	5,844
24 Oct	Halifax	3	24	T: Rae.	5,854
31 Oct	WHITEHAVEN	10	26	T: Walker 2. G: Todd 2.	4,105
7 Nov	Hull	0	8		4,000
14 Nov	Salford	2	12	G: Jones.	2,400
21 Nov	YORK	14	2	T: Stock, Davies. G: Rae 4.	4,150
28 Nov	WAKEFIELD TRINITY	3	0	T: Brown.	7,658
5 Dec	DEWSBURY	2	0	G: Rae.	4,761
19 Dec	Keighley	8	10	T: Walker, Fisher. G: Rae.	3,500
9 Jan	Whitehaven	3	3	T: Smales.	996
16 Jan	LEEDS	8	3	T: Brooke, Rhodes. G: Rae.	4,238
30 Jan	FEATHERSTONE R	5	11	T: Walker. G: Rhodes.	5,923
6 Feb	Leigh CC1	7	6	T: Brooke. G: Clawson 2.	5,000
13 Feb	Batley	25	2	T: Brooke 2, Rae, Rhodes, Clawson. G: Clawson 2.	3,000
20 Feb	Dewsbury	8	2	T: Brown, Brooke. G: Clawson 5.	2,800
27 Feb	WAKEFIELD T CC2	7	10	T: Brooke. G: Clawson 2.	19,905
6 Mar	BRAMLEY	8	0	T: Brown, Metcalfe. G: Clawson.	5,056
13 Mar	Hull KR	17	22	T: Budge, Stock, Metcalfe. G: Clawson 4.	5,800
20 Mar	HUNSLET	16	10	T: Rae, Hardcastle, Metcalfe, Walker. G: Clawson 2.	2,252
27 Mar	Castleford	10	22	T: Rae, Brooke. G: Clawson 2.	6,200
3 Apr	HALIFAX	7	9	T: Rhodes. G: Clawson 2.	7,306
12 Apr	Wakefield Trinity	7	12	T: Stock. G: Clawson 2.	7,219
14 Apr	KEIGHLEY	15	0	T: Clawson, Walker, Rhodes. G: Clawson 3.	4,009
17 Apr	Leeds	7	2	T: Lord. G: Clawson 2.	4,300
19 Apr	HULL	15	9	T: Stock, Rae, Rhodes. G: Clawson 3.	4,441
20 Apr	DONCASTER	23	9	T: Brown 2, Lord 2, Davies. G: Clawson 4.	5,005
21 Apr	Liverpool C	10	0	T: Rae, Walker. G: Rhodes 2.	1,000
28 Apr	Widnes BPO	9	15	T: Ackerley, Lord, Rae.	4,435

186

Appendix 2: Player appearances

1954 –55	A	G	T	Pts
Neil Carter	11		1	3
W Collins	4			
Trevor Foster	29		3	9
Roy Goddard	9			
Harry Griffett	16		2	6
Len Haley	35		10	30
Norman Haley	23			
Eric Hamilton	4			
Dennis Hodgson	14			
Bill (W) Jenkins	24	16	3	41
Gwylfa Jones	23		1	3
Wynne Jones	31		2	6
David Knopf	37		10	30
Jack McLean	22		16	48
Joe Mageen	27		7	21
Joe A Phillips	31	83	5	181
Brian Radford	27		5	15
Bill (W) Seddon	22	12	6	42
Carl Sharrock	6			
Bob (R) Smith	24		15	45
Tony (A) Storey	32		2	6
Eric Sutton	15			
Ken Traill	30		6	18
Barry Tyler	32			
Jack Wilson	4		1	3
Ralph Winnard	1		1	3

1955–56	A	G	T	Pts
Les Belshaw	26			
Neil Carter	4		1	3
Brendan Cope	1			
Derek Davies	1		1	3
Jimmy Glynn	26		1	3
Roy Goddard	4			
Harry Griffett	24		2	6
Norman Haigh	1			
Len Haley	31		4	12
Brian Hambling	42		3	9
Eric Hamilton	10			
Dennis Hodgson	9			
Bill (W) Jenkins	23	8	11	49
Wynne Jones	19		2	6
David Knopf	5		4	12
Milan Kosanovic	7			
Alan Lancaster	6		2	6
Jack McLean	41		60	180
Norman Mackie	31		1	3
Joe Mageen	25		6	18
Graham Oddy	23		3	9
Joe A Phillips	42	119	8	262
Brian Radford	29		3	9
Jack Scroby	16		4	12
Bill (W) Seddon	42	6	13	51

Bob (R) Smith	19		10	30
Tony (A) Storey	4		1	3
Eric Sutton	20		5	15
Rodney Thomas	9			
Brian Todd	5			
Ken Traill	14		1	3

1956–57	**A**	**G**	**T**	**Pts**
Tony Beevers	5	9	1	21
Les Belshaw	10			
Clive Best	4	3		6
Neil Carter	31			
Phil Crabtree	1			
Derek Davies	13		3	9
Malcolm Davies	18		22	66
Jimmy Glynn	7		1	3
Harry Griffett	6			
Gordon Haley	14	9	2	24
Len Haley	33		2	6
Brian Hambling	28			
John Hanley	7			
Bryn Hopkins	20		5	15
Bill (W) Jenkins	17	9	4	30
Trevor Jones	37	1	5	17
Milan Kosanovic	3			
Alan Lancaster	21		4	12
Fred Lee	5	3	1	9
George McLean	2			
Douglas Maclean	19		9	27
Norman Mackie	32			
Joe Mageen	2			
Graham Oddy	2			
Brian Radford	32		8	24
Stan Rodwell	27		11	33
Jack Scroby	37		6	18
Bill (W) Seddon	37	58	7	137
Bob (R) Smith	27		13	39
Eric Sutton	14		6	18
Brian Todd	4			
Ken Ward	5			
Ralph Winnard	26		7	21

1957–58	**A**	**G**	**T**	**Pts**
Tony Beevers	18	17	1	37
Neil Carter	14	1	2	8
Phil Crabtree	12			
Arthur Daniels	28		15	45
Derek Davies	32		8	24
Malcolm Davies	35		46	138
Alan Dawes	2		2	6
Norman Feather	24		2	6
Harry Griffett	4			
Gordon Haley	30		4	12
Len Haley	26	2	3	13
Brian Hambling	4			
Gerald Handley	2			

188

	A	G	T	Pts
Walter Hemingway	20		2	6
Geoff Higgins	1		1	3
Bryn Hopkins	6			
Bill (W) Jenkins	37	47	15	139
Trevor Jones	25	4	1	11
Milan Kosanovic	39		3	9
Alan Lancaster	3		1	3
George McLean	30		2	6
Douglas Maclean	4		1	3
Norman Mackie	4			
Graham Oddy	12		3	9
Brian Radford	38		11	33
Stan Rodwell	3		3	9
Jack Scroby	35	1	5	17
Bill (W) Seddon	6	7	1	17
Bob (R) Smith	43		17	51
Rodney Thomas	2			
Brian Thompson	5	4		8
Ralph Winnard	28		9	27

1958–59	A	G	T	Pts
Peter Baddeley	2			
Tony Beevers	8	1	1	5
Clive Brook	1			
Phil Crabtree	12			
Arthur Daniels	33		20	60
Derek Davies	16		7	21
Malcolm Davies	32		28	84
Jack Doran	10		1	3
Norman Feather	8			
Gordon Haley	11		3	9
Len Haley	22		4	12
Gerald Handley	4		3	9
Walter Hemingway	17		1	3
Steve Hey	26		3	9
Geoff Higgins	30		8	24
Bryn Hopkins	8			
Bill (W) Jenkins	23	23	6	64
Trevor Jones	36		10	30
Milan Kosanovic	36		5	15
Alan Lancaster	3			
George McLean	30		1	3
Douglas Maclean	3			
Graham Oddy	1			
George Penketh	21		10	30
Brian Radford	39		6	18
Stan Rodwell	1			
Jack Scroby	15		1	3
Bill (W) Seddon	26	69	3	147
Phil Walshaw	10	24		48
David Walton	7			
Gerald Welsh	4			
Ralph Winnard	25		7	21

1959–60	A	G	T	Pts
Denis Broadbent	1			
Clive Brook	14		2	6
Derek Davies	29		6	18
Malcolm Davies	5		1	3
Alan Dawes	20		1	3
Ken Dawes	1			
Jack Doran	42		17	51
Norman Feather	17		1	3
Harry Griffett	6		3	9
Terry Griffett	7			
Len Haley	25		3	9
Walter Hemingway	27		3	9
Steve Hey	20		7	21
Geoff Higgins	26		3	9
Trevor Jones	23	13	3	35
Milan Kosanovic	33		2	6
Alan Lancaster	7		3	9
George McLean	12			
Peter Marston	23		3	9
Peter Nunns	2			
Graham Oddy	1			
George Penketh	39		10	30
Brian Radford	20		2	6
Gray Robbins	10			
Bill (W) Seddon	38	86	2	178
Brian Smith	24		11	33
Brian Thompson	4	1		2
Phil Walshaw	3	6		12
David Walton	20		2	6
Gerald Welsh	5			
Ralph Winnard	42		6	18

1960–61	A	G	T	Pts
Denis Broadbent	28	2	2	10
Clive Brook	14		4	12
Phil Crabtree	7		1	3
Derek Davies	35		8	24
Alan Dawes	4			
John De Klerk	4			
Jack Doran	33		14	42
Norman Feather	5		1	3
Duggie Greenall	4			
Terry Griffett	1			
Len Haley	7			
Arthur Hattee	13	19		38
Walter Hemingway	32		2	6
Geoff Higgins	10	1	1	5
Doug Holland	21			
Trevor Jones	11	2		4
Milan Kosanovic	25		2	6
George McLean	18			
Peter Marston	17		1	3
Peter Nunns	17		5	15
George Penketh	24		5	15
Gray Robbins	28		2	6

	A	G	T	Pts
Terry Robbins	17		2	6
Bill (W) Seddon	13	7		14
Arthur Sharkey	1			
Brian Smith	34		15	45
Alan Sutcliffe	1			
Bob (R) Taylor	9			
Eddie Trumble	9	3	3	15
Phil Walshaw	10	22		44
David Walton	9			
Gerald Welsh	13		1	3
Ralph Winnard	20			
1961–62	**A**	**G**	**T**	**Pts**
Goeli Abed	12	21		42
Tony Beevers	3	2		4
J Bentley	1			
Denis Broadbent	15		2	6
Clive Brook	14			
John (W) Coggle	18		4	12
Phil Crabtree	6			
Derek Davies	13		3	9
Lance Davies	17		3	9
Alan Dickinson	2			
Jack Doran	20		7	21
Horace Grainger	29		9	27
Terry Griffett	1			
Len Haley	12		1	3
John Hardcastle	21			
Don Hatfield	26		1	3
Arthur Hattee	12	27	1	57
Walter Hemingway	24		3	9
Steve Hey	5			
Doug Holland	3			
Trevor Jones	10			
Jock McAvoy	9	1	2	8
George McLean	5			
Tony (A) Marker	15			
Peter Marston	7		1	3
Peter Nunns	9		1	3
George Penketh	11			
R Radonic	4			
Terry Robbins	16		2	6
Trevor Schofield	10		2	6
Bill (W) Seddon	21	13	3	35
Brian Smith	2			
Peter Smith	3			
Alan Sutcliffe	25	3	2	12
Dennis Tate	13		2	6
Colin Taylor	14		2	6
Bob (R) Taylor	2			
Rodney Thomas	2			
David Walton	1			
Gerald Welsh	23		1	3
Tom Whitaker	7		1	3
Alan Wigglesworth	14			
Ralph Winnard	17			

1962–63	A	G	T	Pts
Goeli Abed	17	11	1	25
Tony Beevers	7		1	3
J Bentley	10		1	3
Trevor Brewer	2		1	3
John (W) Coggle	27		3	9
Phil Crabtree	1			
Lance Davies	34		2	6
Enslin Dlambulo	12			
Jack Doran	16		2	6
E. Flynn	6			
Derek Foster	4		1	3
George Gomersal	10			
Horace Grainger	2			
Len Haley	4			
John Hardcastle	35		2	6
Rudi Hasse	27		2	6
Don Hatfield	2			
Walter Hemingway	2			
David Horton	1			
Wynne Jones	7			
Tony (A) Marker	4		1	3
Alan Martin	15	13	5	41
Brian Monaghan	1			
Frank Moore	15			
Peter Nunns	14		3	9
George Penketh	31		6	18
Vernon Peterson	6			
A. M. Poxton	5			
John Reynolds	1			
Mick Reynolds	26		7	21
Bernard Robinson	7	2		4
Trevor Schofield	4			
W. (Bill) Seddon	25	29		58
Henry Sharratt	14			
Alan Sutcliffe	13		5	15
Dennis Tate	17		1	3
Colin Taylor	13		2	6
Rodney Thomas	8			
Gerald Welsh	2		1	3
Fred White	2		1	3
Tom Whitaker	2			
Alan Wigglesworth	15			
Ralph Winnard	2		1	3

1963–64	A	G	T	Pts
Goeli Abed	10	19	3	47
Tony Beevers	9	7		14
Trevor Brewer	1			3
Derek (R) Carr	9			
John (W) Coggle	16		10	30
Phil Crabtree	11			
Lance Davies	15		2	6
Enslin Dlambulo	14		3	9
Jack Doran	9		1	3
E. Flynn	1			

George Gomersal	14			
Len Haley	2			
John Hardcastle	13			
Rudi Hasse	4			
Ian Hume	6			
Peter Nunns	6			
George Penketh	4		1	3
Mick Reynolds	15	1	2	8
Trevor Schofield	5			
Alan Sutcliffe	7		3	9
Colin Taylor	13	1	1	5
Malcolm Thornton	5			
Tom Whitaker	1			
Trevor Whitaker	1			
Alan Wigglesworth	15		2	6
Stewart Wilkinson	1			
J. E. Yeoman	1			

1964–65	**A**	**G**	**T**	**Pts**

New signings only. Number in brackets shows substitute appearances included in total.

Terry Ackerley	36		1	3
Keith Ashcroft	25			
Gil Ashton	20(2)		1	3
Ian Brooke	30		8	24
Mike Brown	27		5	15
Garth Budge	23		1	3
Terry Clawson	15	36	2	78
Ian Crawshaw	3			
Stan Fearnley	2			
Idwal Fisher	17		1	3
Alan Hepworth	15			
Bryn Jones	15(2)	1		2
Joe Levula	10(1)	3	2	12
Brian Lord	28(1)		7	21
David Metcalfe	4		3	9
Stan Moyser	3		1	3
Arthur Mullins	1			
Barry Potter	2			
Johnny Rae	35(1)	6	10	42
Alan Rhodes	15	3	5	21
Tommy Smales	17		1	3
Errol Stock	19		4	12
David Stockwell	2			
Brian Todd	12	5	2	16
Albert Tonkinson	22			
Willie Walker	32		10	30
Jack Wilkinson	12(1)			
Keith Williams	10	24		48

Appendix 3: Debuts and departures

1954–55
Debuts
W. Collins
Dennis Hodgson (Wyke)
Eric Sutton (Otley RU)
Jack Wilson (Hunslet junior)
Ralph Winnard (West Bowling)

Departures or final senior appearance
W. Collins
Ron Greaves (Keighley)
Trevor Foster (retired)
Norman Haley (retired)
Gwylfa Jones (struck off 1956–57)
Carl Sharrock (Hunslet)
Barry Tyler (Doncaster)
Jack Wilson (Hull)

1955–56
Debuts
Les Belshaw (Barrow)
Brendan Cope (Batley – trialist not retained)
Derek Davies (Ovenden)
Graham Oddy (Ovenden)
Jimmy Glynn (Hunslet junior)
Norman Haigh
Milan Kosanovic (Pellon)
Alan Lancaster (Cleckheaton RU)
Norman Mackie (Morley RU)
Jack Scroby (Ovenden)
Rodney Thomas (Pellon)
Brian Todd (Halifax junior)

Departures or final senior appearance
Roy Goddard (struck off 1956–57)
Norman Haigh
Eric Hamilton (Whitehaven 1958–59)
Dennis Hodgson
Wynne Jones (Featherstone R 1956–57)
David Knopf (returned to South Africa)
Jack McLean (returned to New Zealand)
Joe Phillips (Keighley)
Tony Storey (Featherstone Rovers)
Ken Traill (Halifax)

1956–57
Debuts
Tony Beevers (Ovenden)
Clive Best (Barrow – trialist not retained)
Phil Crabtree (Baildon RU)
Malcolm Davies (Leigh)
Gordon Haley (Overthorpe, Dewsbury)
John Hanley (Bramley)
Bryn Hopkins (Keighley)
Trevor Jones (Batley)
Fred Lee (Wyke)
George McLean (Clayton)
Douglas Maclean (Wyke)
Stan Rodwell (Wakefield ARL)

Ken Ward (Doncaster – trialist not retained, retired)

Departures or final senior appearance
Les Belshaw (on loan to Leeds 9 April 1957 – joined Doncaster 1957–58)
Malcolm Davies (Leeds)
Jimmy Glynn (Keighley)
John Hanley (struck off 1957–58)
Wynne Jones (Featherstone Rovers)
Joe Mageen (Halifax)
Eric Sutton (Batley 1957–58)
Brian Todd (struck off)

1957–58
Debuts and re-signings
Malcolm Davies (Leeds)
Alan Dawes (Low Moor junior)
Norman Feather (Roundhay RU)
Gerald Handley (Keighley Albion)
Walter Hemingway (Bradford junior – signed 16 August 1956)

Geoff Higgins (Ovenden)
Brian Thompson (Bradford RU)
Arthur Daniels (Halifax)

Departures or last senior appearance
Les Belshaw (Doncaster)
Neil Carter (struck off 1960–61)
Harry Griffett (Hull K R)
Brian Hambling (Hull)
Fred Lee (Castleford)

Norman Mackie (struck off 1958–59)
Stan Rodwell (Batley trialist not retained – struck off Northern register but re-signed 1958–59)
Bob Smith (retired)
Rodney Thomas (struck off 1958–59)

1958 –59
Debuts and re-signings
Peter Baddeley (Doncaster – trialist not retained)
Clive Brook (Lockwood)
Jack Doran (Victoria Rangers)
Steve Hey (Stanningley)
George Penketh (Ovenden)
Stan Rodwell (re-signed)
Philip Walshaw (Batley)
David Walton (Wakefield Trinity)
Gerald Welsh (Burton Sports, Leeds)

Departures or last senior appearance:
Arthur Daniels (retired)
Gordon Haley (Dewsbury)
Gerald Handley (National Service – re-signed 1961–62)
Bryn Hopkins (retired)
Bill Jenkins (retired)
Douglas Maclean (struck off 1961–62)
Stan Rodwell (struck off)

1959–60
Debuts and re-signings
Denis Broadbent (Huddersfield RU)
Ken Dawes (Wyke)
Harry Griffett (Hull K R)
Peter Marston (Keighley)
Peter Nunns (BTA - Bradford ARL)
Gray Robbins (Abertillery/New Brighton)
Brian Smith (York)

Departures or last senior appearance
Malcolm Davies (Bramley)
Ken Dawes
Harry Griffett (struck off 1961–62)
Alan Lancaster (Huddersfield 1960–61)
Graham Oddy (struck off 1962–63)
Brian Radford (retired)
Jack Scroby (Halifax)

1960 –61
Debuts
John de Klerk (South Africa)
Duggie Greenall (St Helens)
Arthur Hattee (Castleford)
Doug Holland (Hull K R)
Terry Robbins (Hunslet)
Arthur Sharkey
Alan Sutcliffe (Underbank)
Bob Taylor (Castleford)
Eddie Trumble (Rochdale Hornets – trialist not retained)

Departures or last senior appearance
Alan Dawes
John de Klerk (Huddersfield)
Norman Feather (struck off 1962–63)
Duggie Greenall (struck off 1961–62)
Geoff Higgins (struck off 1962–63)
Milan Kosanovic (Wakefield Trinity)
Alan Lancaster (Huddersfield)
Peter Marston (Castleford on loan – not retained – struck off 1961–62)
Gray Robbins (struck off 1963–64)
Arthur Sharkey (struck off 1961–62)
Brian Thompson (struck off 1961–62)
Philip Walshaw (Bramley – free transfer)

1961 –62
Debuts
Goeli Abed (South Africa)
J Bentley (Wyke)
John Coggle (Hull)

Lance Davies (Neath)
Alan Dickinson (York – trialist not retained)
Horace Grainger (Hunslet)

John Hardcastle (Maesteg)
Don Hatfield (Hunslet)
Tony Marker (Bramley)
Jock McAvoy (free agent - ex-Workington Town)
R. Radonic (Halifax junior)
Trevor Schofield (Shaw Cross Dewsbury)
Peter Smith (trialist – not retained)
Dennis Tate (Hunslet)
Colin Taylor (Castleford)
Tom Whitaker (Batley)
Alan Wigglesworth (Yorkshire Schools)

Departures or final senior appearance

Denis Broadbent (transfer-listed at £500 1962–63 and 1963–64)
Clive Brook (struck off 1962–63)
Derek Davies (Leeds)
Terry Griffett (struck off 1962–63)
Arthur Hattee (struck off 1962–63)
Steve Hey (transfer-listed at £1,000 1962–63 – Bramley trialist 1963–64 – not retained)
Doug Holland (transfer-listed at £500 1961–62 - struck off 1962–63)
Trevor Jones (struck off)
Jock McAvoy (struck off 1962–63)
George McLean (Batley on loan – not retained - struck off)
Peter Marston (struck off)
R. Radonic (struck off, but re-joined 1963–64)
Terry Robbins (Bramley)
Brian Smith (Huddersfield as 'A' team coach)
David Walton (struck off 1962–63)

1962–63

Debuts or re-signings

Trevor Brewer (Bramley)
Enslin Dlambulo (South Africa)
Derek Foster ('A' team)
E. Flynn (Featherstone junior)
George Gomersal (Hunslet)
Rudi Hasse (South Africa)
David Horton (Doncaster – trialist not retained)
Wynne Jones (Featherstone R)
Alan Martin (Halifax)
Frank Moore (Wakefield T)
Brian Monaghan ('A' team)
A. M. Poxton (Featherstone junior – trialist not retained)
Vernon Peterson (South Africa)
John Reynolds (Featherstone junior – trialist not retained)
Mick Reynolds (Featherstone Rovers)
Bernard Robinson (Doncaster – trialist not retained)
Henry Sharratt (Dewsbury)
Fred White (Hunslet – trialist not retained)

Departures or last senior appearance

J. Bentley (Keighley trialist 1963–64 – not retained. Returned and later granted free transfer)
Derek Foster (struck off)
Horace Grainger
Don Hatfield (retired)
Walter Hemingway ('A' team)
David Horton ('A' team)
Wynne Jones (struck off 1963–64)
Tony Marker
Alan Martin (Bramley on loan 1963–64 – not retained – Huddersfield on loan 1964–65 – not retained)
Frank Moore (retired)
Brian Monaghan
Vernon Peterson (returned to South Africa)
Bill Seddon ('A' team – returned to New Zealand)
Gerald Welsh (Keighley)
Ralph Winnard (retired 1963–64)

1963–64
Debuts
Derek (R) Carr (Featherstone Rovers)
Ian Hume (Leeds – trialist not retained)
Malcolm Thornton (Wyke)
Trevor Whitaker ('A' team)
Stewart Wilkinson (Dewsbury area)
J. E. Yeoman (Bramley – trialist not retained)

Departures or last senior appearance
Tony Beevers (Keighley – free transfer)
Trevor Brewer (Huddersfield – free transfer – not retained)
W. (John) Coggle (Batley trialist – joined Hull KR 10 January 1964)
Phil Crabtree (free transfer)
Enslin Dlambulo (Keighley)
Jack Doran ('A' team)
E. Flynn (free transfer)
Len Haley ('A' team)
Walter Hemingway (free transfer)
Peter Nunns (free transfer - Huddersfield not retained)
George Penketh (Featherstone Rovers)
Malcolm Reynolds
Dennis Tate
Colin Taylor (Castleford and Hunslet)
Stewart Wilkinson (Dewsbury trialist – not retained)
Alan Wigglesworth (York trialist – returned and granted free transfer)

1964–65
Debuts
Terry Ackerley (Workington Town)
Terry Albone (ex-Keighley/ Batley on trial 1963–64 – not retained)
Keith Ashcroft (St Helens)
Gil Ashton (Leeds)
Ian Brooke (Wakefield Trinity)
Mike Brown (Halifax)
Garth Budge (Rockhampton)
Terry Clawson (Featherstone R)
Ian Crawshaw (Greetland)
Stan Fearnley (Clayton)
Idwal Fisher (Warrington)
Alan Hepworth (Doncaster)
Bryn Jones (Halifax)
Joe Levula (Rochdale Hornets)
Brian Lord (Oldham)
David Metcalfe (Cleckheaton RU)
Stan Moyser (Hunslet)
Arthur Mullins (Hull KR – trialist not retained)
Barry Potter (Siddal)
Johnny Rae (Oldham)
Alan Rhodes (Halifax)
Tommy Smales (Huddersfield)
Errol Stock (Rockhampton)
Dave Stockwell (Halifax)
Brian Todd (St Helens)
Albert Tonkinson (Castleford)
Willie Walker (Hunslet)
Jack Wilkinson (Wakefield Trinity)
Keith Williams (Huddersfield)

Departures or last senior appearance
Goeli Abed (Batley)
Terry Albone ('A' team)
Derek (R) Carr ('A' team)
Lance Davies (Bramley 1965–66)
Idwal Fisher (Bramley 1965–66)
George Gomersal ('A' team – struck off)
John Hardcastle ('A' team)
Bryn Jones (Keighley)
Joe Levula ('A' team – Batley on loan 1965–66)
Stan Moyser (retired)
Trevor Schofield (free transfer)
Henry Sharratt (free transfer – Batley 1965–66)
Malcolm Thornton (free transfer – Bramley 1965–66)
Brian Todd (Halifax)
Tom Whitaker (free transfer)
Jack Wilkinson (retired)
Keith Williams (Doncaster)

Appendix 4: The click of the turnstiles
Northern's home attendances 1954–55 to 1963–64

The experience of once having briefly helped man the old turnstiles at Odsal Stadium should have taught me never to believe in the accuracy of published attendance figures. Apart from the problem of controlling the rickety foot pedal, which was meant to register each spectator, there was also the question of how the final figure had been calculated.

Having since been granted access to the RFL's attendance books at Huddersfield University, I now know that there were, in fact, two attendance figures. There was the official paying one, which each club had to declare to the RFL together with a cheque for 10 per cent of the gate for the later redistributed Levy Fund. There was also that given to the press, which included season ticket holders and members. Although a more exact figure was given in the later years, in Northern's case the final published attendance until 1959–60 appears to have been simply rounded up to the nearest 500.

Nonetheless, these press figures clearly give a truer indication of the actual attendance on the day, and, importantly, have been used in the past to determine the season's averages and to chart the dramatic decline in the club's support. From the record average of 17,791 in 1951–52 it dropped by over 50 per cent within three seasons. They are therefore the figures that I have decided to use, although, due to several adjustments, they rarely correspond with those published at the time in the *Telegraph & Argus (T&A)*. The tour games against Australia and New Zealand have been used to calculate the seasonal averages, but not the Lazenby Cup and other friendlies.

Match average gates

1954–55: 8,570	1959–60: 3,010
1955–56: 6,881	1960–61: 1,864
1956–57: 4,691	1961–62: 1,495
1957–58: 4,651	1962–63: 1,257
1958–59: 3,745	1963–64: 1,021

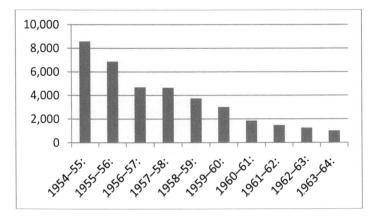

1954–55

Doncaster	6,500
Wigan	15,000
Bramley	8,500
Whitehaven	8,500
Hunslet YC2	8,105
Halifax	16,000
Featherstone R	8,000
Hull	7,000
Wakefield T	6,500
Widnes	2,000
Leeds	8,500
Keighley	7,000
York	5,500
Huddersfield	8,500
Warrington CC1	14,302
Featherstone R CC2	20,575
Castleford	4,500
Batley	3,500
Dewsbury	3,500
Warrington	10,000
Hunslet	8,000

League games (18): 137,000 (average 7,611)
Cup ties (3): 42,982
Total (21): 179,982 (average 8,570)
T&A: 8,577 (league only 7,611)

1955–56

Keighley (LC)	*5,727*
Bramley	5,000
Hunslet YC1	8,939
Batley	5,500
Leigh	10,500
Workington T	8,000
Castleford	7,000
Huddersfield	12,000
Featherstone R	9,500
New Zealand	5,271
Hull	6,000
Hull K R	6,000
Liverpool C	2,400
Keighley	6,000
Wakefield T	6,000
Hunslet	4,500
Leeds	10,000
York	4,500
Halifax	9,000
Doncaster	5,500
Swinton	6,000

League games (18): 123,400 (average 6,856)
Cup ties (1): 8,939
Tour game: 5,271
Total (20): 137,610 (average 6,881)
T&A: 6,911 (all possibly exc New Zealand)

1956–57

Leeds	10,500
St Helens	5,500
Albi (Friendly)	*1,400*
York	4,000
Barrow	4,000
Huddersfield (Exp rules)	*1,084*
Warrington	6,000
Australia	3,000

Halifax	10,000
Hunslet	6,000
Castleford	4,500
Hull	3,000
Featherstone R	2,500
Dewsbury	1,700
Bramley	3,000
Dewsbury CC1	6,646
Wigan	6,000
Widnes CC2	6,959
Doncaster	3,500
Keighley	5,000
Wakefield T	3,200
Huddersfield	3,500
Hull K R	2,700
Batley	2,000

League games (19): 86,600 (average 4,558)
Cup ties (2): 13,605
Tour game: 3,000
Total (22): 103,205 (average 4,691)
T&A: average 4,791 (all possibly exc Australia)

1957–58

Keighley (LC)	*6,200*
Swinton	4,100
Workington	3,000
Dewsbury	3,700
Leigh	4,500
Featherstone R YC2	5,776
Whitehaven	4,000
York YCSF	10,794
Wakefield T	10,000
Hunslet	7,000
Hull	3,500
Featherstone R	4,000
Doncaster	2,300
Keighley	4,500
Castleford	3,500
York	4,000
Hull K R	2,000
Halifax	6,000
Warrington	4,500
Batley	3,000
Huddersfield	5,000
Bramley	2,500

League games (19): 81,100 (average 4,268)
Cup ties (2): 16,570
Total (21): 97,670 (average 4,651)
T&A: 4,645 (all games)

1958–59

Leigh	4,000
Hull	6,000
York YC1	5,168
Warrington	4,000
Doncaster	3,000
Hunslet	5,000
Hull K R	3,000
Dewsbury	2,500
York	2,500
Whitehaven	2,000
Bramley	3,500
Salford	3,000
Huddersfield CC1	6,470

Batley 2,000
Keighley 3,500
Castleford 2,000
Halifax 4,000
Huddersfield 3,500
Wakefield T 7,500
Widnes 3,000
Featherstone R 3,000
League games (19): 67,000 (average 3,526)
Cup ties (2): 11,638
Total (21): 78,638 (average 3,745)
T&A: 3,747 (all games)

1959–60
Workington T 4,250
Keighley 4,250
Hull YC1 4,376
Widnes 2,500
Halifax 5,000
Hunslet 5,000
Featherstone R 2,750
Batley 3,000
Australia 4,126
Castleford 1,500
Huddersfield 1,100
Bramley 1,500
Doncaster 1,000
York 1,300
Hull 2,000
Hull K R 2,000
Warrington 1,550
Leeds 5,250
Leigh 1,750
Wakefield T 7,500
Whitehaven 1,500
League games (19): 54,700 (average 2,879)
Cup tie: 4,376 Tour game: 4,126
Total (21): 63,202 (average 3,010)
T&A: 2,960 (excluding Australia)

1960–61
Featherstone R 3,100
Batley 1,850
Castleford YC1 1,774
Rochdale H 1,600
Leeds 5,500
Castleford 1,500
York 1,350
Keighley 1,600
Hunslet 2,400
Doncaster 950
Bramley 1,150
Blackpool B 1,100
Workington T 1,850
Hull 1,200
Huddersfield 1,800
Dewsbury 1,400
Barrow 1,000
Wakefield T 3,800
Hull K R 500
League games (18): 33,650 (average 1,869)
Cup tie: 1,774
Total (19) 35,424 (average 1,864)
T&A: 1,858 (all games)

1961–62
Keighley 1,718
Leeds 4,075
Castleford 1,470
Widnes 1,306
Wakefield T 5,636
Halifax 2,322
Hunslet 1,493
Liverpool C 563
Dewsbury 1,030
Salford 1,323
Doncaster 790
Featherstone R 904
Bramley 502
Hull 483
York 1,001
Batley 738
Hull K R 722
Barrow 842
League games (18): 26,918 (average 1,495)

1962–63
Huddersfield ED 1,819
Wakefield T ED 2,756
Bramley YC1 1,262
Leeds ED 2,781
Featherstone R ED 1,476
Dewsbury 1,700
Rochdale H 2,027
Liverpool C 631
Salford 744
Doncaster 525
Barrow 632
Wakefield T CC1 2,069
Whitehaven 543
Blackpool B 617
York 782
Hunslet 1,262
Leigh 435
Batley 703
Keighley 1,124
League games (13): 11,725 (average 902)
Eastern Division (4): 8,832
Cup ties (2): 3,331
Total (19): 23,888 (average 1,257)

1963–64
Dewsbury 953
Doncaster 766
Featherstone R YC1 1,005
Wakefield T ED 1,686
Salford 1,044
Huddersfield ED 1,742
Batley 1,235
Liverpool C 699
Rochdale H 934
Barrow 324
Leigh 841
League games (8): 6,796 (average 850)
Eastern Division (2): 3,428
Cup tie: 1,005
Total (11): 11,229 (average 1,021)

Appendix 5: Odsal's pioneering floodlights

Floodlit football had been staged as early as the 1870s, but what has been dubbed the first modern floodlit game under any code of football in the north of England took place at Odsal Stadium on 31 October 1951, when Northern defeated the New Zealand tourists 13–8 before a crowd of 29,072. Before kick-off the players had entered the field of play under darkness and once Odsal's master switch was pulled the onlookers were treated to the surprising spectacle of seeing the players standing in their positions. On this clear autumnal night New Zealanders scored 18 of the game's 21 points, as Jack McLean scored two tries and Joe Phillips kicked two goals, with Northern's other try coming from Len Haley. The New Zealanders, under an agreement to take a £750 guarantee and half the surplus, made about £2,000 on the match, and Northern's share went a long way to paying for the cost of installation.

Odsal's first lights consisted of forty three 1,000 watt adjustable Philips lamps, which were installed in five days by BCS Electrics of Leeds. The majority of the lamps were mounted under the two stand roofs with others on high poles around the perimeters. Although the lights on the Old Stand were considerably lower than those on the New Stand and the system was augmented by the speedway track lights, the players reported no real problems with glare or in fielding high balls. For the Kiwis game the match ball was white, but Northern twice experimented with a black and white striped ball in 1959, first for the Radford-Jenkins-Redman benefit match and also for the Australians' visit. The BBC took pictures of that historic game as research for the future possibilities of screening matches.

But despite the success of that first game, with the exception of Leigh and Wigan, whose floodlit challenge match against Northern at Odsal on 28 November 1951 was cancelled 20 minutes before the kick-off due to fog, most clubs were reluctant to welcome the innovation. True, eight of the game's top teams were lured by the promise of £400 per game (plus profits from the gates) to take part in the ITV Floodlit Trophy at Woolwich Stadium and Loftus Road in London in September 1955, but few clubs were prepared to play Northern under Odsal's lights, fearing some disadvantage; and both Hull and Halifax preferred to play their 1955 Yorkshire Cup semi-final replay on a Wednesday afternoon at Odsal rather than make use of the lights and the benefit it would have given their travelling supporters. In fact, Leigh, in October 1953, was the only other rugby league club, along with Northern, to have invested in floodlights before BBC2 launched the Floodlit Trophy in 1965–6.

The Odsal floodlights in 1951–52. (Courtesy Robert Gate).

Clubs were also reluctant to agree to Northern's suggestion, because of the fading light in midwinter, to kick off games at 3.00pm and play the second-half under floodlights. Keighley were one of the few clubs to see the advantage of this proposal, on Boxing Day 1955, although Blackpool Borough also agreed to this arrangement on a visit to Leigh.

The first floodlit international took place at Odsal on Friday 7 December 1951 when a crowd of 8,568 braved the sleet and snow to see New Zealand beat Wales 15–3; and the first floodlit International Championship game took place on Wednesday 7 October 1953 when a crowd of 14,646 witnessed Other Nationalities beat Wales 30–5. The second half was televised by the BBC and, as an aid to viewers, Other Nationalities played in all-white jerseys. The international in 1951 had produced a slight loss for the RFL, and when only 3,643 turned up to watch a Rugby League XIII beat the 1955 New Zealanders there was further proof that the novelty of watching floodlit rugby at Odsal in the height of winter was wearing thin. Due to technical difficulties with the BBC's hour-long outside broadcast from Odsal, only a few minutes of the latter game were actually seen by television viewers.

Had Great Britain drawn with Australia in the final game of the 1960 World Cup, then the final decider would have been played under Odsal's lights on the following Monday, 10 October, with the crowd limit set at 60,000 – a frightening prospect given the state of the terracing at that time. As it was, the champions, Great Britain, played a Rest of the World side in what amounted to an exhibition game, before a meagre crowd of only 3,908. The last scheduled game under those original lights took place 48 hours later when Keighley transferred their Yorkshire Cup semi-final tie against Wakefield Trinity to Odsal.

The failure to maintain both the stand lights and the speedway track bulbs (the latter which could easily explode during games when rain water hit them) had rendered the 1951 system obsolete within a decade, and what remained of these suffered a buffeting from the tornado that hit the West Riding on 11 February, 1962, when floodlit pylons at both Park Avenue and Valley Parade were blown down. The last competitive use of Odsal's original lighting system was on 22 December 1962, when, due to fog, the referee, Charlie Appleton, asked for the remaining track lights to be switched on during Northern's game against Barrow. It took until 1979 for a new system to be installed.

First team and representative games played in full or part under the lights from 1951

Date	Note	Home		Away		Att.
31.10.51		Northern	13	New Zealand	13	29,072
07.12.51		Wales	3	New Zealand	15	8,568
12.01.52		Northern	38	Cardiff	5	16,000
07.04.52		Northern	12	York	8	14,500
08.10.52		Northern	6	Australia	20	29,287
19.11.52		Northern	43	Hull K R	0	8,063
23.02.53	CC1 2nd leg	Northern	17	Batley	3	16,722
07.10.53		Wales	5	Other Nats	30	14,646
17.02.54	CC1	Northern	11	Rochdale H	2	20,014
24.02.54	Friendly	Northern		Leigh		4,250
24.03.54		Northern	13	Hunslet	5	11,000
06.10.54		Yorkshire	20	Lancashire	10	8,500
20.10.54	RL XIII	Northern	13	Australia	25	17,049
19.11.54		Northern	9	Wakefield T	3	6,500
16.03.55		Northern	26	Batley	4	3,500
25.03.55	Schoolboys	Yorkshire	13	Lancashire	18	
30.03.55		Northern	27	Dewsbury	3	3,500
05.10.55		Yorkshire	14	Cumberland	2	3,370
23.11.55		Northern	6	New Zealand	11	5,271
07.12.55	RL XIII	Northern	24	New Zealand	11	3,643
10.12.55	Last 25 min	Northern	27	Liverpool C	0	2,400
26.12.55	2nd half	Northern	16	Keighley	5	6,000
14.03.56		Northern	5	Leeds	17	10,000
19.03.56		Northern	9	York	4	4,500
11.04.56		Great Britain	18	France	10	10,453
05.09.56		Northern	5	York	17	4,000
03.10.56		Great Britain	26	Rest of League	23	6,477
08.10.56	Ex Rules	Leigh	26	Oldham	12	1,084
08.10.56	Ex Rules	Northern	14	Huddersfield	6	1,084
24.10.56		Northern	11	Australia	23	3,000
25.03.57		Northern	3	Keighley	18	5,000
10.04.57	After 2 min	Northern	9	Wakefield T	23	3,200
30.09.57	YCSF	Northern	2	York	2	10,794
11.03.59		Northern	9	Castleford	23	2,000
16.03.59		Northern	10	Halifax	13	4,000
26.10.59	Benefit	Northern	40	Keighley	34	1,500
04.11.59		Northern	8	Australia	29	4,126
28.09.60		Northern	17	Castleford	18	1,500
10.10.60	World Cup	Great Britain	33	Rest of World	27	3,908
12.10.60	YC SF	Keighley	4	Wakefield T	5	6,892

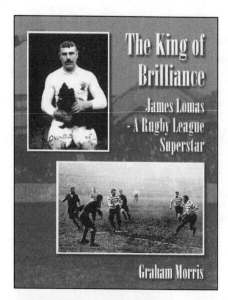

Great new book about one of the
sport's genuine legends. James
Lomas played for Bramley, Salford,
Oldham and York, and won
representative honours for
Lancashire, Cumberland, England
and Great Britain. He captained the
first Lions team to tour Australia and
New Zealand in 1910. This is the
first biography of him.

Published in October 2011 at £16.95
(hardback). Copies available post free at
£16.95 direct from London League
Publications Ltd, PO Box 65784, London
NW2 9NS (cheques payable to London
League Publications Ltd); credit card
orders via our website:
www.llpshop.co.uk or from any bookshop

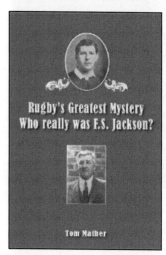

Rugby's Greatest Mystery
Who really was F.S. Jackson?

A true life rugby detective story
This is the story of a man whose life was made up of
mystery, intrigue and deception, but was also a
Rugby Union star before the First World War. He
played for Leicester and Cornwall when they won the
1908 County Championship. He was selected for the
Anglo-Welsh Rugby Union tour to New Zealand and
Australia in 1908. However, the RFU recalled him
from the tour and banned him from the sport over
allegations that he was a professional player, and
had played for Swinton in the Northern Union. The
scandal around his suspension from rugby union
caused great problems for the RFU and almost saw a
further split in the game.
He then played Rugby League for New Zealand,
against the British Lions in 1910. After the First
World War he was reinstated by the New Zealand RU, became an East Coast selector and
saw his son play for the All Blacks. For around 60 years he used the name Frederick
Stanley Jackson, even though it was not his given name. When he died in 1957 he took
to the grave his true identity. Even his family knew little about his early years in England,
or even where he came from. **It was a mystery that remained unresolved until
now.** The book also includes an analysis of the development of Leicester Tigers RFC up
to the First World War.

Published in March 2012 at £12.95. Copies available at £12.95 post free direct from
London League Publications Ltd, PO Box 65784, London NW2 9NS
(cheques payable to London League Publications Ltd);
credit card orders via our website: www.llpshop.co.uk or from any bookshop.

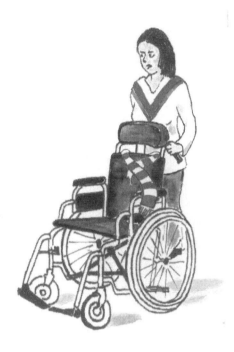

Braver than all the rest

A mother fights for her son

Philip Howard

Dave and Sarah Burgess are devastated when their young son Karl is found to have muscular dystrophy. Then another tragedy hits the family hard. But the family are committed to do the best they can for Karl, who has a passion for rugby league. Based in Castleton, a Yorkshire town near the border with Lancashire, Karl's determination to get the most out of life, despite his disability, inspires those around him, in particular Chris Anderton, one of the Castleton Rugby League Club players, who is coming to the end of his career in the game. A moving novel of family life and rugby league.
Published in 2010 at £9.95, special offer £9.00 direct from London League Publications Ltd. Credit card orders via www.llpshop.co.uk , orders by cheque to LLP, PO Box 65784, London NW2 9NS

Best in the Northern Union

The pioneering 1910 Rugby League Lions tour of Australia and New Zealand

Tom Mather

Fascinating account of the first Great Britain Lions tour of Australia and New Zealand. Published in 2010 at £12.95, special offer £12.00 post free direct from London League Publications Ltd. Credit card orders via www.llpshop.co.uk , orders by cheque to LLP, PO Box 65784, London NW2 9NS

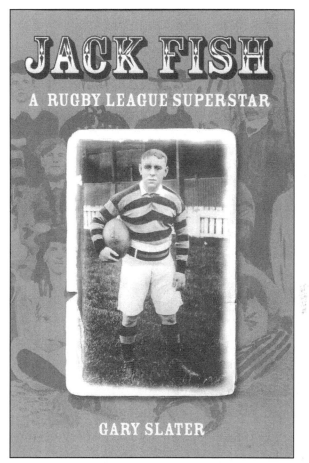

JACK FISH

A RUGBY LEAGUE SUPERSTAR

GARY SLATER

Jack Fish was one of the sport's great players from the Northern Union period. He played for Warrington, Lancashire and England. He played in four Challenge Cup Finals, and scored both tries when Warrington beat Hull KR 6-0 in 1905. He captained the team in 1907 when they beat Oldham 17-3 in the Final.

He scored a phenomenal 214 tries and kicked 263 goals for the Wire. He is still the only player to score 200 tries and kick 200 goals for Warrington.

This book is the first biography of Jack Fish, and was published in April 2012 at £11.95. Order from London League Publications Ltd direct for £11.95 post free . Credit card orders via www.llpshop.co.uk order by cheque to LLP, PO Box 65784, London NW2 9NS

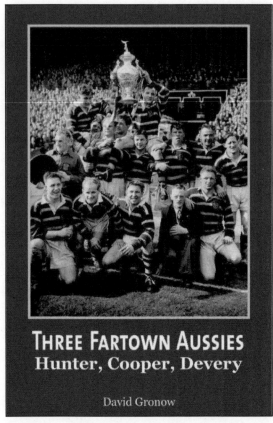

THREE FARTOWN AUSSIES
Hunter, Cooper, Devery

David Gronow

From 1947 to 1953 the Huddersfield rugby league team – 'Fartown' as they were known to their supporters – enjoyed a golden age. The Championship was won in 1949, and the Challenge Cup in 1953, along with the Yorkshire Cup. The Yorkshire League title was also won three times in this great period. These were halcyon days for the Huddersfield club and their supporters.

After the end of the Second World War Huddersfield were a formidable combination under the guidance of Russ Pepperell, but the signing in 1947 of 'Three Fartown Aussies' – Johnny Hunter, Lionel Cooper and Pat Devery – added quality and excitement to the team.

The book also covers Cooper and Devery's appearances for Australia in 1946 and the games they all played for the famous Other Nationalities team and international representative teams. 'Legend' is a word which is used too often these days, but the Three Fartown Aussies were the genuine article.

Published in May 2012 at £12.95. Order from London League Publications Ltd direct for £12.95 post free . Credit card orders via www.llpshop.co.uk order by cheque to LLP, PO Box 65784, London NW2 9NS

All London League Publications Ltd
books can be ordered from any
bookshop, and are also available on
Amazon.co.uk